Applied Theology 2

'TEND MY SHEEP'

TEF Study Guides

This series was first sponsored and subsidized by the Theological Education Fund of the WCC in response to requests from Africa, Asia, the Caribbean, and the Pacific. The books are prepared by and in consultation with theological teachers in those areas. Special attention is given to problems of interpretation and application arising there as well as in the West, and to the particular needs of students using English as a second language.

General Editors: Daphne Terry and Nicholas Beddow

ALREADY PUBLISHED

IN PREPARATION

TEF Study Guide 19

Applied Theology 2
'TEND MY SHEEP'

Harold Taylor

First published in 1983
SPCK
Holy Trinity Church
Marylebone Road,
London, NW1 4DU

Third Impression 1990

The photographs in this book are reproduced by courtesy of Lee/Dennis. Methodist Information (p. 59). The Mansell Collection, London (pp. 12 and 20), and Camera Press Ltd.

Unless otherwise stated the Scripture quotations in this publication are from the Revised Standard Version of the Bible (Ecumenical Edition), copyrighted 1973 by the Division of Christian Education of the National Council of the Churches of Christ in the USA.

ISBN 0 281 04055 9 (net edition)

ISBN 0 281 04056 7 (non-net edition for Africa, Asia, S. Pacific, and Caribbean)

Printed and bound in Great Britain by
Dotesios Printers Ltd, Trowbridge, Wilts

Contents

Preface

When I was asked to contribute a volume on pastoral care and counselling for the TEF Study Guide Series, my first reaction was to say 'No'. This was because of a keen awareness of my limited knowledge and experience in this subject, but more importantly, I felt that any writing which was dealing mainly with Third World situations should come from peoples within those particular cultures. My Western background carried with it ways of thinking and relating to others which were often irrelevant to other cultural situations. I had observed and experienced the mistake of attempting to foist Western methods and concepts of counselling on to Melanesian and Polynesian situations without adequate understanding of the considerable differences which exist between Western and Third World cultures.

Yet I could also see the value of some of the insights which had come in the fields of counselling and pastoral care in Western countries. Over the years I had attempted to integrate some of 'the best of both worlds', at the same time seeking to relate any approaches in counselling to the teaching and example of the Scriptures, and also to the practice of pastoral care which has been present in the life of the Church through the centuries. This book is the result of that rather faltering attempt, and I hope it will encourage more contributions on this subject from within Third World Churches.

The book has become a reality through the kind pressure and unending patience of Daphne Terry, General Editor of the Study Guide Series. Her ability to suggest necessary changes and make the finished product balanced, readable, and usable, have produced in me both gratitude and admiration. The book would not have progressed past the 'good idea' stage without her input and support.

Many others have contributed through suggestions, comments, and in some cases, through relevant examples from different areas of the world, to illustrate some particular points. In this regard special mention is made of the work of Roger Bowen, who has given much detailed help, and with Principal Jeremiah Anondo and other colleagues and students at St Paul's Theological College in Kenya provided many insights and contributed a number of the examples and case studies out of the African scene. Many writers have contributed to my thinking over the years, and it is impossible to acknowledge the many sources from which ideas have come. Certainly the book would not have been possible without these rich sources.

Much of the material in the book has developed in classroom and pastoral situations in Melanesia, and I acknowledge my great debt to the students at Rarongo Theological College, Rabaul, and to the many pastors in the United Church in Papua New Guinea and the Solomon Islands, who, through their willingness to share and learn together, have taught me so much about the meaning of effective pastoral care.

The book is sent out as a contribution to the continuing pastoral task given by Jesus Christ to His Church, to 'tend my sheep' (John 21.15–17; 1 Pet. 5.2).

H. TAYLOR
Bible College of Victoria, Lilydale, Victoria, Australia

Editor's Note:
The plan and use of this book

As explained in the first volume of this Applied Theology course, that book dealt primarily with ministry to people as *groups*, that is, with communities and congregations as such. The emphasis of this second volume will be on the pastoral care of *individuals*, and especially on the role of the pastor as counsellor of those who need help at times of particular crisis in their lives.

Like the first volume, it is based very largely on case studies and examples drawn from real life. These are intended to illustrate the sorts of situation which the pastoral counsellor is likely to encounter, and also to serve as a jumping-off point for the study and interpretation of people's needs and the possible ways of meeting them in the student's own situation. The first volume was related almost entirely to work in a rural and undeveloped area. In this second book the illustrations are drawn from a wide variety of contexts, both urban and rural, in the Third World and in the West.

After a brief Introduction to the general idea of ministry as typified by the work of a shepherd (or other herdsman) looking after his flocks or herds, Part I then deals with the overall ministry of pastoral care. We first look at the biblical conception of the 'Good Shepherd', culminating in the archetypal ministry of Jesus Himself who 'lays down his life for the sheep', and at the development of this idea in the history of the Church. Then we go on to discuss ways in which the pastor can achieve the understanding, both of other people and of himself, which is essential to the role of counsellor.

In Part II we examine the ministry of counselling in all its aspects, ranging from the situation of need in which it is chiefly exercised, the pastor's own approach to this task, and the actual process and methods of counselling by whomsoever it is done, to the spiritual resources available to counsellors in the specifically Christian context.

Part III describes in detail some of the situations in which pastors most frequently have to give counselling help: namely, in problems of marriage and family relationships, in times of sickness, in death and bereavement, and in matters of personal conscience, especially those which arise from the fundamental changes many people are facing today, not only in the social and economic conditions in which they live, but also in the generally accepted ideas of what is right and what is wrong.

Finally, in the Epilogue, we invite readers to sum up and evaluate what they have learnt in the course of studying with the Guide, and suggest some ways in which a pastor can judge the effectiveness of his counselling ministry.

CASE STUDIES AND EXAMPLES

The 65 detailed examples and case studies, mostly in Parts II and III, are without exception drawn from real-life experience, but all individuals described have been given fictitious names. Countries, tribal areas, etc. are specified only where the cultural or political background is relevant to the problem or counselling method under discussion. As many of these examples are relevant to more than one sort of situation, and some consist of lengthy conversations, we were at first undecided whether they should appear as interruptions in the text, or be placed all together as an Appendix. To avoid the inconvenience of continual reference to and fro they have been retained at appropriate points in the text and numbered serially throughout, with cross-references to other passages which they may help to elucidate. A complete list of these examples appears at the end of the book, briefly indicating the contexts to which they relate (p. 286).

SCRIPTURE REFERENCES

In Part III, as well as elsewhere in the Guide, references are given for passages of Scripture suggested as specially suitable for use in counselling. A complete list of these references appears on p. 283, classified according to the situations for which they are appropriate.

STUDY SUGGESTIONS

Questions and suggestions for review, research, and discussion appear at the end of each chapter. They are intended to help readers to understand clearly what they have read and to check their own progress, and especially to relate the ideas and issues raised to their own situation.

The best way to use these study suggestions is *first* to read the chapter carefully once or twice, and *then* do the work suggested, in writing or group discussion, without looking at the chapter again except where it is suggested that you should do so. Please note, however, that these suggestions are only *suggestions*. Some readers may not want to use them at all. Teachers may wish to select only those which are relevant to their particular need, and will almost certainly want to add or substitute questions for discussion or research that relate more directly to their local situation. For some of the longer chapters teachers may want to direct students to undertake some questions as they go along, rather than after completing the chapter.

The *Key* (p. 290) will enable readers to check their own work on those questions which can be checked in this way. In most cases the Key does not give the answer to a question: it simply shows where an answer is to be found.

INDEX

The Index (p. 299) includes only the main subjects which are discussed in the Guide.

QUOTATIONS

In some cases passages from the work of other authors have been condensed in order to save space, or paraphrased rather than quoted exactly when this seems likely to help readers using English as a second language.

BIBLE VERSION

Except where otherwise indicated, the English translation of the Bible used in this book is the Revised Standard Version Common Bible (Ecumenical Edition). Reference is also made to the New English Bible (NEB), Today's English Version or Good News Bible (TEV), Jerusalem Bible (JB), and Authorized or King James Version (AV) in cases where comparing translations can help to show the meaning of a Scripture passage more clearly.

FURTHER READING

Because cultural backgrounds and social customs vary so greatly from one part of the world to another, no attempt has been made to supply a comprehensive list of books for further reading that would be appropriate for all areas. In most places, however, readers are likely to find that the Churches have prepared books or reports on such subjects as marriage, healing, bereavement, and personal ethics, which relate specifically to the local situation.

Most of the volumes listed below, which deal with counselling generally or relate to a fairly wide geographical region, have been used as source material for this Guide, and readers may find it useful to study them in more detail. The first TEF Guide to Applied Theology, too – Al Krass's '*Go . . . and make Disciples*' – though chiefly concerned with Church growth and outreach, contains much that is directly relevant to the work of pastoral care.

Basic Types of Pastoral Counselling. H. Clinebell, Abingdon.
Christian Counselling – A Comprehensive Guide. G. Collins, Word.
Christian Marriage in Africa. A. Hastings, SPCK.

Culture and Human Values. J. A. Loewen, William Carey Library.
Family Counselling in East Asia. S. Southard, EACC, New Day Publishers, Manila.
Healing for You. B. Martin, Lutterworth.
The Healing Ministry in the Church. B. Martin, Lutterworth.
A Helping Hand. M. Brown, Africa Christian Press.
A History of the Cure of Souls. J. T. McNeill, Harper.
The Mental Health Ministry in the Local Church. H. Clinebell, Abingdon.
The Ministry in Historical Perspective. H. R. Niebuhr and D. D. Williams, Harper.
Pastoral Care in Historical Perspective. W. A. Clebsch and C. R. Jaekle, Harper.
Your Healing is Within You. J. Glennon, Hodder & Stoughton.
Christian Psychiatry. F. B. Minirth, Revell.
Biblical Perspectives on Counselling. R. Inwood, Grove Books.
I Married You. W. Trobisch, Inter-Varsity.
Christian Marriage and Family. John Patton and Brian H. Childs, Abingdon.
A Coat of Many Colours: Pastoral Studies in the Christian Way of Life. Michael Wilson, Epworth.
Learning to Care: Christian Reflection on Pastoral Practice. Michael H. Taylor, SPCK.
Love the Stranger: Christian Ministry in Multi-Faith Areas. Roger Hooker and Christopher Lamb, SPCK.
Still Small Voice: An Introduction to Pastoral Counselling. Michael Jacobs, SPCK.
Swift to Hear: Facilitating Skills in Listening and Reflecting. Michael Jacobs, SPCK.
Twenty Questions about Healing. Morris Maddocks, SPCK.

Introduction:
The Shepherd and the Flock

'VARIETIES OF SERVICE'

Jesus Himself used the idea of a caring shepherd looking after a flock, to describe His own relationship with His disciples and faithful followers (Luke 12.32; John 10.7–16), and also the relationship of the disciples and other leaders with all the members of the Church that was to come (John 21.15–17).

The idea was a familiar one to the people of Israel, most of whom owned or worked with flocks and herds of sheep, goats, and cattle; and it was widely used by writers of the Jewish Scriptures to describe religious and political leaders, and even God Himself. We shall look more closely, in chapter 1, at the ways in which this idea was developed in the Bible as a whole, and at the pattern of pastoral ministry to be seen in Jesus's own life and work. Then, as a background to our study of the pastoral ministry today, we go on, in chapter 2, to see how this same idea has been understood in the life of the Church through the centuries.

As St Paul told the Christians at Corinth, within the Church 'there are varieties of service . . . and there are varieties of working' (1 Cor. 12.4–6). The work of the ordained minister is an important one among these 'varieties'. Ordination is the rite by which a Church sets apart, as ordained ministers, people whom it believes to be specially gifted for a ministry of the Word and Sacraments, and for pastoral care of a congregation. When other Church leaders lay their hands on the ordinand's head, it means that he (or, in some Churches, she) is being 'set apart', and 'ordained', i.e. given authority by the Church, to carry out a particular ministry.

But this is not the only ministry or service in the Church. Unordained leaders and lay people also are involved in the service which the Church offers to God. This important point is sometimes forgotten, and then the ordained leader becomes the centre of all activities and takes the role of a 'director' who controls the Church, and is regarded as the 'boss' because he is paid to do this work for the congregation. In later chapters we shall show that the ordained leader is only one member in a team ministry, a fellowship of people who work *together* to carry out God's plan. *Everyone* in the Church has an important part to play.

However, this does not mean that the appointed or ordained leader has no special role. On the contrary, within the fellowship he or she has a very important task: namely, 'to equip the saints for the work of ministry, for building up the body of Christ' (Eph. 4.12).

In different Churches, different titles are used to describe this appointed leader. Three such titles commonly used are 'minister', 'pastor', and 'priest'. Each of these titles emphasizes a different aspect of the leader's work, and reflects the ideas about leadership held by each particular Church. Every Church needs some sort of ministry and organization if the Gospel is to be made known to people in an effective way. But God calls different people to different sorts of ministry: 'some apostles, some prophets, some evangelists, some pastors and preachers' (Eph. 4.11). So we should not be surprised to find many different ideas about how this special ministry developed, and what its special work is today. Questions about the selection, training, and ordaining of ministers, the extent of their authority, and the work they actually do, are answered in different ways according to the traditions of each particular Church, and the situation in which it is bearing its witness to the gospel.

In all Churches, however, there are four chief sorts of work that the leader in any congregation has to undertake, whatever title he is given and whichever aspect of his leadership is regarded as the most important. In the 4th century AD a great Christian leader, Chrysostom, in his writings 'On the Priesthood', described these four essential functions as follows:

1. The ordained leader has *sacramental* functions. He administers the saving rite of the sacraments. In baptism he signs and seals the adoption of new Christians into God's family of the Church; in the Lord's Supper he mediates the body and blood of Christ to a needy world. Chrysostom regarded this as the minister's most important task.

2. He has *disciplinary and administrative* functions. He must maintain the purity of the Church; administer discipline to unworthy members; judge disputes among Christians; and administer the Church's property.

3. He has a *teaching and evangelistic* function. He is the instructor of the people. He must oppose false teaching, and build up the faithful in their knowledge and understanding of the gospel, so that they in turn can proclaim the good news to others.

4. He has a *pastoral* function. He must be able to mingle with people from all walks of life. He must not confine himself to the work of sacraments and preaching. He must move among his people, and 'preside at all the great moments of human life', that is, he must be present and involved so as to bring the resources of the Christian faith to people at every stage and every crisis of their lives.

In this Guide we are chiefly concerned with the *pastoral* function, and especially the work of counselling and caring for those in need or distress of any kind.

Some Churches do not use the rite of ordination as such, yet they do appoint leaders whose work and position in the Church is much the same as that of ordained ministers. In this Guide we shall use the word 'pastor' to mean any person, ordained or unordained, who is recognized by the Church as a leader in carrying out its worship, and in administrative, preaching, teaching, caring, and counselling work. Such a leader may be the only person in a particular congregation who bears this responsibility – and may therefore have great authority over that congregation. Or he may share the responsibility with others, while still remaining as the recognized leader or 'first among equals'. He may work full-time as a pastor, or he may work part-time, and do some other job as well to help support himself and his family. We have chosen to use the title 'pastor' partly because it will remind us throughout our study of the 'shepherding' or 'pastoral care' emphasized by Jesus in His command to Peter: 'Tend my sheep' – and by Peter when he exhorted his fellow elders in the Church to 'tend the flock of God' (1 Pet. 5.2). And we also use it because it is a familiar word in many Churches. However, each reader must apply the title and the ideas it reflects to his own situation. If you are unaccustomed to the term 'pastor' – or 'ordained leader' or 'minister' – then think of the word or title normally used to mean 'leader of a congregation' in your own Church.

INTRODUCTORY EXERCISE:
AS YOU START YOUR STUDY

Before beginning to study the work of a pastor, readers may find it helpful to complete the following questions, basing their answers on their knowledge and experience. Some who study this book will have had many years of experience working in the Church, while others may just be starting their training. The length of experience does not matter. What is important is that you answer the questions from your own thinking at the present time. This will help you to clarify the ideas you already have on this subject before you begin to study some ideas which may be new to you. The questions assume that each reader will have had some experience of life in the Church, and this experience will be the foundation from which your answers to the questions can be given.

For all of the questions, *write down* your own answers, and for those in which you discuss your answer with other people, note also the important points of the discussion.

1. This question is about *your own experience* in the life of the Church.

(a) How long have you been part of the fellowship of the local Church, and in what ways have you been involved? Are you a full member? Do you attend services regularly? Or only occasionally? Have you been involved in any special activity in the congregation, e.g. as youth leader, prayer group member, chorister?

(b) As a result of sharing in the life of the Church, what do you think are the *good* points in your local Church which you have found helpful in your own life?

(c) What do you think are any *weak* points in your local Church which you would like to see improved?

2. This question is about *a pastor's work* in the Church. The following statements on this subject were made by a number of different people. Which of them do you agree with, and which do you disagree with? Think out your reasons for agreeing or disagreeing in each case. When you have finished the question, discuss your answer with at least one other person, and compare your ideas with theirs.

The statements are:

(a) A pastor is the leader responsible for the spiritual life of the Church. He should not have to worry about worldly matters like money and property.

(b) Every pastor needs a good training in a theological college before he can be effective in his work.

(c) There is no difference between a pastor who has been specially ordained and any other Church member who is not ordained. Each has a gift to use in serving the Church.

(d) Everyone is equal in the Church, and a pastor should not expect any special privileges because of his position.

(e) It is best to think of the pastor as the 'overall director' of all the affairs of the congregation.

(f) Most pastors are lazy and care more for getting their money than for caring for the people.

(g) Most pastors are not paid enough for the work they have to do.

3. This question is about *the work of lay people* in the Church.

The following statements were made by people who were discussing the role of lay people. As with Question 2, say whether you agree or disagree with each statement, and think out your reasons. Then discuss your answers with a friend, and compare your ideas.

(a) Pastors should give lay people more jobs to do, and should allow them to share more in the work of the Church. Most pastors do not want others to take any leadership role. They want to keep all the power for themselves.

(b) Most lay people are lazy about doing anything for the Church. They let the pastor do it all, because he is paid for it.

4

(c) There are three main things that lay people in the Church ought to do. They should support the work of the pastor by: (i) praying for him, (ii) giving money to help the Church, and (iii) attending the services regularly.

(d) The work of a pastor seems to be an out-of-date job today. A few years ago it was all right, but few well-educated people would choose it now. A person can do much better work for the Church as an ordinary lay member, because he can really understand what is going on in the world around him.

4. This question is a matter of *judgement*. In your experience you have probably seen both good points and bad points in the work of pastors and also heard other people's opinions on this subject. Use this experience to make two lists, one containing the good points, and the other the bad points commonly found in the work of pastors. Do not name any of the pastors whose work you describe, simply record your own experiences and views about it. When you have completed the lists, show them to another person from your own congregation, and also, if possible, someone from a different area. Discuss the lists with them, and compare and contrast your experiences and opinions with theirs.

5. This question is about *your own feelings* as you begin to study the work of a pastor. Write down your own feelings about yourself as a pastor or would-be pastor in the Church – your hopes, fears, doubts, problems. Then discuss what you have written with two other people – close friends or fellow-students.

6. This question gives you an opportunity to *sum up your own thinking* on some wider questions. Because the joint work of pastor and people is essential if the Church is to grow and develop, and to bear its witness in the world, all Christians, and especially pastors, need to be clear about the aim or purpose of the Church. In your experience, what is the Church really trying to do? How does the work of the Church relate to God's plan in the world today?

In Questions 2 and 3 you considered some other people's ideas about the work of the pastor and of lay people in the Church. In this question, clarify and summarize your own ideas on the subject by completing each of the following sentences:

(a) I think that the *main work of a pastor* is to:

(b) I think that the *main work of lay people* is to:

(c) The three words which best describe *my feelings* as I begin this course of study on the work of a pastor are:

(d) I see the *main task of the Church in the world* as a whole as:

(e) I see the *main task of my own Church* in the local situation as:

(f) The two words or ideas which I feel best describe or explain the meaning of the phrase '*the Church*' are:

7. This question concerns the ideas that *people outside the Church*

have about the work of Christian pastors and lay people. It is partly a research question.

(a) From your own experience, what do you think that most people of other religions (or of none) in your area think about the Church, and about the work of Christian ministers and lay people?

(b) Discuss your answer to (a) with one or two Christian friends or fellow students, and compare and contrast your experiences and ideas with theirs.

(c) *After* completing (a) and (b), try to find out from as many people of other religions as you can, what they really do think about the Church and its work in your area. If you can, persuade the friends with whom you discussed (a) to do the same, and compare results.

(d) How far were the answers given to Questions (a) and (b) correct, as compared with what you discovered that people of other religions *really* thought about the Church, when you came to ask them?

In the Epilogue at the end of this book it is suggested that you do this exercise over again, answering the questions in the light of your work on the Study Guide as a whole, and then compare your answers with those you have given at the beginning. So keep your present answers in a safe place till the time comes to compare them.

PART I
THE MINISTRY OF PASTORAL CARE

1

The 'Good Shepherd' Idea in the Bible

A WELL-KNOWN FIGURE

The shepherd is a well-known figure among many agricultural peoples, and in ancient Israel everyone understood what the work of a shepherd was. Flocks of sheep and goats were important possessions, just as they are in many countries today, and to have large flocks was a sign of wealth and status. The value of a sheep in those times was equal to the value today of, for example, a pig in Papua New Guinea, or a cow among the nomadic peoples of East Africa. The work of the shepherd in guiding, feeding, and protecting the flock was essential if the animals were to be productive and valuable for their owner.

This idea of the caring shepherd was so familiar and meaningful to the people of Israel that many preachers and writers used it, as we see in the New Testament as well as the Old Testament, as picture-language to describe not only human 'shepherds', but also the attitudes of God towards His people.

1. *In the Old Testament* this idea was used in three chief ways:

(a) It was used to describe the relationship between God and the people of Israel. 'He is our God, we are the people of his pasture, the sheep of his hand' (Ps. 95.6–7). 'He will feed his flock like a shepherd' (Isa. 40.11). It was used to show God as the *true* shepherd, who can be trusted never to fail His people; and as the shepherd who cares for each individual, not only the flock as a whole. 'I will seek out my sheep and rescue them . . . I will bring back the strayed . . . bind up the crippled . . . strengthen the weak . . . the fat and the strong I will watch over, I will feed them in justice' (see Ezek. 34.11–15). 'The Lord is my shepherd . . . He leads me . . . restores my soul' (Ps. 23).

(b) Secondly, the idea of the shepherd was used to describe the work of the religious and political leaders in Israel, whom God 'appointed to care for his people' and encourage them to keep His law. God had saved and protected the Israelites on their journey to the

7

promised land, and had made His will clear in the commandments He gave to Moses. But the way of obedience was not always easy. The people needed continuing instruction and care from human 'shepherds': the priests and prophets who led them in worship and taught and counselled them on religious and moral questions, and also the judges and kings who protected them from enemy nations and administered justice in the land. God continued to guide and strengthen these wise elders and leaders: 'The Lord gives wisdom; from his mouth come knowledge and understanding, he stores up sound wisdom for the upright, he is a shield to those who walk in integrity, guarding the paths of justice and preserving the way of his saints' (Prov. 2.6–8). 'Thou didst guide me with thy counsel . . . God is the strength of my heart' (Ps. 119.105).

But not all these leaders led the people in right ways. Among them were 'false prophets' and 'worthless shepherds', 'wise in their own conceit', 'who destroy and scatter the sheep of my pasture' instead of feeding and defending them (see Ezek. 13.3; 34.1–10; Jer. 23.1).

(c) It was in such times of trouble, when God's people were suffering defeat and oppression for lack of good leadership, that prophets like Isaiah and Jeremiah used the 'good shepherd' idea in yet another way. Believing that God would never wholly forsake His people, they looked forward expectantly to the coming of a new leader, the One True Shepherd (Ezek. 4.23), the 'righteous Branch' who would 'execute justice and righteousness in the land' (Jer. 23.5), 'feed his flock and gather the lambs in his arms' (Isa. 40.11). It was as a shepherd as well as a princely ruler that the prophets foresaw the coming of Jesus, the Messiah who would save and redeem God's people (see Micah 5.2–4).

2. *In the New Testament* the idea of the shepherd is chiefly used in two ways.

(a) As we have already seen, Jesus used it for Himself: 'I am the Good Shepherd' who 'calls his own sheep by name . . . and the sheep follow him, for they know his voice.' And 'I am the door of the sheep . . . if anyone enters by me he shall be saved' (see John 10.1–16). The writer to the Hebrews, too, referred to Jesus as 'the great shepherd of the sheep', who overcomes death, having been 'brought again from the dead by the blood of the eternal covenant' (Heb. 13.20), i.e., through His willingness to lay down His life for the sheep.

(b) Again, as in the Old Testament, the idea was used to describe the human leaders of 'the flock of God'. The risen Jesus Himself commanded Peter, on whom He said He would found His Church, to:'feed my lambs . . . tend my sheep' (Matt. 16.18; John 21.15, 16). Paul warned the elders of the Church at Ephesus, 'take heed to yourselves and to the flock, in which the Holy Spirit has made you overseers' (Acts 20.28), and Peter exhorted the leaders of the Churches in Asia Minor to tend the congregations in their charge 'willingly . . . eagerly . . . being examples to the flock' (1 Pet. 5.2, 3).

THE WORK OF THE SHEPHERD

The meaning of this picture-language may not always be clear to people who live in countries where there are no sheep or other herds, or who live in towns and large urban centres. We can only fully understand it if we consider what a shepherd actually does.

In any situation the main tasks of a shepherd or other herdsman are:

1. He guides his flock to good pastures and safe resting places (see Isa. 40.11).

2. He feeds the sheep and provides for all their needs, seeing that they have water to drink and keeping the sheepfold in good repair (see Ps. 23).

3. He guards his flock and protects it from wild animals, or thieves, or other dangers, even when this involves danger to himself (see 1 Sam. 17.34).

4. He searches for any sheep that strays or gets lost, until he finds it, even if this means going into difficult and dangerous places, however dark the night or bad the weather (see Matt. 18.12).

5. He knows and names each sheep individually, so that they too know his voice and follow when he calls (see John 10.1–4).

6. He carefully tends any sheep that are sick or weakly, and takes especial care of the nursing ewes and young lambs (see Gen. 33.13).

Thus we see that being a shepherd means taking a deep personal interest in the welfare of the flock as a whole and of each individual sheep in the flock. It calls for strength and courage, patience and self-sacrifice. The good shepherd must always put the welfare of the flock before his own comfort, even when this means losing sleep, and facing personal danger or even death.

The work of the leaders in the early Church was modelled on this pattern. It included *feeding* the new Christians with the truth; *protecting* them against error and false teaching; *caring* for the needy and distressed; *encouraging* those who had become half-hearted in their faith; keeping *order* and *discipline*; giving *guidance* and *spiritual direction* (see John 21.15–17; Acts 20.28–31; 1 Thess. 5.2–15; 2 Tim. 4.1–5). All these activities are summed up in the idea of '*tending the flock of God*' (1 Pet. 5.2).

FALSE PROPHETS AND WORTHLESS SHEPHERDS

In both the Old Testament and the New Testament, however, we find accusations against 'shepherds' who oppressed and exploited the people, or led them astray with false teaching, instead of doing their work properly. Why were they condemned so strongly?

In Israel shepherds had certain privileges. In return for the responsibility of tending and guarding the flock, they were allowed a share of the milk and wool (1 Cor. 9.5). But some shepherds were eager to take these privileges, while refusing to accept their responsibilities (Ezek. 34.2, 3). In the same way, some of the leaders exploited the people as a means of making profits for themselves, and refused to offer guidance, help, and protection in return. This led to injustice, oppression, and suffering. Ezekiel saw the people as weak, sick, injured, misled, and lost because of this failure of the leaders to carry out their duties properly. Even the strong were enslaved and preyed upon (Ezek. 34.4–6). As the writer Walter Eichrodt puts it, the office of leader or shepherd was clearly 'a very onerous and responsible vocation, requiring unwearying vigilance and readiness for sacrifice. Yet the shepherds of Israel have not only failed to show self-sacrifice in protecting and providing for those in need of their care, but have violently trodden down the stronger sheep, which would otherwise be the pride of the flock, i.e. they have overworked them and taken advantage of them for their own profit.'

Ezekiel warned these corrupt leaders and false prophets that God Himself would 'put a stop' to their shepherding, and rescue the sheep that they had ruled with 'force and harshness' (see Ezek. 34.4, 5, 10). Jeremiah prophesied 'woe to the shepherds who destroy and scatter the sheep', saying that God would cast them away from His presence and would bring them to 'everlasting reproach and perpetual shame' (Jer. 23.1, 39, 40).

In the New Testament, also, there are accusations against leaders who behaved more like 'robbers and thieves', than caring shepherds. Jesus contrasted with the behaviour of a true shepherd, that of a hireling, who neglects the flock and looks after himself. The hireling did not care for the sheep as his own, and was chiefly interested in getting his wages. It seems that Jesus was quoting from the words of Ezekiel in referring to His own work as that of the 'true shepherd'. And like Ezekiel Jesus was denouncing the religious leaders of His time for oppressing and exploiting the people, and leading them astray.

A little later, too, in the early Christian congregations, some of the leaders failed to care for the people as shepherds should. Peter warned against wrong ideas of leadership (see 1 Pet. 5.2, 3). Some leaders were half-hearted, unwilling to give their whole time and energy to their work, or working only because they were forced to do so. Some even used their position as leaders, not to serve others, but for their own gain. Some dominated and lorded it over the common people, rather than being good examples to them.

On several occasions Paul found it necessary to warn the Churches of the danger of being led by 'false apostles and deceitful workmen' (2 Cor. 11.13), or 'false brethren' (Gal. 2.4), or 'the dogs . . . the evil workers' (Phil. 3.2), or those who would 'make a prey of you by philosophy and empty deceit' (Col. 2.8).

So it seems there is always a danger that those whom God calls to 'tend the flock' will fail in their task unless they honestly try to follow the pattern of the *true* 'good shepherd' as set by Jesus Himself.

THE PATTERN SET BY JESUS

The life and ministry of Jesus is *the* pattern for individual Christians, for the life of the Church as a whole, and especially for the life and work of leaders in the Church. Jesus was not only the carrier and bringer of the message; He was *Himself* the message. By His way of living, by the qualities of His character, by His compassion and readiness to come close to people in their need, Jesus set a pattern for His followers. All Christians in the fellowship of the Church are called to be a living expression of these same attitudes, to be 'living letters for everyone to know and read' (2 Cor. 3.1–3, TEV).

As Lord and Master, Jesus was also Servant. Unlike other leaders of His day, Jesus put a new meaning into the idea of leadership. He lived to *serve* those whom He led, not to be served by them (Mark 10.45). So He set a new pattern for all forms of Christian ministry. He can be truly described as the 'servant shepherd' (Luke 22.25–27; John 13.13–16). He told His disciples that they too, and all His followers, were called to be servants (Mark 10.42–44) – servants of Christ Himself (1 Cor. 4.1), servants of God (1 Cor. 3.5), and servants of other people (2 Cor. 4.5). The highest meaning of life is to be found in service of this sort.

In His own life and ministry Jesus showed very clearly what being a 'servant' means. He did so in two chief ways: (a) by the very fact of His incarnation, that is, by being one with people and sharing in the lives of those He came to seek and save; and (b) in His attitudes, that is in the way He behaved towards people.

BEING ONE WITH PEOPLE

Jesus shared fully in the ordinary life and customs of His time. He truly became human, He was not simply pretending. He took the nature of a servant, becoming a man and taking part in the normal patterns of human life. 'He was humble, and walked the path of obedience to death' (Phil. 2.7, TEV). As a servant, Jesus did not keep Himself apart from the needs and burdens that human beings experience. He came

Many preachers and writers used the idea of the caring shepherd to illustrate the pattern set by Jesus for the life and work of leaders in the Church (see p. 7. So did many artists, like the sculptor who carved this figure on a stone coffin in the third century AD.

and lived among men and women (John 1.14). He was like His 'brothers', i.e. the people He lived with, in every way excepting that He did not follow ways which commonly lead to sin (Heb. 2.14–17). As a man He felt temptation (Heb. 2.14, 18). He experienced joy and sorrow, hunger, pain, anger, tiredness, disappointment (see John 2.1–11; 11.33–36). He enjoyed the fellowship of His disciples and close friends. He shared in the deepest possible way in the lives of those around Him, and He knew how and why people thought and acted as they did (John 2.25). But this knowledge of their weakness and sin did not make Him draw back from complete involvement with them. He trusted completely in God as the caring Creator and loving Father, and He knew that love and goodness would conquer sin and death. But this confidence did not stop Him from being a true Jew, a man of Nazareth, a young man who had to die. He has been called 'the man for others', who lived and died so that others might live in freedom and joy. When the risen Jesus prepared His disciples for their mission in the world by endowing them with the Holy Spirit, He told them 'As the Father has sent me, even so I send you' (John 20.21, 22). The pattern of ministry set by Jesus is a ministry of 'incarnation', of 'becoming one with men', a ministry of identification and involvement. Jesus sends His followers into the world, in the same way, to be identified with, and involved in, the life of the people with whom they live and work.

JESUS'S ATTITUDES TOWARDS PEOPLE

It is not possible for human beings to understand fully the character, life, and ministry of Jesus. Even after the most careful study, scholars confess that they cannot plumb the depths or 'get to the bottom of' Jesus Christ. He remains a mystery. But we can understand enough about Him to recognize some of the ways in which He calls His followers to imitate the example He has set. Christians acknowledge Jesus as a master of human relationships. His attitudes towards people give a deeper meaning to the work of a 'servant shepherd', and provide a model for the ministry of pastoral care today, and at all times. And Jesus is more than just a good example from long ago. He provides living inspiration and energy to help His followers show the same sort of attitudes that He showed, in their own relationships with others.

The following summary points to some of the attitudes in Jesus's ministry that pastors today may want to imitate. It does not exhaust or complete the full picture of who and what Jesus was.

1. *Jesus showed a deep concern* that people should live the best and fullest sort of life. He was equally concerned with obedience to God's will and with everything that affects people's lives. Obedience to God is linked with the freedom of every human being. Jesus's mission is to set men and women free from all that enslaves and oppresses them, not

13

to tie them up in a rigid system of written rules (see Luke 4.16–21; and also Isa. 61.1, 2).

All the same, as Jesus told the people, He had not come to abolish the law of Moses, but to fulfill it (Matt. 5.17). In His teaching, Jesus went beyond that law. He showed that what is important is not a slavish obedience to the 'letter' of any particular rule or commandment which God gave as an example of how He intends people to live. What is important is the *attitude* of loving obedience to God's will, and loving concern for other people, which alone can enable men and women to live in that way (Acts 14.38, 39). Jesus freely interpreted some of the particular Jewish laws, for example about the Sabbath (Mark 2.23–35). And again and again He showed His hearers that He was teaching them the true meaning of the Law, with the words: 'You have heard that it was said, "you shall not . . .". *But I say to you . . .*' (see Matt. 5.21–28; 22.35–40).

2. *Jesus felt a deep compassion for all people*, especially those who were 'harassed and helpless' (Matt. 9.35, 36), and 'adrift' in their lives. Compassion towards others is 'feeling great pity for' those in need (Matt. 15.32; Mark 1.40–42).

3. *Jesus's compassion was blended with authority*. His concern for people led Him to speak clearly and strongly about their true needs. He spoke and taught with authority (Matt. 7.28, 29). He criticized and corrected people when this was necessary, but He did it with compassion, and never used His authority as a 'club' to beat people with.

4. *Jesus accepted people as they were*. To 'accept' a person is to recognize that person's worth *as a person*, whether or not one agrees with their ideas or approves of their behaviour. Jesus did not approve of wrong behaviour, but He did not let His condemnation of people's wrong behaviour get in the way of His loving relationship with them, or prevent Him from helping them. He helped the woman caught in the sin of adultery, and at the same time warned her, 'sin no more' (John 8.1–11). He spoke out honestly to people about their sinful ways, and because He loved and accepted them He was able to help and heal anyone who truly wanted His help. Jesus was the friend of people of all classes, some outcasts and sinners (Luke 15.1, 2), some rich and powerful. So He was able to accept, befriend, and help many different sorts of people – the prostitute (Luke 7.36–50), the despised tax-collector (Luke 19.1–10), the beggar (Luke 18.35–43), the upper class religious leader (John 3.1–10). He saw *value* in every person. To Him, no person was without worth, even when others regarded them as useless (Matt. 10.29–33; Luke 12.7). To help people, he broke through all the barriers of race, sex, and social class.

5. *Jesus was impartial*, that is, He did not favour any particular

person or group. He was not more friendly with the rich upper classes or with the influential leaders than He was with poor and unimportant people. He felt at ease with everyone, rich and poor, old and young, from the highest to the lowest ranks of society (Matt. 8.10–14).

6. *Jesus made Himself available* to people in need. He made time to help them even when He was very tired or busy Himself (Mark 1.32–34). He accepted interruptions to His programme with good will (Mark 5.21–40). Yet He also balanced this being available with a disciplined use of time, and often withdrew from the crowds who were besieging Him, in order to pray and meditate, and also to give special instruction to His disciples (Mark 1.35–39; 6.30–32; Luke 11.1–4).

7. *Jesus gave great importance to helping and counselling individuals.* In His early ministry, Jesus's preaching was very popular. He was followed about by crowds waiting to hear His message, and His fame spread far and wide so that He 'could not openly enter a town but was out in the country, and the people came to him from every quarter' (see Mark 1.40–45; 2.2, 13; 3.7–9, 19, 20). However, even when Jesus spoke to the crowds He applied His message to the people's individual needs (Mark 4.1–9), and He seems to have preferred ministering to individuals or to small groups. Most of His parables are concerned with the spiritual problems that individuals experience. Jesus showed that each person is so important to God that 'there will be more joy in Heaven over one sinner who repents than over ninety-nine righteous . . .' (see Luke 15.3–7).

8. *Jesus used different methods in helping different sorts of people.* He did not approach people in one way only. A method He often used in guiding and helping people was *dialogue*, or personal conversation, using questions skilfully to discover the basic problems in people's lives. In this way He was like other philosophers; the Greek thinker, Socrates, for example, used a similar question-and-answer method. But Jesus differed from those thinkers of His time who believed that the intellectual understanding of truth was mankind's most important achievement. Such a belief often limited their dialogue and questioning to the 'head-level' only; that is, it concerned people's *ideas* rather than their aims, feelings, or behaviour. Jesus, on the other hand, directed His questions and conversation to people's whole being – their emotions and personal relationships as well as their ideas. He showed that if people are to live in accordance with God's will, then understanding with the mind must be matched by obedience from the heart. The rich young man who came to Him had an intellectual understanding of the law and he kept the rules, but this was not linked with loving obedience or self-sacrifice in his actual living (Mark 10.17–22). Jesus was able to bring change and transform people, not just by showing errors in their thinking, but by bringing them to repent

15

and commit themselves to the commands of the Kingdom of God (see Matt. 4.17–22; Luke 19.1–10).

A large part of Jesus's method of dialogue was careful *listening*. Often He listened when people expected Him to speak. Many of His parables gained their meaning and force because He ended with a question and then listened while people worked out their own interpretation. When a lawyer asked Jesus how to gain eternal life, instead of giving an answer, Jesus turned the question back to him: 'What is written in the law?'. Then He listened while the man gave the answer for himself (Luke 10.25, 26).

Jesus often urged those whom He taught to 'hear and understand'. Especially when He was training His disciples for their own ministry, He emphasized that people hear, but usually do not listen carefully enough to understand (Mark 7.14–23; 8.14–18).

9. *Jesus was quick to offer encouragement and praise*, especially when He discovered hidden spiritual qualities in people, like the centurion's unquestioning trust and obedience, or the humble faith of the Syro-phoenician woman (Matt. 8.5–13; 15.21–28). He did not praise people to gain their favour, nor to hide their faults. He gave honest praise to people whose actions deserved commendation, and equally honest criticism to those whose faults prevented them from truly knowing or doing God's will. He was especially critical of spiritual hypocrisy like that of the scribes and Pharisees, who kept all the detailed rules for religious observance, but 'neglected the weightier matters of the law, justice and mercy and faith' (Matt. 23.13–28).

10. *Jesus saw a very close connection between the healing of the body and the healing of the soul*. He was not concerned *only* with people's spiritual needs, nor *only* with their physical needs for healing and food. He healed people in order to make them *whole* in body, mind, and spirit. He called for faith in His ability to give both physical and spiritual healing: 'which is easier, to say, "your sins are forgiven" or to say "rise and walk"? But that you may know that the Son of man has authority on earth to forgive sins' – He then said to the paralytic – 'Rise, take up your bed and go home' (Matt. 9.5, 6). Jesus exercised His divine power in both these areas of need. He emphasized the importance of spiritual health, as when He told Nicodemus 'You must be born anew' (see John 3.1–10); and also the connection between physical well-being and spiritual rest and peace: 'Come to me, all who labour and are heavy-laden . . . and you will find rest to your souls' (Matt. 11.28–30).

The New Testament record of the life and ministry of Jesus shows that His power was sufficient to heal people's troubled lives. Today it is still true that the divine grace and energy available to us through faith in Jesus is sufficient to renew and recreate our lives if we will trust ourselves to Him. As the theologian Gerhard Kittel wrote: 'He was not scribe, and not rabbi; not teacher or master of wisdom; what men discovered in Him was exactly this – the healer of souls'.

The attitudes of Jesus that we have described in this chapter do not give a complete explanation of all the pastoral qualities He showed in His ministry. But they are examples of the *pattern* of care we find in all He said and did. From the ministry of Jesus we can discover the basic attitudes that are needed for effective pastoral care and counselling today. As the servant shepherd, Jesus is the model whom all Christians involved in the work of caring for others must try to follow. As Paul said, 'Have this mind among you, which is yours in Christ Jesus . . . taking the form of a servant' (Phil. 2.5, 7). The pattern that Christ sets is not just a vague ideal. Through the work of the Holy Spirit it can become a reality in the lives of His followers who commit themselves to His service and the service of others in the world today.

STUDY SUGGESTIONS

WORD STUDY

1. What do you understand by each of the following words?
   pastor   incarnation   pattern
2. 'Some shepherds were eager to take these privileges, but refused to accept their responsibilities' (p. 10).
   (a) Which four of the following words have the same or nearly the same meaning as 'privilege'?
       principle   favour   benefit   privacy   right   advantage   handicap   priority
   (b) Which four of the following words have the same or nearly the same meaning as 'responsibilities'?
       duties   benefits   obligations   interests   respects   concerns   necessities   tasks
3. Which of the following words would you choose if you were asked to describe what is meant by 'involving oneself' with people?
   caring   disciplining   sympathizing   directing   guiding   sharing   evaluating   teaching   mixing   loving
4. Which of the following phrases mean the *opposite* of 'being impartial' to others?
   treating people fairly; accepting a bribe; favouring your own tribe or group; sharing equally with others; refusing to help anyone at all; seeing that justice is given to all; hearing all points of view in an argument; helping only those who can return your help.

REVIEW OF CONTENT

5. Describe the work of a shepherd or other herdsman and the qualities needed to do that work properly.
6. What do you see as the chief difference between a true and a 'worthless' shepherd?
7. In what chief ways was Jesus *like* other teachers and philosophers of His time, and in what chief ways was He different from such teachers?
8. Describe what happens when someone uses the 'dialogue' method in teaching.

BIBLE STUDY

9. Read Luke 4.16–21, and then give examples from everyday life of what it should mean today for a pastor to
   (a) proclaim release to the captives,
   (b) offer recovery of sight to the blind,
   (c) set free the oppressed,
   (d) preach good news to the poor.
10. (a) According to the following passages, in what chief ways did Jesus share in the human life and culture of His time?
    (b) In what chief ways was Jesus different from the people of His time?
    Luke 2.40–52; John 2.1–11; John 4; John 11.33–36; Hebrews 2.14–17.
11. What sorts of people did Jesus consort with, according to each of the following passages, and what were His attitudes towards them?
    (a) Mark 8.2   (b) Mark 10.17–22   (c) Matthew 8.10–13
    (d) Matthew 19.27–34   (e) Luke 15.8–10   (f) John 4.1–15.
12. According to 1 Peter 5.2–5, what three attitudes are chiefly necessary for the good shepherding of God's people in the Church? How far do you think those same attitudes are necessary for the work of pastoral care today?

APPLICATION, OPINION, AND RESEARCH

13. (a) What are the chief 'responsibilities' undertaken by pastors in your own Church today?
    (b) What are the chief 'privileges' that pastors enjoy in your Church today?
14. What answer would you give to someone who said 'Jesus lived so long ago that I can't see how His example can be of help to people living today. Things are completely different now, and we face completely different problems.'?

18

15. The Church has been described as 'a community patterned after the servant King'. Do you think this is a good description of the congregation to which you belong? Give reasons for your answer.

16. 'Jesus was impartial in His attitudes to people. He did not favour any particular person or group' (p. 14). After reading this paragraph one student said: 'But Jesus did choose a special group of disciples. He spent more time with them than He did with anyone else and gave them special training. And John seems to have thought that Jesus loved him more than the others.' Another student said: 'Jesus told the Canaanite woman that His mission was only to the people of Israel, and He charged His disciples not to go to the Gentiles.' Both students thought those examples show that Jesus was not impartial, and even had favourites. What is your opinion?

17. Imagine that as a pastor you are asked to visit the following three people who need counselling:
    (a) the headmaster of a high school, whose educational qualifications are much higher than your own;
    (b) a lorry driver who works for the local government council and who often gets drunk;
    (c) a mother of three children who comes from an area (and perhaps a tribal group) different from your own.
    How would you feel about visiting each of these people? Would you prefer to visit one rather than the others? Discuss your answers with a friend or fellow student.

18. Are there any groups of people, or individuals, whom you find it difficult to 'accept'? If so *why* do you find them difficult? Again discuss your answer with a fellow student, or, if you can, a pastor.

2

Pastoral Care in the Church

Because the modern pastor or other Church leader belongs to the Christian community, he has the privilege of sharing in a very long history. He comes from a long line of Christian 'ancestors'. Every Christian is part of the wide family of God's 'household', the Church (1 Tim. 3.15; Eph. 2.19). And the fellowship of the Church is like a very big extended family system, a family which reaches across tribal, racial, geographical, and cultural divisions. In extended family systems, even more than in the 'nuclear' family system now common in the West, the present generation is seen to be linked with past generations of relatives and ancestors. The wisdom of the past is available for those living today, and those who lived in the past are believed to retain their interest and concern for those living in the present.

Christian teaching about the communion of saints can bring similar help and encouragement to Christians living at the present time. Christians who have lived before should not be thought of as finished and gone, but rather as 'the great cloud of witnesses' who surround the present-day Church (Heb. 12.1). From the wisdom of those who have served Christ and are now living in His presence, Christians living on earth today can learn much that will help them in their work.

Unfortunately many writers of Church history deal chiefly with its doctrinal, political, and social aspects – i.e. the *organization* of the Church, its relations with the government, its internal disputes about ideas and beliefs, etc. Such writers have paid little attention to the continuing pastoral role of the Church in the community, and so have given the impression that pastoral care was not being done, or was not considered important. But this is not true. Though there were disputes about doctrine, and new ways of running Church affairs were being developed, the work of pastoral care was still being carried on. As the following examples of the work of a pastor from different periods in the history of the Church will show, pastoral care has always been seen as one of the basic tasks of the people of God.

THE EARLY CHURCH AND THE MEDIEVAL CHURCH

The growth of the ministry in the centuries after Christ is very complicated, with the development of various ministerial 'orders', such as bishops, priests, and deacons. The way in which these various orders of ministry developed in different parts of the Church is a special study in itself. In this Guide we are chiefly concerned with the sort of work which the minister or pastor was expected to perform.

We have already noted (p. 2) Chrysostom's analysis of the work of the ordained leader, including in particular 'the cure of souls' or pastoral care. One important example of this sort of work was given at about that same time by St Augustine of Hippo, one of the great bishops of the Church. As a bishop, Augustine was responsible for the wellbeing of the Church in a very large area, so he had to supervise the work of many priests and leaders of congregations. Augustine said that the pastor must be ready to help the following sorts of people in the following ways:

disturbers are to be rebuked,

the *low-spirited* (that is, the unhappy or sorrowful) are to be encouraged,

the *infirm* are to be supported,

objectors (this probably means those who opposed true teaching) are to be confuted,

those *eager to serve Christ but unskilled*, are to be taught properly,

those *lazy in the service of the Church* are to be aroused and awakened,

those who are *contentious* (wanting to argue all the time) are to be treated with patience,

the *proud* are to be shown the path of humble service,

the *oppressed* are to be set free,

the *good* are to be approved and encouraged,

the *evil* are to be 'borne with', and treated with patience and care,

all people, whoever and whatever they are, are to be loved.

During the thousand years that followed, the four functions of the pastor as described by Chrysostom continued, some of them being given more emphasis than others. Other sorts of work were gradually added and developed, for example business functions, as the Church acquired more land and buildings; wider administrative functions, as the number of congregations increased; and some civil and political functions relating to government and commerce, as the Church gained wealth and power and its influence spread. The pastoral function continued, but it cannot be said that pastoral care was always carried out effectively. In some periods it was considered important, and the clergy looked after their congregations well. But at other times between AD 500 and 1500, it was much neglected, and very little compassion and concern for the needy was shown. Often the only real help was provided by the monks, who cared for orphans and travellers, and the sick, the poor, and the hungry. Reforms and revivals were needed to bring about a true pastoral concern for the masses of people in the Church.

One factor which affected the work of the ministry during this long period was the development of the idea that priests were somehow *different* from the rest of God's people. Because of their ordination and their sacramental and disciplinary functions, priests came to be regarded not only as 'set apart' for special work, but as actually 'separated' in kind from those who were not ordained. This idea had arisen quite early in the history of the Church. Gregory of Nyssa, writing at about the same time as Chrysostom, said: 'The same power of the Word makes the priest venerable and honourable, separated. While yesterday he was one of the mass, one of the people, now he is suddenly transformed into a guide, a president, a teacher of righteousness, an instructor in hidden mysteries, raised in respect of his unseen soul to a higher condition.'

As the centuries passed, and the Church grew in political, economic, and spiritual power, the ordained clergy gained a position of great authority. By the thirteenth century they were responsible only to the Pope, and not to any control by lay people. They were free from judgement by the normal civil courts. If they did wrong they were judged by other Church leaders only, and lay people had no say in the way priests did their work. The idea that there was a great difference between clergy and laity became very strong, and was reflected in various practices that grew up, differentiating between them. Some of these were:

At the service of the Lord's Supper the clergy stood, but the people kneeled,

the clergy received the bread and the wine, but the laity received the wine only, not the bread,

it gradually became customary for the clergy to be celibate (i.e. not permitted to marry); new laws against marriage for priests were introduced, and lay people were regarded as inferior in holiness, because they were of course allowed to marry,

the clergy began to dress in a distinctive way which set them apart from the laity.

Thus the priests became a separate 'order' from the rest of God's people. They were the 'rectors' or 'rulers', exercising their authority through control of the teaching and sacramental functions within the Church, and the ordinary believers were regarded almost as their 'subjects'. As this distinction between clergy and laity became clearer, the laity became passive supporters and followers of the very powerful ordained leaders, for whom Chrysostom's four 'priestly functions' were reserved. Many of the leaders neglected the real needs and wishes of the laity, to whom they simply dispensed what seemed like 'magical' formulas for salvation.

THE REFORMATION AND AFTER

With the Reformation of the Church in the 15th and 16th centuries, a new understanding of the ministry developed. The rules about celibacy, and other differences which separated the clergy and laity, were ended in many parts of the Church, and the ordained leaders began to live more closely with their people.

Martin Luther, the leader of the Reformation in Germany, stressed the doctrine of the universal priesthood of all believers, thus doing away with the distinctions between clergy and laity. According to Luther's teaching, every believer in the gospel is a priest, that is, one who mediates the gospel to others. Every believer must pass on the power of Christ which has come into his own life. He must express his faith in loving action, and in this way communicate it to others. In this sense, Luther said, all Christians are 'ministers': 'God has placed His Church in the midst of the world among countless undertakings and callings, in order that Christians should not be monks, but live with one another in social fellowship and manifest among men the works and practices of faith. . . . We are all priests, in so far as we are Christians, but those whom we call priests are ministers selected from our midst to act in our name, and their priesthood is our ministry.'

The leaders of the Reformation often spoke of the ordained minister as 'pastor', but the title they chiefly used was 'preacher'. It was not until the 18th century that the title 'pastor' came to be widely used. This suggests that many people regarded preaching as more important than pastoral care. This may have been true, although many of the leading reformers, including Martin Luther, John Calvin, and Martin Bucer, stressed the need for ministers to give good pastoral care to the people.

In 1656 *Richard Baxter*, a Puritan minister of the Reformed Church, wrote a book called *The Reformed Pastor*, in which he described many of the tasks the clergy ought to undertake. Baxter emphasized the need for a ministry to individual people and family groups as well as to the congregation as a whole. Those who are not Christians, he said, are not to be neglected. Those strong in the faith are to be further strengthened and encouraged. Those weak or lazy, or who have turned away from their faith, are to be given special attention, and should be helped to repent and start again. The sick are to be given constant care, and the dying visited before the time of death is near. Those who have broken the laws of the Church are to be given helpful discipline – first in private, then, if there is no response, other leaders must be asked to help them. If they still refuse to repent, they must be expelled from the Church. But if they do repent from wrong ways, they are to be joyfully restored to the fellowship.

As well as describing the pastoral care and oversight of others, Baxter also wrote about the pastor's private life, i.e. his oversight of himself: 'we [that is pastors] have the same sins to kill, and the same graces to be quickened as our people have; we have greater works than they to do, and greater difficulties to overcome, and therefore we have need to be warned and awakened as well as they.'

Baxter suggested that all pastors should try to ensure that the work of saving grace is really effective in their own lives. They should not rest on their past experiences of God's grace, but keep on growing. They should be careful about their own lives so that their example does not contradict their teaching. The work of a pastor is a special work, not to be treated lightly, so a very high standard is required of anyone wishing to serve as a pastor. 'He that does not delight in holiness; who does not hate iniquity; who does not love the unity and purity of the Church; who does not oppose arguments and divisions; who takes no pleasure in the public worship of God with his people and the fellowship of God's people – this person is not fit to be a pastor of a Church.'

In Baxter's time the main tasks included in pastoral care were seen as teaching and instructing people in the faith; disciplining Church members; visiting people, especially those in need; and counselling those with problems and difficulties in their lives. Baxter was careful to stress that the pastoral office involved much more than just preaching and administering the sacraments. Preaching was important, but by itself was not enough. 'One word of wise advice given by a minister to persons in necessity may be of more use than many sermons. . . . A minister is not to be just a public speaker, but to be known as a counsellor for their souls, as the physician is for their bodies.'

Another protestant leader, John Wesley, founder of the Methodist Church, who lived in the 18th century, wrote about the pastoral work of the appointed leader. He urged Methodist teachers, many of whom were not recognized as ordained ministers, to visit regularly each person in their care; to pay special attention to the needs of children; to encourage the head of each family to accept the responsibility of training children in the faith; to organize meetings for fellowship; to test themselves as to their own faith and love; and to continue studying and reading so as to increase their understanding of how to help others.

Like Baxter, Wesley stressed that anyone undertaking the pastoral care of others must understand his own life and character. He recognized that pastoral care was very demanding work, calling for the very best that any man could give. Wesley himself was a skilful and forceful preacher, and he gave an important place to the work of preaching. But he was equally concerned about the work of caring for others. As he wrote to a friend: 'Oh what it is to have a cure of souls.

24

'John Wesley was himself a skilled and forceful preacher' – as William Hamilton's portrait of him suggests – 'but he was equally concerned about the work of caring for others' (p. 24).

'Chrysostom described these four essential functions of the leader . . . including in particular the 'cure of souls' or pastoral care. . . . During the thousand years that followed, the four functions continued' (pp. 2 and 21). And Chrysostom's teaching continued to be remembered, as shown by this twelfth-century mosaic portrait of him in the cathedral at Cefalu in Sicily.

You and I are called to this – to save souls from death, and to watch over them, as workmen that must give an account to God for our work. If our work meant no more than preaching a few times in a week, I could play with it and so could you.'

In saying this, Wesley was not trying to make preaching seem less important; he was trying to point out the heavy responsibility of caring for people in need.

The words and ideas of leaders like Chrysostom, Augustine, Baxter, and Wesley have continued to be of value long after they were written, because they deal with people's real situations and needs, and they suggest ways of helping people in times of trouble. Many of their ideas have been passed on by missionaries to pastors in the Churches which have grown up around the world in the last hundred years. And although some of these ideas and thought-forms refer to situations that differ from those we know today, many of their underlying principles are still very relevant. Nevertheless, many pastors today are asking: Is it possible to apply these ideas to the work of pastoral care today? Do the basic principles they embody still hold valid for a modern pastor?

CAN WE USE THE IDEAS OF PAST LEADERS?

Times have changed, and while it is certainly true that we *can* learn much from the past, we must be careful not to limit ourselves to the ideas of past times and other cultures than our own. In many countries, ideas about pastoral care and methods of helping people have developed and changed very quickly in recent years, as a result of social and economic changes which have affected the ways in which people live and think.

In the industrial countries of the West, for example, new ideas about pastoral care have arisen as a result of:

(a) The development of new 'sciences', such as sociology, psychology, and mental health, and new methods of social welfare in helping people in need.

(b) New living situations caused by the great rise in standards of living, so that many more people have more money to spend, and more leisure to spend it; by the power of radio and TV to mould people's thinking; and by new methods of transport which bring people closer together.

(c) A great decline in church attendance and religious belief, and a consequent loss of confidence in pastors as helpers in time of need.

(d) At the same time, a new understanding of the Church and its ministry, in which the Church is seen as a working group, a people, the family of God, rather than a 'power structure' with the ordained leaders at the centre ruling over a 'faceless mass' of ordinary Church members.

(e) Recognition of the work of a pastor as one work among that of other 'helping professions', in the community, alongside doctors, magistrates, police, nurses, teachers and many others who contribute to the overall work of caring for people. The pastor has a special role to play, but he is no longer regarded as the only person who can give help and counsel to Christians in need.

In many developing countries of the so-called Third World, pastors have followed the traditional patterns taught by missionaries. But it is also true that many pastors in such countries have developed their own patterns of work which are more truly relevant to their cultural situations. Today, however, many changes, both within the Church and in the community at large, have made it necessary to develop new ideas and methods. For example:

(a) The status of the pastor has declined in some areas. Where governments have taken over the schools, the Church no longer has the place in society it once held as the chief provider of education.

(b) The number of Churches and Christians has increased so that in some areas there are not enough pastors to look after the people.

(c) Political independence has brought new feelings of cultural pride and national 'selfhood', and has encouraged movements for similar independence in the Church. There are strong desires to develop a Church that is truly relevant to its own situation, both in its patterns of ministry and its methods of outreach.

(d) Economic injustice and poverty have caused the Church to rethink many of its ideas about ways of helping people.

(e) Political oppression and violence has made some parts of the Church more aware of people's total needs, and more ready to stand and support them even when this means conflict with the ruling authorities.

Of course many of these changes apply to both industrialized and Third World countries, and some changes apply to some situations more than to others. But wherever change is taking place, the Church needs to ask how much can be learnt from the past. If we slavishly copy past patterns and methods of working, then the answer will probably be we cannot learn very much. However, if we study some of the basic principles and ideas which were found to be valid, and learn from them without trying to imitate them exactly, then the past can give us some very valuable understanding of the meaning of pastoral care, and even of what methods are likely to be effective today.

SOME PATTERNS TO AVOID

At the same time, there are also *lessons to be learnt from some past patterns* of pastoral care which developed in ways *which failed* to reflect the idea of the Good Shepherd as shown in the ministry of Jesus. Four of those patterns, in particular, are to be avoided rather than followed:

1. THE 'MISSIONARY' PATTERN

The missionaries who carried the gospel to many different countries and tribal groups exercised a great deal of authority among the people to whom they went. They spoke as representatives of 'the true God'. In many places they provided the only available education, whether academic or practical, which for many people was the only means of gaining employment and eventually achieving wealth and prosperity. For a long time the missionaries alone were responsible for the efficient running of the Church, including the care of Church money, and the building and upkeep of Church property. They were recognized as 'father-in-God' figures, with responsibility for making decisions which affected many people's lives.

Many missionaries carried all this responsibility and power, and still remained true spiritual guides for their people. Others, however, became very authoritarian and strict. Some became closely involved in the lives, aspirations, and culture of the people; others kept themselves separate and aloof. So, depending on the sort of example given, new pastors appointed in missionary areas themselves began to follow these missionary patterns. Sometimes the results were good, sometimes they were bad.

One such pastor was trained by a missionary who never visited the members of his congregation, or even spoke personally to them, but always sent a messenger with his written messages and orders to them. Naturally the young pastor supposed this was the proper way to work, and when he himself was put in charge of a congregation he rarely visited people in their homes, but would instead write out a message and get someone to deliver it for him. He truly believed that in doing this he was fulfilling an important part of his work. By following the pattern set by the missionary he felt that he was exercising the same sort of authority, and this gave him a sense of security and 'success'.

Another example was that of a newly-appointed pastor who demanded a big house and the use of a car because 'the missionary always had these things'. He felt that if he was to be effective in his work, then he must have the same equipment, and be treated in the same way that the missionary had been treated. He did not stop to consider that the missionary had charge over several widely separated congregations, while he himself had only one. (He certainly did not stop to ask himself if the missionary really needed the large house and the car, either!)

2. THE TRADITIONAL 'BIG MAN' PATTERN

Many national, tribal, and local communities recognize certain leaders as 'the big man' or 'the boss', because of their wealth, their special skills or wisdom, or their status according to a hereditary system of leadership. People respect, listen to, and obey the 'big man'; he has chiefly authority in all the affairs of the community. As Christianity spread, the appointed Church leaders came to be regarded as 'big men', perhaps because they were more educated than the people, or had the support of the colonial power. In some places the minister or pastor became the religious advisor to the traditional chief or paramount leader, and in such a position could exercise great authority. As representative of the true God his words and actions commanded respect and obedience. In some countries many pastors followed this 'big man' pattern. More recently, however, this pattern has become less widespread. In many communities the pastor is no longer better educated than others, and many people have greater skills and wealth than he. Today many pastors find they no longer enjoy positions of such status and authority as in the past. Many regard this as a good thing, but some regret it, and try to cling to this pattern for their work because of the power it can give them.

3. THE 'POLITICAL STATESMAN' PATTERN

In many newly self-governing and independent countries, the roles of political leaders have become very important. They represent and speak on behalf of many people. As members of the government or other political groups, they receive certain privileges, and many people petition them for help in furthering particular policies. To keep the support of their electors, politicians must try to 'look after' the electors' interests. Sometimes politicians have to refuse their support for legislation that seems likely to harm their constituents, or to antagonize voters.

Politicians not only need to be well-informed about the affairs of their country, they also face strong temptation in the form of bribes and other rewards offered in return for their favour. Many of the younger leaders in newly-developing countries regard the status and authority of being a politician as most desirable. They need great honesty and integrity of character to overcome the temptation to gain support by any means that seem likely to be effective.

In the same way, a pastor is sometimes tempted to become a sort of politician within the Church, and to seek support for his ideas and policies from influential people in the congregation. It is not wrong to want to influence people's opinions in ways we believe to be right, but we must always be careful not to let our influence turn into 'pressure' on people to support us against their will. A politician who obeys the law and truly represents and *serves* his people sets a good example. But a dishonest politician can do a great deal of harm if he tries to use the people for his own benefit or to further his own ends. Any pastor seeking to follow this sort of political pattern in his work must take care that he does so in a good way, not a bad way.

4. THE 'POLICEMAN' PATTERN

As a representative of the government, and entrusted with the work of interpreting and enforcing the law, the policeman holds a position of authority and importance in most communities. In his role as defender of justice and law, he has the right to ask questions and probe into people's activities. It is part of his job to restrain – by force if necessary – anyone who is disobeying the law. People often forget about the positive work of the police in keeping law and order, and merely think of them as waiting to 'catch' those who do wrong. A mother will discipline her children by threatening that if they are disobedient: 'the policeman will get you'.

Some pastors tend to behave rather like policemen. They seem always to be looking out for people's faults and scolding them for their misdeeds, instead of praising their good qualities and encouraging them to do right. Such pastors try to *enforce* the law of the Church, sometimes without properly understanding the situation. One lay leader in a congregation said: 'I couldn't possibly tell the pastor about my feelings and temptations. He would only accuse me, and make me feel so ashamed that I could not find any help or forgiveness. When I do wrong I keep away from him, in case he finds out about me.' If a pastor follows this pattern, the time will come when mothers are warning their children: 'the pastor will get you!'

A PATTERN TO AIM AT

William Clebsch and Charles Jaekle, in their book, *Pastoral Care in Historical Perspective*, have studied the many different ideas and methods of pastoral care practised in the Church from the time of the apostles down to the present. Based on this study they have defined pastoral care as: 'Helping acts, done by representative Christians, directed towards the healing, sustaining, guiding, and reconciling of troubled people.'

According to this definition, then, pastoral care is:

1. *A ministry done by representative Christians*, that is to say, it is generally done by people appointed to some official position in the

Church. They may be called elders, pastors, ministers, priests, or by some other name. But other members of the Church also may be involved in the work, even though they do not hold any official position. The important thing is not so much *who* does this work, but the fact that whoever does it brings the resources and wisdom of the Christian faith and life to people in need. They seek to help troubled people by offering them the resources of faith, love, wisdom, authority, and fellowship which are found in the Christian community of believers. The emphasis is not so much on the person who gives this help, but on the sort of help given. Whoever brings this help *represents* the whole Christian fellowship.

2. *A ministry to troubled people*, who are unable by themselves to solve or cope with difficulties in their lives, and who seek help from those who may bring some answer for the problems they are experiencing. This does not mean that people who are 'well and strong' in their lives have no need for pastoral care. A good pastor cares for *all* the flock, not only those who get into deep trouble, just as the good shepherd cares for the healthy sheep as well as the sickly ones. It is true that troubled people have always been given the greatest attention, because their need is the most obvious and the most urgent. But a good pastor, like a good doctor, will try to keep the flock healthy. And by giving continuing care to all, he can help to prevent at least some sorts of trouble from developing.

3. *A fourfold ministry* consisting of:

(a) *Healing*, which helps to make people 'whole' or 'healthy' both in their physical bodies, and also in their spiritual and social attitudes and relationships.

(b) *Sustaining*, which helps individuals and groups to face difficult situations. This may mean helping them to bear some burden which threatens to break up their lives. It may mean giving support in times of grief, sorrow, sickness, fear, and loneliness. Those in need are sustained, strengthened, and encouraged to find resources in God, in others, and in themselves.

(c) *Guiding*, which helps people to choose between different ways of thinking and behaving. It may be in decisions about marriage, work, pleasure – anything that causes people concern. It also means helping people to *grow* in their moral and spiritual understanding, and to apply this understanding to different aspects of their lives.

(d) *Reconciling*, which helps people to agree together, or be restored to friendship and fellowship, with God, with others, and often with their own feelings and desires. The relationship between God and men is continually being broken, and feelings of guilt, shame, and sorrow are real in people's lives. Personal relationships become twisted and torn through harsh words, actions, and attitudes. But

31

broken relationships can be restored through acceptance and forgiveness, and new relationships can be formed.

This definition of pastoral care does not explain *how* these different sorts of care are to be given: there are many different methods and ways of approaching people. But it does provide a helpful summary of the main purpose of pastoral care as this has developed in the Church. The idea of a fourfold ministry of healing, sustaining, guiding, and reconciling can serve as a useful guideline as we develop our understanding of pastoral care in the Church today. In the two chapters that follow, we set out to explore, first how we can develop our understanding of others, and then how we can also learn to understand ourselves.

STUDY SUGGESTIONS

WORD STUDY

1. Explain the meaning of each of the following 'technical' terms:
   (a) 'a cure of souls'   (b) 'order' of ministry   (c) the 'laity'
   (d) the 'priesthood of all believers'   (e) celibacy
   (f) an 'administrative' function.

REVIEW OF CONTENT

2. In what ways did Augustine of Hippo say that a pastor should treat the following sorts of people?
   (a) low spirited   (b) contentious   (c) eager but unskilled
   (d) evil.
3. (a) What were some of the reasons why the clergy became 'separated' from the laity in the medieval Church?
   (b) What were some of the differences between clergy and laity which marked this separation?
4. What did Martin Luther chiefly teach concerning the ministry?
5. (a) What was the title of Richard Baxter's book about the work of a pastor?
   (b) Describe three of the ideas about the work of a pastor which Baxter explained in that book.
6. (a) Who was John Wesley, and what is he chiefly remembered for?
   (b) In what ways were Wesley's ideas about pastoral care like those of Richard Baxter, and in what ways were they unlike?

BIBLE STUDY

7. Which of the 'patterns' of pastoral care described on pp. 28–30 do you think Paul was warning Church leaders against in each of the following passages?

(a) 1 Timothy 5.1, 2   (b) 1 Timothy 3.1–5 and 6–10
(c) Philippians 3.2–11.

APPLICATION, OPINION, AND RESEARCH

8. Richard Baxter and John Wesley both thought pastoral care just as important as preaching. What do you yourself think about the relationship between pastoral care and preaching? Do you agree that preaching and pastoral care are equally important? Give reasons for your answer.

9. Each culture has people who specialize in helping others (see p. 27).
   (a) In your own cultural situation, what sorts of people give help to people in trouble?
   (b) In what ways does the help they give compare with the four sorts of pastoral care given by the Church?

10. What do you consider the chief disadvantages of (a) the missionary pattern and (b) the policeman pattern of pastoral care (see pp. 28, 30)? What advantages if any do you see in either of these two patterns?

11. Read again the lists of social and economic changes which have occurred in recent years in industrialized countries on the one hand, and in developing countries on the other.
    (a) Which of these changes have occurred in your own country?
    (b) What other changes, if any, that are *not* included in those lists have affected the work of a pastor in your country?

12. 'Ideas about pastoral care have developed and changed very quickly in recent times as a result of social and economic changes' (p. 26).
    (a) List three ways in which ideas about pastoral care have changed in industrialized countries.
    (b) List three ways in which ideas about pastoral care have changed in Third World countries.

13. Which of the four sorts of pastoral care listed by Clebsch and Jaekle (healing, sustaining, guiding and reconciling – see pp. 30, 31) are given most attention in your Church? Which, if any, are neglected, and what do you think are the reasons for such neglect?

14. Discuss with two working pastors what they see as the chief purpose and meaning of their work, and any changes in that purpose and meaning which they have experienced since they were first appointed. If possible, do this with one pastor of many years' experience, and one with only a few years of experience. Notice any similarities and differences in their approach to their work.

3

Understanding People

WHAT IS 'MAN'?

In any sort of work we need to know and understand who or what it is that we are working with. If we want to do a job well, we need to gain the necessary skills, and learn how to use the proper tools. (The word 'we' is used in this chapter to mean ourselves as Christians and also all other people.)

For most forms of ministry some understanding of people is necessary. For a pastor this is especially important, because *people* and their thoughts, feelings, doubts and fears, their hopes and joys, are his chief concern. Pastoral care depends on the pastor's ability to work with people, so a pastor needs to know people, and understand the lives they lead, if he is going to help them in any effective way. He needs to develop the skills of good personal relationships.

How we deal with people and treat them depends on what we believe about them. If we believe that people are useless and a nuisance, we tend to treat them as such. If we believe that people are valuable and of great worth, then we show this in the way we treat them. So it is very important that every pastor should work out his own answer to the question asked by the writer of Psalm 8: 'What is man?'

The word 'man' as used in the Psalm means 'mankind' – all the races and tribes and nations of human beings in the world. But it also means individual men and women, boys and girls – the people we meet each day, the members of our Church, those who live in our village or neighbourhood or town. We usually find it fairly easy to think well of mankind in general, yet we often treat the people we meet each day in ways which show that we do not think very highly of them.

If someone asks us what a particular person is like, we usually describe them in ways that reflect our own opinion of them or relationship with them. We say, 'Oh, he is a silly boy', or 'she is a pretty girl', or 'he is a good carpenter', or 'she is a bad-tempered old grandmother'. But there are many different ways of studying and describing people which can help us to understand them better.

(a) *The biological way*: This deals with the physical side of our lives, the material and chemical nature of our bodies which we share with other living creatures. This can show some of the reasons why people behave as they do, for example when they are hungry, or sick, or just going through a particular phase of their physical development.

(b) *The sociological or anthropological way:* This is concerned with the cultural environments in which we live, and with our traditional customs. It can help to explain people's attitudes, and show why the different classes and castes and other groupings of society organize their lives as they do.

(c) *The psychological way:* This deals with our emotional reactions, how we develop our ideas, and form relationships with other people. It is closely related to both the biological and the sociological ways of describing people, and is especially important for helping people in times of personal crisis and stress.

(d) *The religious way:* This deals with the spiritual side of our nature, with our relationship with God the Creator, and with the effect of our religious beliefs and practices on our relationships with one another.

A Christian pastor needs to study people in all these ways if he is to understand them as fully as possible. But he needs to go further: he needs to remember that there is a distinctively *Christian* way of understanding human beings. As C. F. Kemp explains in his *Pastoral Counselling Guidebook*:

'The pastor does all his counselling (and other pastoral care) from a particular point of view. He approaches all persons from the perspective of a Christian faith and a Christian view of man. It is very easy to forget this and slip into the habit of seeing man from other points of view. Psychiatric, psychological, and sociological interpretations can be so interesting, clear, authoritative, and helpful, that it is easy for a pastor to forget that he has a distinct and all-important view of his own.'

This distinctive Christian view of human beings takes careful notice of the various 'scientific' ways of understanding people we have mentioned, but its foundation is God's revelation of His purposes for all mankind and the world. This is based on the Bible.

THE BIBLICAL VIEW

The Bible is a collection of writings containing many different sorts of material, from many different sources, which were gathered and put together over a period of many hundreds of years. So we should not be surprised to find that it contains many different answers to the question 'What is man?' Nevertheless there are certain basic truths about human beings which all the Bible writers express in one way or another:

(a) *Human beings are made in the image of God.* 'God created man in his own image, in the image of God he created him, male and female' (Gen. 1.26–28). These verses have been explained in many different ways, for example:

We have a special place in God's creation. In many ways we are like

35

the animals, but our brains are more highly developed. We are able to think and to reason.

God gives us the ability to share His thoughts and plans. We can choose either to love and serve Him, or to refuse His way and choose our own.

Because we are able to think, and to be in fellowship with God, He has given us the responsibility of controlling His creation and using it according to His purposes.

Because we have this special relationship with God, we cannot find true fulfilment and meaning in our lives if we separate ourselves from Him and refuse to accept His plan for us and for His world. St Augustine said, 'You have made us for yourself, oh God, and our hearts are restless until they find their rest in you.'

(b) *Human beings are both good and evil.* We want to serve God and to obey Him. But we also want to go our own way and control things for ourselves. As Paul said: 'When I want to do right, evil lies close at hand. I delight in the law of God in my inmost self, but I see in my members another law making me captive to the law of sin' (Rom. 7.21–24). Each of us spoils God's plan in our lives. This 'sinful nature' prevents us from knowing God truly and being fully in fellowship with Him.

This does not mean that God's image has been completely destroyed in us, but it has been damaged. Our lives are like a mirror that is cracked, or a pond where the surface of the water is ruffled by the wind. Our lives do not truly reflect God's plan for us. But they can be restored through Jesus Christ who truly reflects the image of God in His life (see 2 Cor. 4.4; Col. 1.15). Things are not right 'within' us. 'Out of the heart of a man' come evil thoughts which cause trouble and confusion in our lives and in the lives of others (Mark 7.14–23). But even so it is possible for us to do good, and to live in ways which give a good example to others, if only we are willing to be changed.

(c) *Human beings can be changed.* Two examples of such change in the New Testament are Paul and Nicodemus. Each was a respected religious leader, living a 'good' life and carefully following God's law. But when Paul saw himself in the light of Jesus Christ, he knew that he was 'the chief of sinners'. As a result he changed from 'ravaging the church', and 'amazed all who heard him by proclaiming that Jesus was the Christ' (1 Tim. 1.15; Acts 8.3; 9.1–6). And when Nicodemus, a teacher and ruler of the Jews, came to Jesus, Jesus told him that he must be 'born anew' (John 3.1–12).

So long as we are alive, we have not finished our development and growth. We are still 'becoming'. This means we can look back in our lives to the past from which we can become free, and we can also look forward to the future towards which we are moving. Our past life influences us, but it need not hold us a prisoner. As we grow, we can change direction, like a plant that turns towards the light. We can make decisions; we can respond to love; we need not remain as we are. Jesus sees possibilities of growth and development in the life of every person. He sees what men and women are really like, and also what they can become. Two examples are Zaccheus and Peter. Most people hated and despised Zaccheus, the greedy and dishonest tax collector. But Jesus saw great possibilities of growth and change in him. Jesus offered His friendship to Zaccheus and as a result Zaccheus grew into an honest and generous person (Luke 19.1–10). Peter was a very impetuous man, easily swayed by his feelings, but Jesus saw that with love, good instruction, and strong friendship, Peter could become a 'rock' (John 1.42; Matt. 16.18). Growth in knowledge and character is possible when a person becomes united to Christ (2 Pet. 3.18).

(d) *Each human being is a unity:* Several words are used in the Bible to describe different aspects of our human nature: body, soul, spirit, mind, flesh, etc. The Bible writers did not describe people in modern psychological terms, and some of the words and ideas they used are different from the words a doctor or psychologist would use to describe people today. But like the doctor or psychologist, the Bible writers saw each person as a unity, as one living being. We can say that we have a physical side, a mental side, and a spiritual side, but these different aspects of our total being are all interrelated. Our physical condition can affect our attitudes to other people, or a poor spiritual relationship can cause actual physical pain or sickness in our physical bodies. Here is an example:

Example 1: James and Cynthia were a middle-aged couple. Their children were already grown-up when James began to have a number of adventures with other women. For several years his wife knew nothing of this, and when she did find out James promised to reform. But again and again he failed, seeming to lack the necessary will-power. At this time he complained of severe stomach pains and digestive trouble. He went to the doctor, but medicine did him no good.

James's sister and Cynthia's mother also made things worse by constant interference and advice. In the end James and Cynthia went to their pastor, who told them that their real need was a sense of God's forgiveness and a new relationship with Him and with each other. He suggested they read John's Gospel together. Almost at once James's stomach trouble cleared up. Almost certainly it had been caused by his feelings of guilt and his sense of failure over his first efforts at reform. This was an example of physical sickness having a spiritual cause.

As Bishop Stephen Neill explains in his book *What is Man?*: 'God is interested in the whole man, and not just a part of him. We often speak of man as made up of body and soul – and we often think that the part of him that has to be religious is his soul. It is true that the Bible does make this distinction – a man is made up of body, soul, and spirit. Does this mean that we can speak of man as being made up of two of three parts? The Bible always speaks of man as a unity. He is not a spirit shut up in a body. He is always a unity. He is body. He is mind and soul. He can be spirit. It depends on how we are speaking about man. By means of his body man is related to the world around him. Through his mind he is related to other human beings. He also has an inner life of his own in which he thinks and speaks within himself. This perhaps we could call his soul. But if he enters into his true life and comes to know God, who is Spirit, then man can also be called "spirit", because the Spirit of God is dwelling in him.'

The pastor needs to understand the various aspects of a person's total being, but he has to treat each human being as a unity.

(e) *Because of their relationship to God, human beings are valuable and of great worth*. Our characters are not always good, but our value does not depend on our goodness. Our relationship to God is what makes us valuable. We have seen that Jesus emphasized this idea in His ministry. Each person is so valuable to God that even the very small things that happen in our lives, including our deepest personal feelings, are all known to Him. He knows, loves, and cares for each one of us. (See Ps. 139.1–6; Matt. 10.31; 12.12; Luke 12.7.)

We see God's love for us most clearly in His self-giving love in Jesus Christ. The cross is not only the sign of His love for all sinful people (Rom. 5.8). It also shows us that all people are of value to Him, whatever their race, sex, or culture. Our value to God does not depend on our knowledge or our achievements, or even on our moral character. It depends on the fact that He loves and wants us (John 3.16). When we realize this, our attitude to other people changes because we suddenly recognize every other person as our 'brother' or 'sister' for whom Christ has died.

Tom Skinner, leader of a black gang in New York, was filled with hatred for white people. Then he became a Christian, and his knowledge of Christ completely changed his attitude. In a football game a white came up and kicked Tom hard as he lay on the ground, saying, 'Take that, you black —'. The old Tom Skinner would have taken terrible revenge, but the new Tom just stood up and said, rather to his own surprise, 'I love you, because of Jesus.'

These five biblical truths about human beings provide the foundation on which to build our understanding of the people in need of our pastoral care. These facts are true for every person we shall try to help:

Each one is made in God's image,
each one is both good and evil,

each one can be changed,
each one is a unity,
each one is valuable to God.

The Christian pastor can learn many facts about human beings from the sciences of biology, sociology, anthropology, and psychology. And in the light of these biblical truths he can also add other important ideas which will give him a more complete understanding of people's lives. These modern ideas are related to the biblical ideas, but are usually developed and expressed in different ways. The biblical ideas in turn need to be understood and applied in the light of facts that we learn from these other areas of knowledge.

Three such important facts which a pastor needs to understand are:

1. There are certain basic needs which all human beings experience and seek to satisfy;

2. People's ideas and behaviour are strongly influenced, but not controlled, by their social and cultural surroundings as well as their inherited characteristics;

3. People do not always think and act rationally; they are also influenced by inward and hidden motives and feelings.

We shall discuss each of these facts in detail.

PEOPLE'S BASIC NEEDS

As we have seen, people's ideas and behaviour are affected by many different factors, and psychologists, sociologists, and anthropologists describe these factors in different ways. Perhaps the most helpful way of thinking about them is to relate them to the basic *needs* (the psychologists call them 'drives') which all people have. We all seek to satisfy these needs in order that our lives may continue, and may have meaning and purpose.

The needs themselves are listed in different ways by different writers, but for pastors it is probably most useful to list them under five headings as follows:

1. *Survival:* These needs are the same for everyone: the *physical* needs for the things we all must have in order to survive as individuals and as members of the human race. They include food, water, air, shelter, sex, sleep, etc.

2. *Security:* These are the needs for *safety* and *order*, the need to be able to live without constant fear of foreign enemies or violent groups within society. Many writers include justice and freedom from oppression as basic needs to be listed under this heading.

3. *Belonging:* These are often called the 'social' needs: the need to *belong* to various groups – family, friends, neighbours, workmates, etc.; to have satisfactory relationships with others within these groups,

and to feel that we are accepted, understood, and loved as the case may be.

4. *Esteem:* Once our survival and security needs are met most of us also feel the need for something more than just being accepted as belonging to a group. We need to feel that we are actively respected and needed by others. We need to feel that we can behave as mature and responsible people, and 'stand on our own feet'. We need to be able to *succeed* in some way, however humble. We need to be able honestly to *respect* ourselves, and not to feel that we are what the Melanesians call a 'rabisman' (rubbish-man – that is, someone who is useless and so without value).

5. *Fulfilment:* Some writers refer to the needs for esteem and fulfilment as 'higher needs, which not everyone feels. But if we really believe that everyone is of value to God, then we must also believe that we should all have the opportunity for self-fulfilment, the opportunity to achieve some purpose and to use our abilities in the activity we are most suited for. Under this head, too, we would include the 'spiritual' needs for faith and for a right relationship with God, and also the need of artists of all kinds to express themselves and communicate with others, and perhaps even the ambition of potential 'leaders' to work for the benefit of society as a whole.

In thinking about these various sorts of needs, there are three important facts we must remember:

(a) *People are not all the same.* Not everyone feels all five sorts of needs equally. Some people may not feel some of them at all. Adventurous people, for example, feel less need for security; ambitious people need the esteem that follows success; artists and musicians feel the need for fulfilment. In particular countries or cultures, too, some needs may be felt while others are not.

(b) *The needs differ in importance.* Survival needs are basic to us all and so to a great extent are security needs. But we *can* live without social contacts, even if not very happily, and large numbers of people live their whole lives without being esteemed by others or enjoying the experience of self-fulfilment. In any case, if a man is hungry or in great danger, he will try to satisfy his need for food and safety before he starts to worry about what other people think of him or his opportunities for self-expression.

(c) *The needs themselves may take different forms in different situations.* Social acceptance, for example, can be expressed in many different ways, and an action which shows acceptance or respect for others in one culture may be regarded as silly, or even rude, in another culture. In some societies the needs of each individual person are given less importance than those of the community as a whole, so that ideas like self-esteem, self-fulfilment, and purpose may not have much meaning as related to individuals. In these cultures the need will be for success and fulfilment as members of the community, and for the welfare of society as such.

INFLUENCES FROM 'OUTSIDE'

It is true that all peoples and nations are one before God. 'He created every race of men of one stock, to inhabit the entire earth' (Acts 17.26, JB). However, this basic unity of all people does not mean that all races and groups are exactly the same. Each person is made 'in the image of God', but cultural ideas and patterns of behaviour vary greatly in different parts of the world.

These differences of race and culture are part of God's plan for the world. Each race and nation brings its own special ways of thinking and behaving into the one family of God's people. God has created us as brothers and sisters, each with our own experiences and interests, not as slaves forced into being and doing the same thing. This 'oneness in diversity' is one of the signs of God's victory in Jesus Christ (Rev. 7.9–17).

CULTURE AND TRADITION

The Church lives and grows within the societies and cultures in which people live, and people are strongly influenced by the laws, ideas, and patterns of organization of those societies, even though they do not all react to these influences in the same way. Our cultural environment provides security and meaning for our lives. It shapes our habits and ideas. When people are separated from their usual surroundings and from the ideas and traditions to which they are accustomed, they feel insecure and become upset.

This does not mean, however, that we have to be slaves to our environment. These 'social' influences are strong, but usually we are still able to act and think in ways which are different from those of the society or group as a whole, though this may sometimes be difficult. It may even require courage, especially in a very rigidly organized community, or under a totalitarian political regime. As we have seen, in some societies people normally act and think as members of a group rather than as individuals. In other societies people are less controlled by the thinking and actions of others. A Christian pastor must recognize both of these situations. He has to treat people as members of a group, and yet at the same time as individuals.

Throughout the history of the Church, individual Christians have challenged the accepted ideas of their society, and have refused to 'conform' to its laws, when they believed that these cultural ideas and laws were contrary to the law of God. This is one of the continuing tasks for every Christian – to be shaped and moulded by the patterns and values of Christ rather than the values of the surrounding world. This is what Paul meant when he wrote: 'Do not be conformed to the standards of this world, but let God transform you' (Rom. 12.2, TEV). Someone who did this was Svetlana Alliluyeva, daughter of Joseph Stalin. She wrote in her book *Letters to a Friend*: 'It is simpler to divide people into believers and unbelievers. By the time I was thirty-five and had seen something of life, I, who had been taught from earliest childhood by society and my family to be an atheist and materialist, was already one of those who cannot live without God. I am glad that it is so.'

We must also remember that similar actions or events can have different meanings in different societies. This is especially true of marriage customs. It is unwise, therefore, to apply ideas from one cultural situation to a different situation unless we fully understand the meaning of a particular idea or action in its particular social setting.

INDIVIDUAL CIRCUMSTANCES

It is not only essential for a pastor to recognize and understand the cultural environment of the people he serves. He also needs to ask *who* is this particular person who is seeking for help, and *what* are the particular circumstances of that person's life. The more we understand of any society, the easier it becomes to understand the people who belong to it. But within any society there will be division, for example between rich and poor, between old and young, between those who live in the city and those who work on the land. These divisions and differences, too, influence the ways in which people think and behave. If the pastor is to help people, he has to be able to think and feel *with* them. He has to practice the 'incarnational' principle which we see in the ministry of Jesus. Paul was describing this principle when he wrote, 'I become all things to all men, that I may save some of them by any means possible'. (See 1 Cor. 9.19–23.)

Kosuke Koyama, a Japanese theological teacher, gave a modern example of this incarnational principle when he was working in Thailand. (Koyama was referring to the importance of this principle in preaching, but what he says is equally true and important as applied to pastoral care.)

'On my way to the country church, I never fail to see a herd of water buffaloes grazing in the muddy paddy field. This sight is an inspiring sight for me. Why? Because it reminds me that the people to whom I am to bring the gospel of Christ spend most of their time with these water buffalo in the rice field. The water buffaloes tell me that I must preach to these farmers in the simplest sentence structure and thought development. They remind me to disregard all abstract ideas and to

'A Christian pastor has to treat people as members of a group and also as individuals . . . to think and feel with them as 'persons' not 'things' (pp. 41, 42 and 50).

At a ceremony in Papua New Guinea competitors celebrate their victory in a race. Members of the Tanzanian National Service give a display at a youth festival. What might help a pastor to 'think and feel' with these different groups as 'individual persons'?

use objects that are immediately tangible. "Rice", "banana", "pepper", "dog", "cat", "bicycle", "rainy season", "leaking house", "fishing", "cock-fighting" – these are meaningful words to them. "This morning," I say to myself, "I will try to bring the gospel of Christ through the medium of cock-fighting."

'Proceeding to the country church on my Japanese motor cycle, I once more recite mentally the Scripture text that is to be used, and I try to formulate the approach to the intended message. Then I ask myself, "Is this introduction understandable and realistic in terms of their daily experiences? Is this message digestible and nutritious to their ethical and theological needs?" When I reach the church, I count how many older people there are. How many younger? Are there new faces, sick persons, pregnant women, crippled? Then I say to myself, "I am sent to this congregation today." I begin speaking from where they are (i.e. cock-fighting). From talking about the human situation, I go on to call God into this real situation. It is not I, but my audience, who determines this approach of "theology from below". The truth of "self-emptying" ("Jesus Christ who . . . emptied himself", Phil. 2.5–7) in the God incarnate means, to me, to begin my sermon with "rice" and "cock-fighting" when preaching to my people, farmers of northern Thailand.

'I decide to subordinate great theological thoughts to the intellectual and spiritual needs of the farmers. I decide that the greatness of theological works is to be judged by the extent and quality of the service they can give to the farmers to whom I am sent. I also decide that I have not really understood these great theological writings until I am able to use them for the benefit of the farmers. I am called to work in northern Thailand. God has commanded me to be a neighbour to these farmers.'

THE PEOPLE AROUND US

Another strong influence on people's behaviour is the example, advice, and opinion of those around them – their family, friends, and workmates, their 'heroes'. This is chiefly because of the two needs for 'belonging' and for 'esteem'. Nearly everyone needs and enjoys the society of others, and most of us behave in ways that are acceptable to the various groups to which we belong, because we do not wish to be regarded as 'different'. We do not wish to be laughed at or rejected. Young people tend to follow the example of those a little older than themselves, and behave in ways that make them feel 'grown-up'. They follow – or rebel against – the advice of their parents, or they try to imitate the achievements and appearance of their favourite footballer or pop star. Older people too are influenced in their opinions and behaviour by their relationships with, and reactions to, the other people in their lives. We cannot understand people by studying them in isolation. So a pastor needs to learn as much as he can about people's family background and their friendships. He needs to be sensitive to their relationships with others.

INFLUENCES FROM 'INSIDE'

EMOTIONS

Human beings are sometimes described as 'rational'. This means they can use their knowledge and their powers of thinking to express ideas, to understand what is happening around them, and to make decisions and take action which will affect others. This is true. People do have the ability to think and reason about a situation or a problem. But people also have emotions, feelings, and motives in their lives which sometimes prevent them from acting in accordance with their knowledge. Feelings and emotions have a strong influence on what people think and do. We do not always act from rational knowledge only – we also act according to our inner motives and feelings.

We often hear stories about people in need who are suffering from hunger, poverty, sickness, etc. We receive appeals to help them. But even though we know the facts, we do not respond, because our feelings and emotions are not stirred. Knowledge of 'external' facts alone is not enough to produce action.

Example 2: A young man called Jonathan quarrelled with his father and left his home village to work in a town some distance away. He was very angry with his father, and would not forget the argument which had taken place. His father wrote to him, asking him to come home, but Jonathan refused to answer any of the letters. Then he heard that his father was very sick, and likely to die. He asked some of his friends to find out about his father's condition, but still he would not go home to see his father, even though one of his cousins offered to pay the fare. His father died without seeing his son again. This young man had knowledge of the situation and he really loved his father, but he allowed his very strong feelings of anger and resentment, rather than his knowledge, to control his actions.

THE UNCONSCIOUS

We have seen that people are influenced by emotions, habits and prejudices, and ways of thinking which they have absorbed as members of a certain society. Our ideas and behaviour also depend on other factors which we may not be aware of. Many feelings and emotions and attitudes are hidden deep in our minds. They may be the result of experiences in our childhood which we have now forgotten. Some psychologists believe they may even derive from forgotten

45

events in history that have shaped the traditions and customs of our tribe or our nation. These emotions can strongly influence the way we think and act, even though we may not be conscious that they exist.

Psychologists explain these hidden influences by pointing out that our minds work at three quite distinct levels. They describe these levels as the conscious mind, the subconscious mind, and the unconscious mind.

(a) The *conscious* mind is what we use in all the activities of our waking life. It works when we are thinking, listening, talking, working, playing, studying, solving problems, etc.

(b) When we go to sleep, this does not mean that our mind stops working altogether. It continues to think about some of the things we have been thinking about while we were awake. At this second level, the *subconscious* mind continues to be active even when our conscious mind is resting. Part of this activity causes our dreams. Our minds also operate at this level when we are awake, in activities like walking, riding a bicycle, and 'mechanical jobs' which have become automatic so that we do not have to think consciously about how to perform them.

(c) The *unconscious* mind is the level at which our memories and ideas are stored. We forget much of what happens to us as soon as it is over. But our mind is like a big warehouse or filing system, or like a data bank in a computer, where memories of past experiences are stored away so deeply that we are not aware they are there. Sometimes we remember things that happened many years ago, while other events are forgotten. Sometimes we push an idea down into our unconscious mind because we want to get rid of it. We try to 'repress' or 'keep under' thoughts and memories that we want to forget. But they still all remain in the storehouse, and may suddenly return to our conscious mind, and influence the way we behave. Ideas, thoughts, and memories can pass from one level of the mind to another.

The African writer, A. Omoyajowo, compares the mind to a housewife who has three cupboards in her kitchen. In the first cupboard she puts the cups, pots, and plates she uses every day. She can get them at any time, and they are continually in use. This is like the conscious mind. The second cupboard is filled with pots and bowls which she uses only occasionally. Some are smart and new, but others may be marked, and she may not like them very much, but she knows that she may sometimes need to use them. This is like the subconscious mind. In the third cupboard are packed away all the things which the housewife never expects to use. She even dislikes some of them. Some are old and ugly dishes which she wants to keep packed away. Others are old cracked dishes which might spoil her cooking. She even forgets the sort of things which are there. But they are there, and if someone opens the cupboard door, then they will fall out. This is like the unconscious mind.

We are conscious or aware of most of our ideas, customs, habits, and opinions. But there are always some we are not aware of, although they have become part of us, and these 'hidden' things do influence us, perhaps especially in time of stress or trouble. Often we think and act without understanding *why* we think as we do. When we become angry, or our emotions and feelings are upset in some way, we find ourselves 'unconsciously' thinking, saying, and doing things that are quite unlike our ordinary 'rational' behaviour.

DEFENCE MECHANISMS

People also develop ways of thinking and acting which can prevent them from facing up to difficult situations. These are called '*defences*' or 'defence mechanisms', because they protect or 'defend' us from things that upset our sense of security or belonging, or our self-esteem. Often, when we are criticized, we refuse to admit that we are wrong, and so we develop defences against criticism. These defences are also used in times of difficulty, disappointment, or sickness, to protect us against whatever it is that is causing pain in our lives.

The Bible contains many references to people who put up such defences to protect themselves. The seven examples given below are some of the defence-mechanisms which people still frequently use today:

1. Adam used the defence of *avoidance* (Gen. 3.8). He did not want to face God and admit his wrong action, so he hid himself, hoping to avoid the consequences. Sometimes a person seeks to avoid a difficult situation or problem by running away, or by simply pretending it doesn't exist. Or if others are talking about something we find painful to hear, we try to change the subject.

2. Adam also used the defence of *projection*. He did not succeed in avoiding God, but he was unwilling to accept blame, so he 'projected' the blame on to Eve instead (Gen. 3.12). A common way of protecting ourselves from blame for a wrong action is to blame someone else, and make excuses for ourselves. We 'project' or 'throw' the blame on to others.

3. *Withdrawal* is rather similar to avoidance. People use this defence when they find themselves in a difficulty. They 'withdraw' from the situation, and refuse to become involved. Pilate gave an example of withdrawal when confronted with the demand that he should condemn Jesus, whom he had already declared innocent (Matt. 27.22–24). Pilate did not want to anger the religious leaders by deciding to free Jesus, so he 'withdrew' and 'washed his hands' of the

problem. He could not actually run away, but he refused to take any responsibility for the decision to put Jesus to death.

4. *Self-justification* is another defence against having to accept responsibility for a difficult task. People find reasons or excuses to support their desire to escape from something they do not want to do. When God called Moses to go to Egypt to deliver His people, Moses did not want to go. He may have been frightened of Pharaoh. He may have felt unwilling to face responsibility and hardship. Or he may have truly believed himself unfitted for the task. Whatever the reason, he made excuses (Exod. 3.11—4.10). Moses did not want to obey God, so he 'justified' himself, answering God with 'good reasons' for his unwillingness. These 'reasonable excuses' covered up the real reason: Moses did not want to go.

5. When Ahab could not get possession of Naboth's vineyard, he felt sorry for himself, and acted in a childish way. He sulked in his room, and refused to eat (1 Kings 21.4). This was *'regression'*. People are said to 'regress' or 'go back' when they respond to a situation in ways which belong to a child rather than an adult. Sulking, temper-tantrums, screaming, kicking, and slamming doors – these are all examples of the defence we call regression.

6. *Rationalization* is a very common defence which people use. This is when we give misleading arguments and reasons to support something we wish to do, or perhaps to escape from an action we ought to do but do not wish to. It is similar to the defence of self-justification, but usually when we rationalize we are deceiving ourselves as well as trying to deceive others. We are using cover-up arguments to hide the real reasons why we will or will not do something.

The Syrian army captain, Naaman, wanted to be cured of his leprosy. He wanted Elisha to perform a miracle cure by calling on the name of God. When Elisha told him to wash in the Jordan river, Naaman's pride was hurt. Had he come all the way to Israel just to be told to wash in a river? So he argued that the rivers of Damascus were better than the waters of the Jordan. Why couldn't he wash in *them*? (2 Kings 5.1–14). Naaman gave what seemed to be a rational common-sense answer so as to avoid the threat to his pride.

7. Another very common defence against criticism or conflict is *lying*. When Peter was in danger of arrest and possible punishment, he denied that he was a follower of Jesus (Matt. 26.69–75). A person who is lying sometimes speaks very strongly and loudly, so that his words will sound true. He may also add swearing and cursing in order to sound more effective.

Most people use defences to protect themselves in a difficult situation. However, one defence often turns out to require another, and we can end up in a much more complicated and difficult situation than at first. Using defences also weakens our ability to accept responsibility, and can stop us from facing the need to examine our attitudes and actions. Defences are often a sign of selfishness, and result from a lack of care for other people. They are one of the most usual expressions of our sinful nature.

CONSCIENCE

As we have seen, most people fail to live in harmony with God's purposes. But almost everyone is aware that there is a difference between right and wrong ways of living. This sense of right and wrong, and the feeling that we are 'guided' as to what we 'should' do or 'should not' do in a situation, is known as our 'conscience'. But though conscience is a valuable guide, it is not an absolute standard. Conscience is itself formed and influenced by people's own experience and surroundings. The values which conscience suggests are shaped by our culture, customs, family examples, and education. An action may be approved by conscience and regarded as morally 'good' in one culture, while in another culture the same action may be regarded as quite wrong. The idea of vengeance, for example, or protecting the members of your own group against others and avenging every wrong, is binding in some cultures today; we see this in the tradition of 'vendetta' among Italian and Greek people of the Mediterranean area, and the law of 'payback' in Papua New Guinea. People in those areas have learned from their childhood that this is 'what should be done'. In other countries, however, it is regarded as a wrong way to act.

So we see that conscience can be mistaken, and can lead to wrong actions. Often it needs to be made clean (Heb. 9.14). We cannot take it as an absolute standard. Conscience does not necessarily pass correct judgements on behaviour as if God was speaking to us. It speaks according to how it has been trained, and it needs to be trained according to the standards shown in Jesus Christ. False training will result in the conscience giving us false guidance.

For Christians, Jesus Christ is the only true standard for human living. Not only does the life of Jesus show God's plan for all people; Jesus Himself enables us to make this plan real in our own lives. He is both the standard by which we can judge what is right behaviour, and also the enabler, the energizer who makes such behaviour possible. Often the standards set by Jesus will agree with those of our society and friends; at other times they will conflict, and then we have to decide which standard we shall try and follow.

Jesus is the only person who has lived a truly human life in obedience to God. Only through Him can people become truly human, and be freed from the crippling effects of self-centredness. The pastor will always see people as needing the controlling standard and influence of

Jesus, so he will do all he can to help people relate to Jesus, and share in the fellowship of His body – the Church.

THE PASTOR AND HIS PEOPLE

A pastor needs to study and understand all these facts about people and the ways in which they think and behave, as a basis for effective counselling. He needs to recognize both the conscious and the unconscious factors which affect people in their daily surroundings. Very often their repressed or forgotten thoughts, feelings, and wishes 'come to the surface' as a result of talking to a counsellor.

The pastor's own relationship with the people he is to counsel is also something he needs to understand. Although he must recognize the defences which people put up to protect themselves from painfiul situations, he must not allow this knowledge to give him a feeling of pride, or think of himself as superior to those he is trying to help. He must always try to treat people as 'persons', and not as 'things'.

Many of us gain our living by working with *things*. A builder works with bricks. A clerk works with paper and pen or typewriter. We have control over these impersonal, unfeeling objects, and can use them as we wish. If we are not careful, we sometimes find ourselves thinking of people too as if they were things. When this happens there is a danger that we shall treat people as if they were less than human.

A factory manager starts thinking of his workers in the same way that he thinks of his machines – as objects to be used for profit until they run out.

An office manager may treat his staff as though they had no minds of their own, and never allow any of them to take any decisions or responsibility.

A teacher treats his students as objects to be 'filled up' with knowledge; he never answers any of their questions or allows them to think for themselves.

A husband is treating his wife as an object when he forces her to obey his orders and beats her if she fails to please him. (A wife, of course, sometimes does the same sort of thing to her husband!)

These are all examples of a relationship in which people fail to treat each other as *persons* who are to be respected and cared for and loved as brothers and sisters. When people have this attitude towards each other, one person or group will often speak of another in ways which show that they regard them as inferior. In biblical times, Jews spoke of Gentiles as 'dogs'. Some Europeans and Americans still speak of adults of other races as 'boys'. People of one race or tribal group refer to those of other groups as 'redskins', 'white devils', 'longhairs', 'bushies', etc. People of one nation may even regard all 'foreigners' as either inferior to themselves, or necessarily hostile. When this happens they begin to think of people of other nations as 'objects' to be destroyed. In World War II Hitler ordered millions of Jewish people to be killed merely because he regarded all Jews as inferior and not fit to live. Today the super-powers of the world fight out their 'ideological' battles in smaller countries whose people they regard as of no value.

Some theologians call this sort of relationship an 'I-it' relationship, instead of the personal 'I-thou' relationship which should exist between human beings. God Himself sets an example of this I-thou relationship in the way He acts towards people. Jesus, who shows the divine attitude (John 14.9), saw great possibilities in each person and situation, even though evil was also present. He never tried to control people for His own benefit. On the contrary, He became a 'servant' in order to help people to develop into mature men and women in their relationship with God and with each other.

As a servant of Jesus Christ the 'chief servant', a pastor is committed to a personal I-thou relationship with all those whom he serves. But he will always be faced by the temptation to deal with people on an I-it basis, because that is so often easier, quicker, and makes fewer demands on his time, patience, and understanding.

So we see that although human wisdom and scientific knowledge are necessary for a pastor in his work of helping people, the answer to their deepest problems cannot come from human wisdom alone. Those who have such wisdom and knowledge are themselves affected by the same problem of wrong relationships with God and with others. Jesus knew the value of human wisdom but He pointed out its limitations (Luke 6.39). And a pastor has to be willing to accept and acknowledge his own limitations if he is to develop the 'incarnational' attitude he needs in order to carry out his work as effectively as possible.

FROM THEORY TO PRACTICE

How can a pastor use all these facts about people in his daily work? How can these ideas become 'alive' in relation to the actual men, women, and children a pastor is concerned to help and serve?

Here are six practical suggestions:

1. If there is already a list of members of your congregation and of people connected with the local Church, then study this list carefully. If not, then begin to draw up a list of the people under your care. Start with actual Church members and families you have met. Do not try to include everyone at first. As you meet more people and enter into some sort of relationship with them, you can gradually add more names and more details. In this way you will have some knowledge of the people who are connected with you as their pastor.

2. Spend time thinking about the people in the list. Try to visualize each particular family, or person, in their own situation. For example, 'James Wilson is a regular member of the Church congregation. He is a farmer. He is married. His wife's name is Mavis. They have four children. His uncle is Zakia, who owns the trade store, and his relatives seem to be important people in the village.' Or again, 'Agnes is a young school-teacher, working away from her home area. She is keen on sports, and spends her free time training the school-girls in basket-ball and hockey. Her father is a pastor in their own area. Agnes is becoming friendly with one of the young men in the congregation, and seems to be forming a deeper relationship with him.'

If you do not know people well enough to say much about them, then try to know them better, perhaps by visiting them, or by taking an interest in some of the activities they enjoy.

3. When a particular person seeks your help, try to apply some of the general ideas discussed in this chapter to that person as an individual. For example if Michael, a rather troublesome young man, comes to seek your help, then try to remind yourself that he is a person of great value to God, that he is capable of growth and development, that like all human beings (including yourself) he is self-centred in his thinking and living, that he is one for whom Jesus died and as such is your brother before God.

4. In your times of quietness, pray regularly for the people in your care. Some of your prayers can be general, for all the congregation, or for a larger group. In some you should concentrate on one person or perhaps a particular couple or family.

5. Try to behave to others in ways that show your concern for them. Your patience, respect, honesty, truthfulness – these all help people to feel that you understand their real feelings and needs, and value them as persons who are loved and wanted by God, not as 'things'.

6. Try to apply the ideas we have been discussing to your own life also. Do not try to become an expert judge of others only. First, evaluate your own life, and acknowledge your own needs, especially your need for God's help. In this way, you will come to people not as a judge or critic; you will come to them as a person who has his own difficulties and problems but who has good news to pass on to others. At the practical level, the evaluation of your own life may mean that you have to rethink the way you live in relation to your people: your house, your means of transport, your standard of living, your readiness to work alongside people, your hospitality – anything which in any way helps or hinders your attempt to be 'all things to all men'.

STUDY SUGGESTIONS

WORD STUDY

1. Explain what is mean by a person's 'cultural environment'.
2. The word 'society' can be used to mean several different things. What is it chiefly used to mean in this chapter?
3. What do you understand by the 'unity' of each human being?
4. What do psychologists mean by the word 'defences'?

REVIEW OF CONTENT

5. The *Christian* view of man is one way of describing and understanding people. What are three other ways?
6. (a) On what five truths is the Christian view of man chiefly based?
   (b) For what chief reason should a pastor regard each individual person as being of 'value'?
7. Why are personal relationships important in the work of pastoral care?
8. For what chief reasons do people use 'defences' in their lives?

BIBLE STUDY

9. Each of the following pairs of passages teaches an important truth about human beings. Say in each case (i) What is that truth? and (ii) What is its chief meaning for the work of pastoral care?
   (a) Genesis 1.26–28 and Psalm 8.3–5
   (b) Psalm 14.2–3 and Romans 3.23
   (c) John 3.3, 16, 17 and 2 Corinthians 5.17
   (d) Matthew 10.29–31 and Matthew 12.9–12.

APPLICATION, OPINION, AND RESEARCH

10. The sight of water buffaloes grazing in a rice field helped Kosuke Koyama to understand the people he wanted to serve (p. 42). What sight might help a pastor in the same way:
    (a) in an African township?
    (b) in an industrial area in India?
    (c) in a village in Britain?
    (d) in your own particular situation?
11. (a) Explain what it means to treat people as 'total beings'.
    (b) Give two examples from your own situation which show this 'total concern' for people.
    (c) Give two examples which show a *failure* to treat people as 'total beings'.
12. Give four examples of particular 'defences' which you have seen in the lives of others, or have experienced in your own life.

13. (a) Discuss with a fellow student or a friend their understanding of the 'I-thou' and the 'I-it' relationships.
    (b) Give two examples of each of these relationships between people.
    (c) In what ways might a pastor be in danger of treating people as 'things' rather than persons.
14. A teacher of pastoral care once wrote: 'Who is this person who comes to the pastor with a burden, bewilderment, perhaps a flaming hatred? For the Christian, the person is Christ Himself standing before the pastor. The Christian faith is that wherever there is human need, there Christ is present.' (See Matt. 25.34–40.)
    (a) What is your opinion of this idea that the person who comes to the pastor for help is really Christ Himself?
    (b) If you find difficulties in the idea, what are they?
    (c) If you accept the idea, what effect would it have in the work of pastoral care?
15. The Chinese philosopher Confucius once said: 'Men's natures are alike – it is their habits which carry them far apart.' Do you agree or disagree with this idea? Give reasons for your answer.
16. Give two examples from your own experience of Christians who have challenged the accepted ideas and customs of the society in which they lived.

4
Understanding Oneself

WHAT AM I? WHO AM I?

We saw in chapter 3 that a pastor needs to ask and answer the question: 'What is Man?' He also needs to ask and answer: 'What am *I*?', and 'Who am *I*'. He needs to apply his understanding of people generally to himself and his own situation, he needs to gain a clear 'self-image', and a clear idea of his role as a pastor.

The ancient Greek philosophers taught that one way to gain wisdom is through self-examination and self-knowledge: 'Man, know thyself' they said. Paul too urged Christians to examine and evaluate their faith and their lives: 'Examine yourselves . . . . Test yourselves' (2 Cor. 13.5).

In thinking about these matters it is useful to distinguish clearly between the term 'self-image' and the term 'role'. In this chapter we shall use 'self-image' to mean the picture each one of us has of what we are in *ourselves*, that is, the way in which we see our own particular characteristics, qualities, faults, habits, attitudes. We could say that our self-image helps us to answer the question '*What* am I?'. We shall use the term 'role' to mean the picture each of us has of what we are *in relation to other people*. We could say that the idea we have of our role helps us to answer the question '*Who* am I?'. In both cases the picture we have may be a fairly true one, or we may be mistaken about ourselves. In both cases the picture we have of ourselves is quite likely to be different from the ways in which other people see us and the picture they have of our relationship with them.

SELFHOOD AND SELF-IMAGE

What we think and how we act depends largely on how we understand the world around us, and our place in that world. Each of us sees and understands the world in our own particular way, and this way varies according to our age, culture, experience, situation, and personality, because all these factors affect our ideas and interests and attitudes.

For example, when we have reached the age of forty-five or fifty we are likely to evaluate events in ways that are quite different from the ways in which we evaluated events at the age of twenty to twenty-five. Similarly, one group of people in society have certain ideas about the world around them, and they seek to live and work in ways which reflect their ideas and beliefs. Another group sees things differently, and regards the attitudes and actions of the first group as a danger to their own interests and way of life. This clash of interests may produce conflict, because of different 'perceptions' or 'understandings' of the world.

Even within the Church there are different groups, each of which understands the life of the Church from a particular viewpoint. Each sees the world in a certain way, and this affects the way in which they think about themselves and their relationships with others, that is, their sense of identity, or their 'self-image' as a group.

The same is true of individuals, though people may never express their idea of themselves in words or discuss it with other people. People who think about themselves a lot, and especially those who are ambitious, may have a very clear self-image. But most of us have no clear self-image because we give the subject little thought. We simply live out in our lives what we understand ourselves to be, rather than actually thinking about what we are like or what other people think of us.

The 'self' is a person's recognition of his or her own existence and experience. Each individual human being has a unique combination of needs, desires, ideas, and emotions, separate and distinct from those of other human beings, and behaves in certain ways as a result. The self is the 'I' who thinks, acts, feels, and experiences life as a separate individual. This 'selfhood' begins when we are babies and gradually start to sense ourselves as persons. As we grow up, so we start to understand what sort of person we are – our habits, attitudes, beliefs, abilities, are gradually shaped. This developing understanding is strengthened and influenced by the way other people treat us – how they speak to us, the names they give us, and by any other continuing factors in our situation. So we build up a picture of ourselves, a 'self-image'.

We also begin to understand ourselves in relation to our families, our home, our possessions. Other people have a strong influence on what we think about ourselves and how we ought to behave. Our parents and family in particular influence our ideas of what we *ought* to be like, what we ought or ought not to do. These ideas are made stronger by rewards for 'good' behaviour or punishment for 'bad' behaviour. So we begin to build up not only our self-image but a 'self-ideal' – the picture of the 'ideal' self we would like to become.

ROLES AND RELATIONSHIPS

The sense of selfhood remains constant in a person even though the actual self-image may change as the person develops and changes over the years. But our 'role' will vary at any one time in different situations and according to the different people we are involved with and the activities we engage in. As with the sense of self, we begin to develop 'roles' from the time we are babies. As we become conscious of ourselves and our surroundings, we begin to understand our place in the family set-up. We become aware of the different members of the family and of our relationships with them. We see how they feel and act towards us, and we respond to this. We begin to learn what other people will expect of us. We learn that if we behave in a certain way, people are likely to react accordingly.

As we grow up and make friends, as we go to school and then to work, we learn our place or role in each situation, We gradually discover and understand the relationships which exist and the sort of behaviour that will fulfil our needs, provide satisfaction, and avoid punishment or rejection by others. Just as our self-image may change with time, so our role differs according to our situation and the people around us. Within the family, for example, each person has a particular place or role to fulfil. There will be many things they share in common, but what is expected of each, their duties and responsibilities, will be different. The role of the mother will differ from that of a child. The role of an uncle will differ from that of a son. Each person will also have a different role in relation to different members of the family. My role as a son towards my father is different from my role as elder brother towards my younger brothers and sisters.

And roles will change with time. When a girl is a younger daughter, she has certain attitudes and responsibilities towards her parents as she is growing up. When she marries and has children of her own, she still has the role of a daughter to her parents, but she will express this role in different ways now that they have become old. Now she will look after them, instead of being looked after by them as she was when she was a child.

Thus each individual can have many different roles, yet remain the same person. At school we behave in certain ways towards the school staff because we are their 'students'. But we act in quite different ways towards our classmates and others of our own age group.

Even though we are often not aware of it, it is our self-image, and our experience in various roles, that help us to develop ways of behaviour which are suitable for the situations in which we live. For example, in an industrial situation a man with little training may remain in a subordinate role at work all through his life. But if that same man is also a first-class athlete, say, or an expert trumpet player, then perhaps he may also have an important role as team captain at the local sports club, or as leader of a music group. And we behave in different ways to match the roles we have in each different situation.

Thus a clear understanding of our self-image and of our various roles will help us to clarify and define our relationships with others. We can learn how to behave towards others in a constructive way, and how others can be expected to behave towards us. Our status, privileges, and responsibilities become clearer to us. Situations become more stable and predictable, and this helps to fulfil our need – and the need of others – for security and satisfaction.

GROUP IDENTITY AND SELF-IMAGE

As we have already noted, groups of people as well as individuals experience a sense of self. As members of a family, or a school, a work team, or a sports side, we have our individual self-image, but we also share in a sense of *group* identity. We see ourselves as part of a group self-image, and this is very important for the welfare of the group as a whole. A tribe or nation, consisting of many different groups of people, can also have a sense of selfhood, which is sometimes called its national identity, or national image. In times of change we see groups and nations, as well as individuals, either searching for a true identity, or trying to emphasize the identity which they feel belongs to them. For example, when Papua New Guinea became an independent nation in September 1975, feelings of national identity were strong and the theme of 'nationhood' was constantly heard over the radio and in other news media. An example of this emphasis appeared in a national newspaper report: 'An Arts and Craft exhibition to promote cultural heritage and identity was held at Hagara Primary School recently. This project was in line with the Education Department's recently announced drive: "Keep our national identity".'

CHANGE AND CONFLICT

When a familiar role is upset and we are placed in a situation where our role is not clear or new roles have to be worked out, then our sense of security is threatened and we suffer from anxiety. This happens especially at times of 'crisis' in our lives, for example when there is a death in the family, when we move to a new area, or start a new job. But many of us become anxious and distressed *whenever* we are faced with a new situation. We become uneasy because we are confused about what we ought to do, or unsure of what our new role is to be. If a new role brings new responsibilities, we may feel inadequate for it, and this brings the fear of failure. All of these feelings will affect our self-image. They will also affect our ability to fulfil the roles expected of us, and our relationships with other people.

The great drive for national independence, which has brought about so many changes in Africa and Asia in recent years, must be seen as part of a world drive for personal and national first-class status, for a sense of personal and national security and self-identity. Many people are experiencing a desperate need for a positive self-image, as they

'Each individual can have many different roles, yet remain the same person. . . . Because a pastor's work consists of helping others, it is especially important for him to understand his role' (pp. 57 and 60).

An ordinand in Benin changes his role of student for that of father as he teaches his little daughters the alphabet, and an experienced pastor on a refresher course in Singapore takes the role of student again as the tutor corrects his work. Which of these two changes of role might be the more difficult to understand?

have entered a period of rapid change, especially in their religious beliefs, in the social structure within which they live, and in their general 'world-view'. The effects of changes like these on people's lives and on their ideas about right and wrong, and the role of the pastor in 'using' the authority which the Lord has given him for building up and not for tearing down (2 Cor.13.10), are discussed more fully in chapter 12.

THE PASTOR AND HIS SELF-IMAGE

We turn now to the pastor's own self-image, his understanding of the role of a pastor, and his confidence in his ability to fulfil that role.

As we have seen, a sense of identity, a positive self-image, and a secure role or roles in life are important for groups of people and also for individuals. If we feel that we are 'second class', lacking in ability and opportunity, and with little or no possibility of change, then our self-image will affect the ways in which we act towards others, and the attitudes of others towards us. A weak self-image weakens our confidence in ourselves and in our work, and this in turn weakens people's confidence in our ability to help them. A positive self-image, on the other hand, helps us to accept ourselves for what we are. This in turn helps us to accept responsibility, and gives others confidence in us, because we see and understand ourselves in a positive way.

Because a large part of a pastor's work consists of helping others, it is especially important for him to understand his role, and to see himself as a person capable of performing that role. If he sees himself as inadequate and inferior he will lack confidence in his ability to be a good pastor. This will affect the work he does and will actually bring about the result that he fears: people will lack confidence in him. His self-image as a pastor will be so weak that he will not be able to help them cope with their problems.

A pastor must be like a good doctor, who has confidence in his own ability and in his medical knowledge. This confidence is conveyed to the patient, who will be confident that the doctor can help him to regain health. If a doctor lacks confidence in his knowledge of medicine or his ability to help his patients, then few people will seek his help and those who do will not follow his advice. Of course if a doctor is over-confident, if his self-image is good when his ability is really poor, then he is likely to harm his patients instead of helping them, and the same is true of a pastor. Our self-image must be a true and valid one if we are to make the best use of the capacities we do have.

A pastor must have knowledge, faith, and training as a basis for his confidence in his ability as a counsellor. In other words, he needs to have a positive self-image *as a pastor*. This does not mean, however, that he should deceive himself, or pretend to be what he is not. Having a good self-image does not mean forgetting or hiding our weaknesses. It means recognizing and accepting the truth about ourselves. Then we can work successfully within our limitations, and make the most of our talents. A good self-image must be based on honest self-examination and self-evaluation.

If this self-evaluation is to be of value it must in turn be based on valid information. We gain such information from three chief sources:

    (a) from what we know about ourselves – our self-knowledge;

    (b) from what others know and tell us about ourselves;

    (c) from God's evaluation of our lives.

Source (a) and source (b) are both subject to human error, and therefore must be evaluated carefully. Source (c) is not subject to human error. God has given us the life of Jesus Christ as the standard by which we can truly evaluate our own self-knowledge and other people's opinions of us.

WAYS TO SELF-KNOWLEDGE

Students in the subject of human relations sometimes use a method of gaining self-knowledge which many Christians too have found useful. It is known as the 'Johari Window' (from the names 'Joe' and 'Harry' of the two Americans who invented it). See Figure 1, p. 62.

Through this 'window' we see our lives as consisting of four main areas:

1. *A Clear or 'public' area* – this is the part of our life that we know about and that others know: the part we share with them. This area contains, for example, our name, the place where we live, our family, our personal appearance, our work and our leisure activities, the sort of house we live in, our shared experience with others, our qualifications and capabilities – all the things in our lives that are 'open'.

2. *A Hidden area* – this is the part of our life we ourselves know about, but others do not know. We keep it hidden and do not tell others about it. This area contains, for example, our secret thoughts, feelings, and hopes – the fears we overcome, the pride we hide, perhaps the dislike we feel for certain people, the thoughts and actions we keep secret because we are ashamed of them, or because they are too precious to us to be shared.

3. *A Blind area* – this is the part of our life which others know but we ourselves do not know. This includes the things other people think about us, the attitudes and qualities they see in us, of which we are not aware – perhaps our boring talk, our bossy behaviour and rude habits, the hurt we inflict – and perhaps also some good qualities, or the comfort and support we give to others without realizing it.

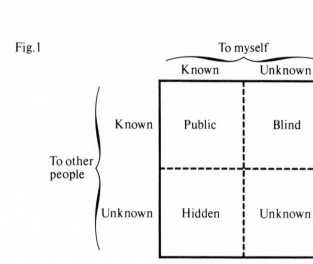

Fig.1

To myself

Known   Unknown

To other people

Known   Public   Blind

Unknown   Hidden   Unknown

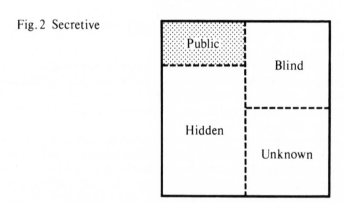

Fig. 2 Secretive

Public

Blind

Hidden

Unknown

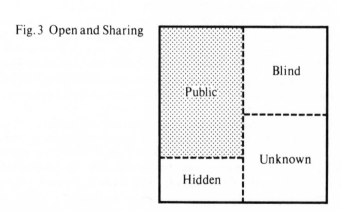

Fig. 3 Open and Sharing

Public

Blind

Unknown

Hidden

4. *An Unknown area* – this is the part of our life that we do not know about, and that others do not know about either. Only God sees and knows this area in us. This area contains our deepest feelings and prejudices, the reasons why we behave and feel as we do, our total personality – perhaps our future destiny and our place in God's plan.

In each person's life the window is different, according to how that person relates to others.

If we are secretive, and find it difficult to share our lives and ideas with others, our window will only have a small public area and a large hidden one. See Figure 2.

If we are open to others, and ready to share our ideas and feelings with them, the hidden area will be reduced and the public area increased. See Figure 3.

If we are unwilling to listen to any criticism from others and stubbornly refuse to think honestly about our lives, then the public area is reduced and the blind area increased. See Figure 4, p. 64.

If we are both secretive and deaf to criticism then both hidden and blind areas will be increased, and the public area will be very small indeed. See Figure 5.

The purpose of the 'Johari Window' is to help us evaluate our lives and gain self-understanding, and improve our relationships with others by increasing the public area and decreasing the hidden and blind areas in our lives. We can do this by:

– *sharing* our ideas, thoughts, and feelings with others (so shedding light on the hidden area);

– *listening* to others, especially about what they see in our lives (this helps to shed light on the blind area);

– *thinking* about and trying to understand some of the deeper areas of our lives: our motives, prejudices, desires, etc. (this helps to open up and shed light on the unknown area).

For Christians there is also another way of opening up the window and gaining a better understanding of the unknown area: that is by seeking to understand how God evaluates our lives. This understanding may come through some sort of 'revelation', or sudden insight and new understanding of ourselves resulting from some crisis in our lives. It may come through a new understanding of some of the psychological processes which operate in our lives, but which are usually hidden from us. It may come to us through Christian teaching, or from our study of the Bible, or from the example of others, and then it provides a standard by which we can evaluate our own and other people's understanding of ourselves. We begin to understand God's evaluation of us in the light of the standard He has shown us in the life of Jesus. The more we are ready to accept God's evaluation of who and what we are, the more we are ready to open up our lives and listen to others,

Fig. 4 Deaf to Criticism

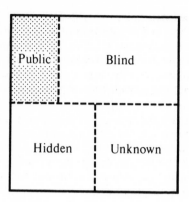

Fig. 5 Secretive and deaf to criticism

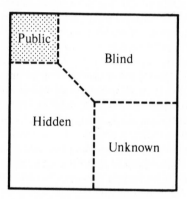

Fig. 6 Open, sharing, listening, understanding

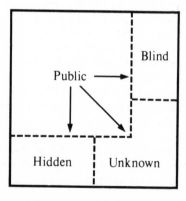

and so achieve good relations with them. As Christians, therefore, we try to open up the public area of the window, and reduce the hidden, blind, and unknown areas as far as we possibly can. See Figure 6.

Of course we can never get rid of the blind, hidden, and unknown areas entirely. Only God knows us completely. Our knowledge of ourselves will always remain incomplete. But we must try to understand as much as possible.

'IN THE LIGHT OF CHRIST'

A pastor's self-knowledge will grow as he involves himself with others, and so gradually opens up the hidden and blind areas of his life. Too often, however, we are unwilling to be open with people, to share with them, or to listen to them. We are afraid that if we do so, we shall be hurt or deceived or 'used' by them. So we remain hidden and secretive. We protect and defend ourselves against others, and even against our own thoughts, for fear our lives may be upset or changed. This tendency to hide from the truth about ourselves affects all people. We see it in Adam, when God called him and instead of responding he hid himself, because he was afraid (Gen. 3.10). Many people have inner 'scars' because they have been hurt or afraid in the past, and this blocks their ability to share with others. The Swiss psychologist Paul Tournier wrote: 'We conceal our person behind a protective barrier. We let it be seen only through the bars. We display certain of its aspects, others we carefully hide.'

Another problem which often prevents good relations with others is that our self-image may be a false one. Perhaps we believe that we are a certain sort of person, but others can see that we are mistaken, and that the picture we have of ourselves is not the true one. We may be too proud of our achievements, and so 'think of ourselves more highly than we ought to think' (Rom. 12.3). Or we may see ourselves as weak and inadequate when really we should be thankful for the good and strong things in our lives. We should think carefully about our lives, and listen to what others say of us. But what we learn of ourselves in this way may need to be corrected by God's evaluation of us. Only 'in the light of Christ' can we gain a true and balanced self-image. All the various aspects of our lives gain true meaning and significance when we see them in this light.

The way to do this is to apply to our lives the truths about human beings generally which we studied in chapter 3 (pp. 35–39). A pastor needs to accept and act upon these as being true for himself. Here are some reminders which may help you to do so:

1. You bear the image of God. You stand in a special relationship to Him and share in some of His qualities: you have the ability to be creative, to communicate, to love and comfort people, to be fair and

just. You are free to make choices, to experience meaning in your life.

2. You are self-centred. In spite of being in God's image you are still a human being. You are sinful, and sin is not just 'bad behaviour', it is separation from God and from His plan for you. The basic cause of sin is self-centredness which spoils the image of God in us and spoils our relationships with other people. In Christ we are renewed, and the Holy Spirit begins to redirect our lives away from self-centredness and towards our true goal of being 'conformed to the image of Christ' (Rom. 8.29). But as human beings we can never wholly escape from the conflict which sin produces in us; and some theologians would say that for committed and 'renewed' Christians this conflict is particularly hard (Rom. 7.25).

3. You are accepted by God. As a pastor, the most important thing to remember is that even though we are sinful and self-centred, God accepts us (2 Cor. 5.17–19). Human beings often accept each other because of their goodness and attractiveness, or their obedience to each other's wishes and plans. But God loves and accepts us whether we are accepted by our fellow human beings or not.

It is very important to recognize yourself as the object of God's undeserved love. You cannot *earn* God's approval and love by your own efforts. You will always fall short. But because of the work of Jesus Christ, God does not condemn you. He freely accepts you as His child, a fellow heir with Jesus. In Jesus you are declared accepted and adequate (Rom. 8.1, 16, 17). *You* have to accept the fact that God accepts you in Jesus Christ. That fact is what makes you want to work to become what God intends you to be.

Many people find the idea of being accepted (or 'justified') by God difficult to understand, because this relationship with God is so different from what happens in our human relationships. Among human beings, people receive rewards for achievement or good behaviour, and are punished for doing wrong. But God's steadfast and sustaining love is a gift of His grace, not something we can barter for, or buy, or earn by our good work (Eph. 2.8, and see Rom. 1.17; 3.24). God does not measure our achievement according to the values of human society and culture, nor according to our ability or the amount of work we do. He measures our achievement according to our faithfulness to His will and purpose (1 Cor. 4.2).

To see yourself as a recipient of God's grace is to gain a new self-image and understanding of yourself. We see a clear example of this in the life of Paul. Paul saw himself as a Jew, a Pharisee, a persecutor of Christians (Acts 22.3, 4, 27, 28; 23.6). But then his eyes were opened and he recognized himself as the recipient of God's love. He began to see himself differently: 'By the grace of God I am what I am' (1 Cor. 15.10). 'Paul, a servant of Jesus Christ' (Rom. 1.1). Paul did not deny or try to hide his sinful weaknesses (Rom. 7.24). He knew that he faced difficult situations; but he accepted the fact that his ability to meet the situations, and his status in relation to other people, did not depend only on his talents and skill and achievements. They depended on God's grace. In the light of God's love for him, Paul gained a deeper understanding of himself which he could never have gained without the grace of God operating in his life. When you recognize yourself as the recipient of God's love, you will also recognize that:

(a) You are a *known* person. God knows and understands you completely – every motive, conflict, idea, and every tendency to behave in a particular way (see Ps. 139.1–6). So you can be honest with Him, and that will help you to be honest with yourself and with other people. You can be open to those who need your help. There is no need to hide from them. You can also be open to receive help from them (2 Cor. 5.10, 11).

(b) You are an *ambivalent* person. You are both good and evil, so you have mixed emotions and motives, and conflicting ideas and feelings. To be 'ambivalent' means to be 'strong on both sides'.

Sometimes we may like a person and want to show our affection for them, yet at the same time we may have some feelings of hatred and unkindness towards that same person, and want to show those feelings also. We often have ambivalent feelings when we are ill. We don't like the illness, so we want to seek help from the doctor. But we also know that the treatment he will give may be painful, and so we are afraid. Sometimes when we are worried about a problem we seek the help and advice of another person, but at the same time we are afraid to tell of the problem because it will be painful to uncover some of the 'sore spots' in our lives. We often have feelings of ambivalence when we have difficult choices to make. Paul experienced ambivalence and conflict in his inner life (Rom. 7.15). Jesus himself struggled with ambivalence as He faced the cross (Luke 22.42). This feeling is very strong when we have to choose between two good and worthwhile alternatives. So ambivalence is not necessarily a sign of failure: it can show our awareness of the problems we have to face. But we have to accept our ambivalence and if necessary seek guidance in order to resolve it.

(c) You are a *'common'* person. Like every other human being, you are unique. But you also share your human nature with all other people. There is no difference between your standing with God and theirs (Rom. 3.9, 19–23). In spite of cultural and personal differences, nearly everyone experiences the same sort of feelings and ideas. The need for good relationships with God and with each other is common to all people, even though it may be expressed in different ways. There is no human experience which God cannot recognize and help with. To share ourselves with others is to find we are building on common ground. It was because of this common bond that Paul tried to be 'all things to all men' (1 Cor. 9. 19–23). This is the meaning of Christ's work as our living High Priest (Heb. 2.14–18; 4.14–15).

(d) You are a *forgiven* person in Christ. Therefore you do not need to be discouraged by your own failures, broken promises, harmful actions and thoughts, unfulfilled wishes and dreams. Your weaknesses have been forgiven and forgotten in Jesus (Heb. 10.14–16, 19–23).

Some pastors have a false self-image, and this affects the way they approach their work. They may lack confidence, thinking of themselves as failures or unfit for the job. Or they may be over-confident, with an exaggerated sense of their own importance. In both cases their self-image needs to be changed before they can be effective as pastors.

All these facts that we have noted above provide the foundation on which you can build a valid and positive self-image. If you have feelings of fear, worthlessness, or inferiority, remember that in Jesus Christ a new strength is possible. In Jesus you can become truly human as God intends. Or if you have feelings of superiority to others and pride in your own ability and success, then remember that even Jesus spoke of Himself as 'one who serves' (Luke 22.27).

THINKING POSITIVELY

How is the change from a negative or false self-image to a valid and positive one to be achieved? Here are six suggestions:

1. Think truthfully and clearly about your life. Do not think too highly or too lowly of yourself. Do not exaggerate your importance, and do not continually describe yourself as weak, sinful, and lacking in ability. Evaluate your abilities honestly in the light of the job expected of you. In this way you will gain a realistic understanding of your life in both its good and its bad aspects (Rom. 12.3).

2. Study and believe the teaching of the Scriptures about your relationship with God in Jesus. Accept these facts even though you may not *feel* their truth. Human feelings change and waver, but God's love is steadfast and will sustain you. Study especially Romans 5.1; 8.1,16,17; 2 Corinthians 5.21, and meditate on the meaning of these passages for your own life.

3. Try to practise a way of living which is open and honest with God, with yourself, and with others. Start with your relationship with God. Acknowledge to Him your personal struggles, doubts, fears, hopes; your failures and your successes. Do not overrate your successes, but do not become tied down in your past failures either. Forget what is past and reach forward to new opportunities (Ps. 32.1–5; Phil. 3.13, 14).

Confession enables you to know yourself, and in Jesus Christ to discover forgiveness and healing. Knowing that God accepts you will give you courage to be more open with others and to overcome the fear of rejection. By understanding yourself better, you are better able to understand other people.

4. Accept the fact that even when you fail you are valuable to God. Faithful service is more important to Him than success. If you measure your value by the amount of work that you do, or by the money you raise for the Church, or by the size of your congregation, you will probably find yourself competing with others, especially with fellow pastors. This can destroy good relationships with them.

5. Acknowledge your abilities and your successes before God with humble thanks. Do not pretend that you have no abilities or gifts. Try to see why God has given you these strengths and how you can use them in His service. Perhaps you have strengths and resources which you are not using, or there may be new things which you could be doing for God (Eph. 3.20).

6. If you wish your ministry to be more effective, work out the objective you wish to achieve, and then desire it, and think and pray about it. Make sure the image you desire for yourself is in harmony with the example and teachings of Jesus. Try to overcome your special difficulties – for example if you find it hard to talk to people, then work at it by actually going to people and talking to them. With God's help, try to make your new self-image a reality in your life.

You may find it helpful to remember the example of other Christians who have gained a clearer understanding of their lives through a new relationship with God and with others in Jesus Christ. Here are three examples of the understanding gained by people who began to see new possibilities for themselves in this way:

Tom Skinner, the American negro we mentioned on p. 38, who was also a leader in the fight for racial equality, wrote: 'Christ has given me true dignity. I am a Son of God. As a Son of God I have all the rights and privileges that go with that rank. I have the dignity that goes with being a member of the royal family of God.'

James Mallory, a European psychiatrist, wrote: 'I belong to God. Jesus Christ is alive and His spirit lives in me. An exciting process has begun which makes it possible for me to reach my rightful destiny and be fulfilled as one created in the image of God. I am a person of extreme value to God. I am a unique person, and uniquely created by God for a unique reason, and I have a unique sphere of influence.'

Johann Kepler, a German astronomer, said: 'I have the privilege of thinking God's thoughts after Him.' (See 2 Cor. 3.4.)

STUDY SUGGESTIONS

WORD STUDY

1. Which *three* of the following words are nearest in meaning to the word 'role' as used in this chapter?
   money ability place respect possessions position attitude occupation relationship
2. Complete the following sentences:
   An 'ambivalent' person is one who . . .
   Something is described as 'unique' when it . . .

REVIEW OF CONTENT

3. What is the difference between:
   (a) A person's 'self', and
   (b) A person's 'self-image'?
4. Draw a Johari Window for:
   (a) A person who is willing to share *all* his feelings and thoughts with others;
   (b) A person who finds it difficult to share his own thoughts and feelings with others, but is always anxious to hear their opinion about him.
5. (a) Explain what it means to be 'accepted' in Christ.
   (b) Give an example of this sort of acceptance in human relationships.
   (c) In what ways is acceptance in Christ different from any human relationship?

BIBLE STUDY

6. In each of the following pairs of passages we can find a particular idea about the relationship of human beings with God. For each pair, say what is that idea, and what is its meaning for the work of a pastor.
   (a) Romans 8.1,2 and Colossians 2.13,
   (b) Romans 6.5 and 1 Corinthians 6.17,
   (c) Romans 8.16,17 and Galatians 4.4, 5.
7. Each of the following passages emphasizes a different aspect of the 'oneness' of all people before God. What particular aspect is emphasized in each case?
   (a) Matthew 15.27,28   (b) Luke 18.15–17   (c) Acts 15.8
   (d) Romans 3.21–25
8. The passages Ephesians 2.4–9 and 2 Timothy 1.8, 9 both state that salvation depends on God's grace. But Ephesians 2.10 and James 2.14–17, 24–26 emphasize the need for human effort and 'works' to make salvation a reality. How would you answer someone who

said 'These two pairs of passages contradict each other, so I cannot believe that salvation is possible'?

APPLICATION, OPINION, AND RESEARCH

9. Describe:
   (a) At least three ways in which your own role in relationship to the members of your family has changed since you were a child.
   (b) At least three ways in which your self-image has changed as a result of changes in your situation since you were a child.
10. Mallory said: 'I have a unique sphere of influence.' In your own present or future situation as a pastor:
    (a) In what ways, if any, do you see your sphere of influence as being 'unique' – i.e. are there any special opportunities or possibilities, any special problems, or anything which you see as 'unique' in your situation, which provides a big challenge for your ministry?
    (b) What dangers are there, if any, in regarding oneself as 'unique'?
11. The negro Tom Skinner found a new freedom through his relationship with Jesus Christ. In what ways does becoming a Christian help a person in the struggle to become a 'first-class citizen'; and in what ways, if any, can Christianity be a drawback to achieving true human dignity?
12. (a) In what ways, if any, is the idea of the Johari Window specially helpful in your own cultural situation?
    (b) In what ways, if any, does it conflict with any strongly held cultural ideas about human relationships?
13. Write a brief statement of your own self-image as a pastor. Share this with a friend or fellow student and ask them how far they agree or disagree with your picture of yourself.
14. How would you answer someone who asked: 'What is the most important desire that you carry in your innermost heart?'

For a group exercise on the Johari Window see p. 277.

PART II
THE MINISTRY OF
COUNSELLING

5
People's Need for Counselling

RECOGNIZING NEED

The ministry of counselling is an important part of the work of pastoral care. It is not a 'special' ministry in the sense of being separate or apart from other aspects of a pastor's work. Even if a parish or circuit minister concentrates on counselling, he is nearly always involved in some other aspects of ministry as well. But anyone who wishes to do counselling work needs to understand the meaning of counselling, and to learn the skills that are required. He will also need to consider the relationship between counselling and the other aspects of his ministry.

As we have seen, pastoral care means helping people to meet the various crises and changing situations which come about in their lives. It is likely to involve:

Healing people, by helping them to become 'whole', both physically and in their personal relationships;

Sustaining people, in times of difficulty, frustration, and sorrow;

Guiding people, as they seek to clarify their thinking and decide on the way to act in different situations;

Reconciling people, challenging them to face the weakness and guilt of their broken relationships and find reconciliation and restoration, both with God and with other people.

In all this work of helping people, counselling will play an important part.

Why do people need counselling? Here are two 'case studies', or examples of counselling situations which actually occurred. Read them through carefully, and as you think about each example, ask yourself these questions: What sort of help is being given, and how is it being given? Is it through advice, or instruction? Are people being corrected? encouraged? guided? comforted? – or what is it that the pastor is offering them?

Example 3: Pastor Richard, who was also chaplain in a university college, records a conversation he had with Jerome, one of the students there:

'I noticed that Jerome seemed to be doing a lot of daydreaming, and had lost his usual high spirits. He just seemed to hang on. I went to see him when there was no one else around, and tried to have a conversation with him. First we talked about everyday things, but Jerome did not take the opportunity to come up with his worries. So I asked him: 'Jerome, what is the matter? Are you sick or only lazy?' He seemed confused, but answered:

Jerome: I – Oh, I am not sick. But I did not go for a holiday last Christmas, so I feel a little homesick.

Pastor: You are thinking about your home, aren't you?

Jerome: Yes I am. Not only about my village, but also about my parents and friends there.

Pastor: And now you feel unhappy here. Your thoughts are with your people all the time?

Jerome (smiling): Yes, but I am not only thinking about my parents. Something else is bothering me. (He seems afraid to talk about his problem.)

Pastor: This problem really worries you?

Jerome: Very true. (His eyes seem to be looking into the far distance; he does not want to talk.)

Pastor: Yes, Jerome, you find it hard to talk about it to another person.

Jerome: I do not want to hide it from you. I am thinking about my girlfriend. Last year I did not think so much about her. When I left home she gave me her picture, and I gave her mine. But now I do not know – is she waiting for me, or has she got married? If she could read and write, I could send her a letter, but she is illiterate. So I keep thinking about her, and I am very absent-minded during classes. I do not take in what the teachers are talking about. So I am worried about my work too.

Pastor: So you feel it's a big problem?

Jerome: Yes, it's a great problem. I don't know what to do about it.

Pastor: You can't make up your mind. (A long pause follows.) You like this girl and now you are thinking perhaps she has forgotten you – perhaps she has married some other fellow.

Jerome: I don't really think she has married, but she might have forgotten me. It makes me really worry.

Pastor: Yes, Jerome, you are in suspense. You would like to know what the girl is thinking and what she wants to do. But you are far away from her here, and it is difficult to find out. What do you think you could do now?

Jerome: It's not so easy to say. I'm not so sure. I suppose I shall have to wait until I get home. There are only three months of this semester left. I think I can overcome my worry, but it's not easy to control my thoughts.

Pastor: You're afraid you will not be able to master your thoughts, and this may interfere with your final examination? Is that it?

Jerome: Yes, that's the trouble.

Pastor: Jerome, you would like very much to graduate in three months time, wouldn't you?

Jerome: Yes, I very much want to graduate. I think I can forget my worries for the time being. I had better go back to my studies.

Pastor: So you think you can let your problem rest for a while?

Jerome: Yes, I think I can. It's only a short time to graduation. After that I go back home. Then I can find out about my girlfriend.

Pastor: It's like when you want to start a new garden. You have to work hard, and when the work is nearly finished you feel you want a rest. Your body is aching and you're thirsty, but you don't really want to stop working altogether. So you take a breath and start working again until the work is finished. Do you feel like that?

Jerome: Yes, I do. You are right. I will try.'

Example 4: In this situation the pastor was present, but the actual counselling was done by the village elders and other villagers. That is, there was group counselling, and three people were being counselled.

Something was happening in the village which made everyone unhappy. Everyone was talking about it. So the chief called for a meeting, and everyone, including the women and the pastor, had to be present. The meeting was held in the local government council house. The chief started the meeting:

Chief: I think all the people are here and we should start the meeting.

Villagers: (Some nod their heads, some say 'Yes', some cough, some clear their throats, etc.)

Chief: I am not happy to hear about the situation of Foto and his wife Susi with Foto's younger brother Job. Our people do not want this thing to happen here. So we will talk about the matter and see if we can do something about it.

Villagers: (Some murmur, some say 'Yes' clearly.)

Chief: Before we go further, I want to ask the member of the village council whom we call 'Custom Boss' to question the people concerned in the situation.

Council Member: Thank you Chief. I understand that everyone in this village had heard about Susi and Job going together, and a few of us have found them sleeping together.

Susi: (angrily): Eh? Eh? Who said that? Where did you find us doing that?

Council Member (turning to the people): OK, who found them?

A Villager (speaking loud and clear): Samuel found them. Come on Samuel, speak up.

Samuel: Yes, I found them sleeping together when Foto was out one day. And more than once.

Susi: No, Samuel is telling lies. That is not true.

Villagers: Oh yes, that is a true story.

Council Member: All right, all right then. We had better ask Foto. Foto, how do you find your wife these days?

Foto (reluctant to talk at first, but then in a clear smooth voice): Since we were married ten years ago, we were good to each other. We loved each other very much, and through having children we came to know each other well. (Pause.) But since we had our fifth child Susi does not show the same love to me as she used to.

Council Member: What do you mean when you say that?

Foto: I mean that she does not want me sleeping with her. I sleep in the kitchen now.

Susi (interrupts Foto): There is no room inside with so many children, that is why you sleep in the kitchen.

Foto: But also when she wants to go out anywhere she doesn't tell me. Sometimes I come home and she is not there, and I have to cook.

Susi: Foto, you are telling lies. Look, we have a lot of children. You are a grown up person telling lies.

Foto: I was just telling people about my feelings.

Council Member: That is good, Foto. But Susi, what is your feeling?

Susi: All this talk is lies.

Council Member: Maybe we should hear what Job has to say. Job, is it true that you have been sleeping with Susi?

Job: (Puts his head down and does not want to talk.)

A Villager: Job you had better talk, otherwise we shall know the story is true. (Job still bends down – almost kissing the floor. A roar comes from the women, indicating that Job was actually forcing Susi to go with him. Job stays bending down.)

Another Villager (kneeling down towards Job): Tell us Job, is it true or not?

Job: It is not true.

Villagers (shouting one after another): You are telling lies.

A Villager: He doesn't want to talk about it, because he did it.

An Older Villager: Job and Susi have been going together for two years now, and that fifth child of Susi's does not belong to Foto but to Job.

A Woman Villager: Yes, that child does not look like his brothers and sisters, he looks like Job.

Older Villager: Are you going to talk or not, Job?

Chief: Job, you'd better say what you want to say, otherwise we will punish you.

Job (looking up for the first time): I didn't do it.

Villagers: Why don't we ask Rhotha, Foto and Susi's elder daughter?

Rhotha: Yes, it's true. Job sleeps with mother while father sleeps in the kitchen.

Villagers: Now we have the truth – now let's punish them.

Susi: Rhotha is telling lies. (She gets up to walk away, but several people grab her and tell her to sit down. She's crying now and doesn't want to listen.)

Pastor: Maybe we should let her go out for a while, and then call her in again.

Council Member: That is a good idea, Pastor, but she won't come back. I think we should finish the matter now.

(The people murmur, but their words are not clear.)

Council Member: Foto, is it true that Job is sleeping with your wife?

Foto: Yes, I think it is true.

Council Member: Well, why don't you fight him then – are you a woman too?

Foto: I can't fight him, he is my brother.

Villagers: Oh well, stupid! (They murmur and shout.) Let him help his brother with his wife. (Some burst out laughing.)

Council Member: Job, Foto says it is true that you are going with his wife.

(Job stands up, shaking all over. He admits that he has been going with Susi for two years. Then he sits down and everyone is quiet. No one knows what to say. Susi is still crying, and refuses to talk or listen.)

Council Member: Now we know the matter is true. According to custom, Job must give a custom feast as a sign of compensation and of reconciliation to Foto and his family.

Chief: Yes we must settle the matter. Job, we are happy that you admit your wrong. Never do it again. No one in the village must do silly things like this. Susi, have you anything to say? (Susi is still crying and refusing to look up.) Susi you must go now and you must not do this bad thing again. During the custom feast, you must apologize to everybody.

(Susi gets up and moves away, still crying. The villagers go back to their houses. When the time came for the custom feast, Susi and Job apologized to all the villagers, and the matter was regarded as settled.)

In both these examples the counselling was offered as a means of helping people in a problem situation. But the two situations were very different, and the sort of counselling differed too.

In Example 3, the counsellor helped Jerome chiefly by patient listening. He gave *guidance* and *encouragement.* He led Jerome to a clearer understanding of the situation, so enabling him to find a solution to his problem. But it was Jerome himself who had to make his own decision to try to concentrate on his work.

In Example 4, Foto and Susi and Job were in a more complicated situation. Several people were involved, and instead of one person acting as counsellor, a group of people together tried to clarify the problem and find a solution. *Right relationships* within the family and in the village as a whole were restored as people were *confronted* with their wrong-doing. Hard words of *correction* and *rebuke* were offered to those concerned before any *solution* and *reconciliation* was possible.

WHAT IS 'COUNSELLING'?

People use the word 'counsel' to express several different ideas. Writers in the New Testament used several different Greek words to describe the various different aspects of what we understand as counselling:

(a) *Nouthesia* means *'giving advice or instruction'* to someone who needs help. It may include the idea of *teaching* or *admonishing*, and also the idea of *warning* or *correcting* people. Paul wrote of his satisfaction that the Christians in Rome were 'able to instruct one another' (Rom. 15.14 – JB has 'give advice to one another'). Paul also summarized one of the aims of his ministry as 'warning' and 'teaching or 'counselling' every man (Col. 1.28). And with the same word Christian leaders were urged to 'admonish' the idle and careless, i.e. to rebuke, correct, and straighten out, their ideas and their attitudes (1 Thess. 5.14).

(b) *Paraklesei* means to *'exhort, comfort, encourage, strengthen'*, and writers in the New Testament used the word above all to describe the work of the Holy Spirit. The Holy Spirit is the 'Paraclete', who comes alongside another person to *guide, comfort, advise* and *strengthen* them. So the Holy Spirit is described as the 'counsellor', 'comforter', the 'helper' (John 14.16,26, TEV and RSV). *Paraklesei* suggests the idea of active involvement and sharing in the troubled situation. The helper or counsellor stands closely alongside the person in need, not apart from or far away from them. We see this in the ministry of Jesus, who shared fully in the living situation of men and women in order to help them. Jesus showed Himself to be the 'Wonderful Counsellor' – the name given to the promised Messiah by the prophet Isaiah (Isa. 9.6).

(c) *Parmutheomai* means to *'cheer up, to encourage'* someone who is timid or easily discouraged; to *'console or comfort'* someone who is sorrowful, as in John 11.31; 1 Thessalonians 2.11 and 5.14.

(d) *Antechomai* means to *'cling to'* or *'hold fast to'* something or someone, as in Matthew 6.24 to *'cling to'* money or be devoted to it; or as in Titus 1.9 to *'hold fast'* to the true message. In counselling it means to hold on to or to hold up spiritually and emotionally someone who is weak.

1 Thessalonians 5.14 gives a good example of these four words used together, as different ways of helping others. They are all linked with another word, *'makrothumeo'*, which means *'to be patient'* or to have patience with others when you feel like giving them up. Taken together these words give a good summary of the meaning of counselling.

From these New Testament examples we can see that the word 'counselling' may contain many ideas, and its particular meaning in any counselling situation will depend on the sort of help needed, and the aim of the counsellor. Thus in Example 3 above, guidance and encouragement are emphasized, but in Example 4, correction, rebuke and advice were given. Yet both were true counselling situations.

During the past twenty-five years, many books have been written on the work of counselling, mostly by authors in Western countries. Courses on pastoral care and counselling are now a regular part of theological education. In several countries 'clinical' pastoral training is given in which students learn the special skills required. However, counselling is not a new or recently discovered skill, but a very old skill which appears in almost every culture. The modern emphasis given to counselling only reflects something which the Church has practised for a very long time.

In 1968, at the Bangkok Conference on Marriage and Family Counselling, many different methods of counselling as practised in the different countries of Asia were discussed. Every cultural group represented at the conference had its own traditional methods, and nearly everywhere these old methods were being weakened and altered because of the new ways of life and the changes which were taking place. But the conference recognized that, in spite of all the differences, 'every culture had its clients and its counsellors, its troubled people, and its priests and pastors'. We should remember this, because some people think that counselling is a new skill developed in the West. It is true that much of the recent study and analysis of counselling methods has been done in Western countries. But there have been skilled counsellors giving help to people in many countries for many centuries. We can find examples from everyday life in all parts of the world.

COUNSELLING IN THE BIBLE

SHARING THE WORK OF COUNSELLING

When Moses was leading the Israelites throught the wilderness, he was visited in the camp by Jethro, his father-in-law, who was himself a priest. Jethro saw that Moses was overworking. Besides leading the people on the journey and in battle, Moses was wearing himself out in administering the law and settling the people's disputes. Jethro advised him to appoint helpers to share in the work of counselling the people, and so lighten the burden of it. Jethro also told Moses what sort of people he should select. (See Exod. 18.1–2.)

WISE COUNSELLORS IN ISRAEL

In Israel, three important groups gave help to the people: the priests, the prophets, and the wise men or elders who were also called 'Judges'. The priests performed the sacrifices and instructed the people in the meaning of the law; the prophets declared the word of the Lord; and the elders gave counsel, teaching and advising people on the meaning of life and helping them to face their everyday problems and difficulties. These wise men or Judges often gathered at the city gate, where it was easy for anyone to find them (Deut. 25.5–10).

IN THE MINISTRY OF JESUS

Jesus presented many examples of counselling – with the Samaritan woman at the well (John 4); with the sinful woman (John 8.1–11); with Zaccheus (Luke 19.1–10); with Simon the Pharisee (Luke 7.36–50). We shall study the counselling methods of Jesus in more detail in chapter 6.

PAUL AS COUNSELLOR

In many of Paul's letters we find references to his counselling of needy people in different ways: comforting them (2 Cor. 1.3–11); instructing and correcting them (Acts 20.31); warning and teaching them (Col. 1.28).

COUNSELLING IN THE CHURCH

We have already noted in chapter 2 some of the examples of pastoral care in the past life of the Church. There has always been a ministry of counselling in the Church, and many Christian writers, both before and after the Reformation, have emphasized people's need for good counselling, especially at times when great changes were taking place in society.

One of these writers was Martin Bucer, a German priest who followed Zwingli as leader of the Reformed Church in Switzerland, and was later a professor of divinity at Cambridge University in England. He believed that if the Church was to be a community of love, ministers must guide and instruct their people through a regular plan of visiting. He said: 'One must not confine Christian teaching and exhortation to the church service and the pulpit, for there are many who interpret and understand it with respect to others rather than with respect to themselves. Therefore it is necessary to instruct the people at home and to give them individual Christian guidance.'

This method of instructing and guiding individuals in spiritual and moral matters was called 'catechizing'. Some ministers found it more valuable than preaching to a large group of people. Richard Baxter (see p. 23) wrote: 'Daily I am forced to wonder at how ignorant many of our people are, that have been my hearers for ten or twelve years, while I spoke as plainly as I was able to speak. But in one hour's familiar instruction of them in private they seemed to understand more than they did in all their lives before.'

At that time, the pattern of society in England was changing quickly, just as it is in many countries today. People felt they needed help in making decisions and finding answers to their personal problems. One writer compared the work of the pastor or minister to that of a lawyer or doctor: 'As the lawyer is a counsellor for their estates and the doctor for their bodies, so the minister is a counsellor for their souls.' Many people were experiencing a deep feeling of anxiety and despair, caused by a sense of 'lostness' in a new society where ways of thinking and behaving were changing too quickly for them to understand what was happening. Those who suffered in this way often kept to themselves, brooded about their feelings, and sometimes even attempted to kill themselves.

Many manuals and handbooks were therefore produced to help ministers counsel such people effectively. The advice usually given was that each person should be seen and counselled individually, and should perhaps be sent to a doctor in case they were physically sick. If they were not, then they were to be encouraged to share their secrets and distress with the minister. After careful listening, the minister could help to resolve their doubts, pray with them, and comfort them with some Scripture promises. They should also be advised to work hard, and to try and help other anxious and despairing people. The minister must be very patient. He must identify with people, sharing their sorrows and tears. He must be a good listener, and a good keeper of secrets. Above all, he must not get discouraged himself.

One problem which faced pastors at that time, and which still faces them today, is that although many people need help, they are often afraid to come to the pastor. Henry Scougal, a Puritan minister writing in the 17th century said: 'Our greatest difficulty is in dealing with the wills of men and making them want to be cured. They have the disease, but shun the medicines like poison, and have no desire to be well. So they do all they can to keep us strangers to their souls, and try hard to conceal their problems. It is hard to do anything towards a cure when they will not let us know the disease.'

TRADITIONAL OR 'CULTURAL' COUNSELLING

In many non-western societies counselling is an important part of the traditional social structure. We sometimes call this sort of counselling 'cultural' counselling, because the methods used relate directly to, and only have meaning in, the particular culture and customs of the people. This is especially true in countries where there are many different languages and many different tribal groupings and customs. Cultural counselling covers all sorts of social and religious matters and is sometimes aimed at settling problems that concern the whole community, not only advising and instructing individuals.

The following is a description of traditional cultural counselling

'Although many people need help, they are often afraid to come to the pastor' (p. 80).

Lonely and jobless men queue for a free meal at a relief depot in New Zealand. A Zambian girl with a big decision to make finds comfort in talking over her problem with a professional fortune-teller. In what ways, if any, might a pastoral counsellor have given these needy people more effective help?

methods in Papua New Guinea, but the points made could apply equally in many African countries today, as well as in other parts of Asia and the Pacific region. The help given was not *called* 'counselling' (which is a modern word), but it did have many of the characteristics of counselling as it is understood in the Church today.

1. Counselling was, and is, part of the traditional *educational system* of the community, by which the advice and wisdom of the elders is passed on to younger generations.

2. Because it was an important part of the social structure, the methods of counselling usually followed traditional social patterns. Society was built on a *chain of authority*, from the chief or 'big man' at the top down through various leaders and people with special responsibilities, to the ordinary members of the community, and their children. Counselling was given by people who were recognized as having authority to speak and advise – the clan chiefs, leaders, fathers, mothers, magicians, those who knew the secrets of the spirit world, etc. This work of counselling was not limited to one particular person or group. Certain individuals might give advice on particular problems because they were known to have a special knowledge of that subject. Often, however, several people would give advice on such a problem, and all would be heard with respect.

3. Skill as a helper or counsellor did not come from learning 'techniques' of counselling out of a textbook. It was based on *wisdom and experience*. A person would be regarded as a wise helper if he or she showed a deep understanding of people's experiences and difficulties, and if the advice they gave worked out well for individuals and for the community as a whole. Skill in counselling was judged on experience and results, not on taking a course or passing an examination.

4. Because of the accepted patterns of authority in the society, counsel given by an older and more experienced person to a younger person was always to be *obeyed*. It was not expected that younger and less experienced people would refuse to listen or disobey the advice given. If they did disobey, then the welfare of the whole community was affected.

5. Advice and counselling instruction was usually given *to* people *as members of a group, usually a family or clan*, rather than as separate individuals. Even though a person might seek help for a particular individual problem, the counselling given usually related that person to the community as a whole. And groups would be counselled and advised together, even though an individual might be at the centre of the problem. Individuals' problems were seen as problems within the family or community group, and any individual problem was regarded as less important than the security and welfare of the whole commun-

ity. Thus in the problem of adultery, or any action involving more than one person, the individual solution to the problem was related to the effect of that action on the community.

6. Counselling was also often given, not just *by* one counsellor, but *by a group*. In a case of adultery, the whole family would talk over the matter. In disputes between individuals or groups the whole village or neighbourhood would meet for discussion, and different people could give their opinions and ideas. The final decision or summing up was usually given by the head man or other leader, and so the matter would be settled. Everyone would have the opportunity to listen, and perhaps to speak as well, and the decision and solution would be known to all (see p. 76). This 'group counselling' did not prevent individual help from being given to people deeply involved in the problem; but unlike most Western counselling, traditional 'cultural' counselling was counselling in the community context. Any solution had to be acceptable to the community as a whole, and individuals 'adjusted' to the community, not the other way round.

7. Counselling involved *more than just giving advice*. Talking, as described in points 2, 5, and 6 above, was very important, and a problem would be discussed at length until everyone had had their say. But words were not always enough. Often the problem could only be fully solved by some *ritual action*, of purification, cleansing, or compensation, especially when one person had wronged another or had done something affecting the whole community. If a man committed adultery, then he would be advised, corrected, and rebuked and would also have to pay a suitable compensation to others involved. This was part of the help given. In some situations the payment of compensation, whether money or goods, was the most important part of the solution. Once this was paid, the matter was regarded as settled. There might still be feelings of strife or anger between the individuals concerned (e.g. between Foto and Susi in Example 4). But as far as the community was concerned, the matter was settled.

In many developed countries today, professional counsellors are specially trained for the job. 'Counselling' is a profession, a job in which a person gains his livelihood. This is not the case in cultural counselling, although people look to the recognized leaders for advice in times of need, and the idea of appointing trained counsellors is now spreading. In many countries the ideas and methods of traditional counselling are being replaced by new ideas and techniques learnt from Western textbooks. People are being trained as counsellors – welfare workers, educational counsellors, training officers, pastors – and these people sometimes replace the traditional counsellor or work alongside the traditional methods.

Many people, especially the young and those in urban situations, no longer find the traditional ways of counselling helpful. They find it difficult to accept the authority of older people who may not have experience of the new situations. And many older people, with less education, find that they cannot offer much help to younger people growing up in the rapidly-changing society of today.

For some detailed examples of problems arising in situations of rapid social change, and discussion of the sort of counselling they call for, see chapter 12.

COUNSELLING TODAY

In recent years much research has been done in different parts of the world, to try to discover the methods of counselling most likely to be effective. Various definitions of counselling have been put forward by experts, which may help us to summarize some of the basic facts being emphasized in the present understanding of the subject.

1. *Counselling is a relationship between two or more people*, in which one person (technically called the 'counsellor') seeks to advise, encourage, help, and support another person, or persons (technically called the 'client') to deal more effectively with the problems of life.

2. *Counselling is a series of direct contacts with a person*, with the aim of offering him (or her) assistance in changing attitudes or behaviour.

3. *Counselling is a changing and purposeful relationship between two people* in which methods vary according to the client's need. Both the counsellor and the client share together in this relationship, which aims to help the client to understand his situation and decide what should be done.

4. *Counselling is an active process which joins the client and the counsellor*, when the client wants assistance, and the counsellor is able to give it. The aim is to help the client to learn to deal more effectively with the reality of his environment.

From these definitions we can see that counselling is a *relationship* betwen two or more people. It is not a legal or business transaction, but a *personal* relationship. It is also a relationship which is *alive and active*, in which whoever gives the help and whoever receives it are sharing together. We see too that counselling has an *aim* or purpose, which may vary according to the situation. It may help people to gain a better understanding of their difficulties and so deal more effectively with them. It may help them to change their attitudes and behaviour. Finally, we see that the *methods* used in counselling will depend on the need of the client, the situation, and the type of problem to be solved. And although these definitions relate chiefly to situations in which an individual counsellor works with an individual client, they are equally true of situations in which counselling may be undertaken by a group, or where an individual has to be treated as part of a group within the community as a whole.

Here are some examples of the many different types and methods of counselling that will be needed in different situations.

(a) *Clarifying counselling.* This helps to 'open up' or 'clarify' the situation before a problem can be solved or a decision made. People often find it difficult to recognize the real problem confronting them, or they may fail to understand what the consequences will be, when they have a choice or decision to make. Often the counsellor's job is simply to help people think things out for themselves.

Example 5: Peter and Mary had attended the same government secondary school, and become close friends at university. Peter was already promised to marry a young woman from his home area, and his parents and relatives had begun to make plans about the bride-price to be paid. He was not happy with these arrangements because he was in love with Mary and wanted to marry her; however, he did not want to offend his parents. Mary had other difficulties. She liked Peter very much, but she was not happy about his attitude towards her faith. They were both Christians, and Mary was a keen Church member, but Peter had little real interest in the Church. Mary wondered whether she would be wise to marry someone who did not share her faith deeply. So they both needed help in seeing clearly what was involved in their problem. A pastor should be able to give the sort of 'clarifying' counselling that would enable each of them to make a wise decision about their future.

(b) *Educative counselling.* This is called for when people need to know more about the Church's teaching, or want to get their ideas and their facts straight so as to understand and cope with their problem or situation.

Example 6: A young married couple, Harrry and Deborah, have come to talk about the baptism of their first child. They are not regular Churchgoers, and they need instruction about the meaning of baptism, and about their responsibility towards the child and the Church.

Example 7: Jacob is leaving school, and although he has attended career guidance classes, he is still not clear where his real aptitude lies, or what he really wants to do. He needs some help in thinking about his future work, and whether he should try for a job at once, or seek further training.

Educative counselling could help each of these people to think more clearly about their situation.

(c) *Supportive counselling.* This gives a person or a group support and encouragement for some decision they have made, or when they face some difficulty.

Example 8: For many years Thomas had been a bad husband. He had neglected his wife and children, and wasted most of the family money on drink and gambling. But now he had experienced God's call to change his life. He wanted to become an active member of the Church, and to be a better husband and father. He believed that with God's help he could do this, but was finding his old habits very hard to break. His friends were always asking him to drink with them, and made fun of his desire to be a different person. Supportive counselling would help Thomas to stand firm in his new desire to be better. So the pastor suggested that he should reaffirm his baptismal promises, and told him of the strength he would receive from coming regularly to Holy Communion, and from making new friends within the Church.

This is the sort of situation in which other Church members can be encouraged to back clients up in their new resolution, and assure them of help and support. Supportive counselling is often most effective when it is carried out by a group.

Example 9: Mr Batoga moved into town with his wife, in order to start a new job. Soon after arriving, however, he was hurt in an accident at work, and was told he would be several weeks in hospital. Mrs Batoga was terribly worried, wondering how to look after the family in his absence. She was far from her family and friends and felt very lonely in facing this new difficulty. But the pastor assured her that she would find many new friends among the Church members, who would stand by her and help her in this time of trouble. This made it much easier for her to face the future with courage rather than fear.

In both these situations the *words* of counsel given by the pastor as an individual, were backed up and supported by the *actions* of the Church members as a group.

(d) *Crisis counselling:* A 'crisis' occurs when something happens to upset a person's life or relationships, which they find difficult or impossible to cope with. It may be sickness, the death of a close relative, adultery of a marriage partner, loss of a job, etc. A group of people, too, can experience a crisis when something suddenly upsets their security. If the crisis is very severe, people may break down in their lives unless they are given help. On the other hand, if support and comfort is provided through a concerned counsellor, the person or group may actually grow in their lives as the result of the crisis.

Example 10: After heavy rains there was a land-slide near to a village in the highlands of Papua New Guinea. Several of the villagers were killed, many families lost their homes, and the whole community was saddened by the shock of what had happened. A sympathetic pastoral counsellor was able to offer comfort and support to the villagers both in his preaching and his advice to those who had lost members of their family. He arranged for those who had lost their homes to be given temporary shelter in the school, and encouraged other families to offer them hospitality while their houses were being rebuilt. In this way he was able to comfort individuals and the village as a whole in its time of crisis.

(e) *Confronting counselling.* This has to be undertaken when people need to be challenged to face up to wrong actions in their lives, to seek forgiveness from God or from others, and to make what restitution they can. Or sometimes a person needs to be shown clearly the way his life is heading. He needs to be 'confronted' with the probable result or effect of his way of living and thinking. As we have seen (p. 48), people are not always honest about their problems. Sometimes they accuse others so as to cover up their own failures and wrong-doing. They may refuse to accept responsibility. They may try to avoid discussing their situation. Then they need to be confronted with the facts. A great biblical example of confronting counselling was when Nathan challenged David to acknowledge his wrong-doing with Bathsheba, and to accept the responsibility for his actions (2 Sam. 11 and 12). To 'confront' means to come 'face to face' with something or someone. In counselling it means that people come 'face to face' with the truth about themselves, and look honestly at their situation.

Example 11: Grace came to arrange for her baby to be baptized, but she was not married, and the pastor felt she needed to discuss herself rather than the baby. As he explained to her, the mother is the biggest influence on a baby's life. The pastor found that Grace knew the Bible well, though she had not attended church for some years, ever since she had been involved with the child's father. Now the pastor showed her that the way back to God was open to her through Jesus, and she became deeply moved, clearly wanting to put her life right. He asked her if she wanted to tell God anything else, and she broke down completely, speaking of an abortion she had had earlier which had made her feel guilty of murder. She was clearly repentant, and the pastor assured her that God's forgiveness was offered to her for that sin, as for any other. After speaking of all that was wrong with her life, Grace said that this was the first time she had felt any happiness for many years. The next Sunday she came to Holy Communion, and from that moment she felt accepted by God and His people, and her life became one of increasing progress, blessing, and confidence.

(f) *Preventive counselling.* The purpose of counselling is not only to help people get out of trouble. Sometimes the aim is to *prevent* them from getting into trouble. Some problems can be seen before they actually arrive, and often a problem which already exists can be prevented from becoming worse.

Example 12: The students in the higher forms of a Jamaican school were very interested in the subject of boy-girl relationships. They were keen to discuss the problems which might arise, and the school chaplain knew that several of them had difficulty in understanding and controlling their growing sexual desires. To help them in this he organized a small group to talk about such things together. He also arranged that any of them who wanted to discuss such questions more privately could come and see him individually. This sort of preventive counselling can help people to avoid the problems which can result from the possible wrong use of sexual desire.

(g) *Spiritual counselling.* The pastor is a representative of the Church, and there is always a religious or spiritual aspect to his ministry of counselling. There are often spiritual issues involved, even when the problem is not directly concerned with religious matters. Many people are troubled by guilt, loneliness, fear of death, and many other thoughts and feelings relating to the deep spiritual issues of life. Often they want to ask questions about salvation and forgiveness. A pastor may have the opportunity of helping people to commit their lives to Christ as a result of his counselling. Spiritual problems and issues should never be treated as less important than other sorts of difficulty. Similarly, it sometimes happens that what seems to be a spiritual or religious problem is merely covering up some difficulty which may not be related to spiritual issues at all. The pastoral counsellor needs to be aware of the reality of spiritual issues when he is counselling people in need. But at the same time he should not make the mistake of regarding *all* problems as spiritual and religious ones.

Example 13: Elizabeth had graduated at Nairobi with high honours, and was married to a surgeon there. She had been called 'Elizabeth' after her grandmother, who was a medicine woman. When Elizabeth's husband went on a course in Europe, she began to suffer from nightmares, always about dead and mutilated bodies. At first the dreams came one or two at a time, but later in series of about thirty together, so that she was afraid to go to sleep. The worst thing was that the series of dreams stopped when a death took place in her family. It seemed that Elizabeth had a gift (or curse) of clairvoyance, and her family told her that she must go home and accept initiation as a medicine woman in her tribal village, for the dreams showed the spirit of her grandmother at work in her. As a Christian, Elizabeth was unwilling to do so. She prayed and read the Bible daily, but it did not seem to help her. She said 'I am not saved, though my mother was saved some years ago.' The pastor counselled her by reading some Scripture passages. He prayed for her and laid hands on her, asking Jesus to send away the spirits. He then told her not to be afraid if she got one or two more bad dreams, but she would not get the long sequences again. He showed her that he himself believed she was certainly 'saved' in God's sight, and pointed out to her the marks of the presence of Christ in her life. He advised her to gather a group of friends to pray and read the Bible with her. After some weeks Elizabeth came back to the pastor to say she felt at peace, and a year later she told him that her bad dreams had never come back. Elizabeth had known that her problem was a spiritual one, but was unable to solve it by herself.

WHO SHOULD DO THE COUNSELLING?

People sometimes ask: Is the ministry of counselling open to anyone who is willing to try to help others? Or should it be reserved for those who have been specially trained in counselling techniques, either by the Church or the secular authorities? Is the pastor always the best person to give counselling help?

We have already seen that the sort of counselling needed, and the methods most likely to be effective, will vary according to people's cultural situation and the nature of the problems they are facing. In the same way, the particular situation and type of problem may determine *who* is the best person to give counselling help.

Usually the most effective counsellor is one who, like the pastor, is recognized as having the necessary qualifications and skill, and who is respected by the people for his experience and wisdom. Sometimes, however, someone more closely related to the person in need may be more suitable. For example, if a man gives more respect and attention to the words of his uncle or older family members than he does to a young pastor, then the uncle would probably be the best counsellor. Or if a woman wants to discuss matters relating to the care of babies, or perhaps her emotional relationships with her older children, then the pastor's wife or another woman would be the best person to give counsel. In situations like these it may still be the pastor's responsibility to ensure that counselling help is given; and he will almost certainly want to offer the counsellors any support and advice they may need, while remaining well in the background so far as the client is concerned.

In many cultural situations it would be very unwise for a pastor to try and counsel any woman without his wife being present. In Churches where women are ordained or appointed to the pastorate on the same footing as men, or take a leading role in the congregation, there may be a recognized system of referring particular sorts of problem to them, while for other sorts of problem the counsellor is normally a man.

There are also some areas where the pastor may not be recognized as a counsellor at all, except where specifically spiritual or religious problems are concerned. In many village situations the pastor's role is seen as relating to 'Church' matters only. Everyday problems like family disputes, marriage difficulties, adultery, stealing, etc., are dealt with by the community as a whole, with recognized community counsellors taking the lead. The pastor has his place in the community and can make his contribution along with the rest of the people, but will only be recognized as a counsellor in matters directly affecting the Church. This attitude was apparent in Example 4, where the people involved were counselled and rebuked by the village as a whole, with the recognized counsellor known as the 'custom boss' leading the discussion. The pastor was present, but no one asked for his advice. It was a community problem and the community dealt with it in the traditional way.

The pastor may of course need to call in professional help from other people, if the problem is very severe, or if the client appears to be either physically or mentally sick, or perhaps even a danger to himself or others. Then the expert help of a doctor, psychiatrist, or qualified social worker may be required, and the pastor's job will be to try and ensure that the person in need receives it.

We have seen in this chapter that people need counselling in many different situations. We have also seen that the sort of counselling required, the best person to give counsel, and the methods to be used, all depend on the particular situation and on the person or group whose problem it is. A child will usually need a different method of counselling from an adult. A person who has little will-power or strength in themselves will need a different sort of counselling from someone who feels secure and confident about handling the situation. It is impossible to make definite rules for any single type of counselling which can be used in every situation. Effective counselling has to be 'flexible', and a good counsellor will be able to adapt his methods to meet many different sorts of problem. In the next chapter we discuss what sort of approach the pastor should take in order to be a 'good' counsellor.

STUDY SUGGESTIONS

WORD STUDY

1. List *four* ideas which are included in the meaning of the word 'counselling'.
2. Counselling is described as a 'relationship between two or more people', a personal relationship. Which five of the following words express the idea of a positive personal relationship?
   friendship agreement contract sharing discussion
   communication trust anger partnership loneliness demand
3. Explain the meaning of each of the following:
   (a) Educative counselling (b) Supportive counselling (c) Crisis counselling.

REVIEW OF CONTENT

4. What were the important ideas about counselling which were noted at the conference about Marriage and Family Life held at Bangkok in 1968?
5. 'There are many different types of counselling' (p. 85). Read again Examples 3 and 4. What type of counselling was given in each of these examples?
6. Seven facts about cultural or traditional counselling were listed in the chapter. Compare the methods described with the counselling methods traditionally used in your own country. (Explain any points which are similar, and any which are different.)
7. What aspects of counselling, if any, would *not* be found in a 'traditional' counselling situation?

BIBLE STUDY

8. Read again Exod. 18.10–27. This passage describes three different instances of counselling. In each case, say (a) who was counselling whom, and (b) what type of counselling it was.
9. Read Mark 2.1–12 and 10.17–22. In what ways were the problems of the paralytic and the rich man like that of Grace in Example 11? What type of counselling did Jesus give in each case?
10. Read the following passages and say in each case:
    (i) Who is counselling whom?
    (ii) Is the counsellor acting chiefly in the sense of '*paraklesei*', (one who stands *in* the situation, alongside the needy person, to give them comfort and support), or chiefly in the sense of '*nouthesia*' (one who corrects and admonishes)?
    (a) Mark 9.33–42 (b) John 8.1–11 (c) Gal. 1.6–10
    (d) Gal. 3.1–5
11. Paul gave as the aim of his counselling ministry: 'to present every man mature in Christ' (Col. 1.28, RSV). Read Col. 2.2, 3; Eph. 4.13–15; 1 Cor. 2.6, 7; and then explain what Paul meant by 'maturity in Christ'.
12. The Holy Spirit is described as the 'Counsellor' (John 14.16). Explain the work of the Holy Spirit as counsellor from the following verses (i.e. what does the Holy Spirit *do*)? John 14.16, 17; 14.26; 15.26; 16.7–13.

APPLICATION, OPINION, AND RESEARCH

13. Is there a special need for counselling in your country or in your neighbourhood today? Give reasons why or why not.
14. Some people see little or no value in learning about counselling ideas and methods from the past. They regard such ideas as

irrelevant to the situation today. What is your opinion? What are some of the values of studying past ideas and methods? What are some of the dangers of doing so?

15. Both Martin Bucer and Richard Baxter stressed that pastors should have a teaching ministry to individuals and families, as well as a general preaching ministry to the whole congregation. Do you think this is a good suggestion for pastors today? Give reasons for your answer.

16. The Puritan Henry Scougal complained that people would not bring their problems to the pastor, but tried to hide them. Is this a problem for many pastors today? If so, why do you think people want to conceal their problems? What can a pastor do to encourage people to 'want to be cured'?

17. In Example 9, other Church members were willing to care for Mrs Batoga and help her in her time of trouble. In what special ways do you think members of your own Church could help someone in a situation like that?

18. If you yourself have already had experience either as a counsellor, or of being counselled, how do you feel about the ministry of counselling? How far was the counselling you have experienced a success or a failure? What other effects did it have, if any, besides solution of immediate problems?

6

The Pastor's Approach to Counselling

As we have seen, counselling can involve both individuals and groups.

In *individual* counselling one counsellor works with one 'client' to discover possible ways of dealing with the client's problem or problems.

In *group* counselling either one counsellor tries to help a group of people who have a common problem, or a group of people try together to help one person or another group to sort out a problem or situation that concerns them all. The 'group' in either case may be a family, a clan, a group who are jointly experiencing a particular problem, or even a whole congregation, village, or tribe. In some situations both individual and group counselling may be needed, perhaps because an individual's problem cannot be solved apart from the welfare of the whole group, perhaps because the pastor needs the support of other members of the Christian community in order to help the client effectively.

In this chapter we discuss chiefly the approach of the pastor as an individual person counselling individuals. We shall study some of the attitudes and ways of working which help towards effective counselling, and consider some of the feelings involved in the counselling situation for both the counsellor and the client. However, these attitudes and feelings apply, to a greater or lesser extent, in group-counselling also.

It has been said that the most important person in the counselling situation is the counsellor himself. Certainly the counsellor's approach to the task and his attitude to the client are of basic importance. So we must ask what sort of approach and attitudes are most likely to lead to effective counselling. We shall consider these under four headings:

1. The counsellor needs to have an *aim*.
3. This aim must be based on an *awareness and understanding* of the facts and the feelings involved in the situation.
3. The counsellor needs to *have positive attitudes*, that is, to approach people and their problems in an open and hopeful way.
4. The counsellor needs to recognize and *avoid negative attitudes* which can prevent good counselling.

THE AIM IN COUNSELLING

Before going further, it will be helpful if readers write out what their own personal aim or purpose would be in offering counsel to people. You could do this by completing the sentence: 'When I counsel another person, my aim is –' What you have written can then be used as a basis for your answer to Study Suggestion no. 13 on p. 113.

In thinking about the aim of counselling we must distinguish between the counsellor's *general* purpose in offering to help people, and the *particular* aim he may have in counselling an individual in a particular situation.

First, the counsellor needs to be clear about his *general* aim. He needs to answer the question: 'What am I trying to do when I go to help people, or when they come to me for help with their problems? What is my *aim* in helping them?' The answer to this question will influence his general attitudes and approach to people in counselling.

In answering these questions, one pastor said: 'My main aim is to try and understand what is troubling the person and preventing him or her from being "free" in life. When I understand what is causing the problem, then I want to try to show how they can deal with it, and if possible lead them to find the meaning of life which Jesus offers.'

The counsellor's *particular* aim in any situation, however, can usually only be set after he has listened to the client and evaluated the problem. It has to be directly related to the client's needs and attitudes, and the client's freedom of choice and action has to be respected. There is always a danger that in setting his aim a counsellor will become more interested in achieving his own purpose than in actually helping the person in need. The aim should not be allowed to control and dominate the counselling situation. The counsellor must never try to push the client into a certain way of thinking, or force him to act against his will. When this happens, the counsellor becomes a controller, not a helper.

On the other hand, if the counsellor has no aim, then he can be too strongly influenced by the client. He may find himself pushed in many directions according to the way the client thinks and acts, like a boat without a rudder. Then the result, for both counsellor and client, will be a sense of frustration, and of going round in circles and getting nowhere.

In many situations, of course, the pastor may not be able to achieve the aim he sets. He may fail in some way in his approach to the client, or the client may refuse the help he offers, so that no satisfactory solution is possible. The important thing is not that the counsellor should necessarily *achieve* the exact aim he has set, but that he should have a reasonably clear idea where he wants to go in his counselling. As we have said, to be able to do this he needs a clear understanding of the situation. But he is unlikely to gain a true understanding unless his attitude is a positive one from the start. We shall therefore discuss the sort of attitudes which are useful in counselling, and those which should be avoided, before we look in detail at the ways to awareness and understanding.

POSITIVE ATTITUDES

The counsellor's effectiveness will depend on his attitudes towards the person in need. What attitudes, then, are required for effective counselling?

Some people use the word '*acceptance*' to sum up the basic attitude required. Acceptance has been defined as 'a non-critical, helping, non-judging approach to the client, which applies in all counselling situations'. But there is a danger of misunderstanding this idea of acceptance, and interpreting it in a wrong way. Some counsellors take it to mean being so kind and loving that they are ready to 'accept' any standard of conduct in the client as good enough. Such counsellors think they must accept whatever the client says or does, they never disagree with the client or take a critical approach to his behaviour, they regard the sort of life the client leads as the client's concern alone. A counsellor who has this 'free and easy' attitude does not try to evaluate ideas or attitudes or actions. But this is not the true meaning of 'acceptance' as the Christian counsellor should understand it.

Three basic ideas or attitudes are included in a Christian understanding of 'acceptance': (1) *respect* for the client, (2) *honesty and sincerity* on the part of the counsellor, and (3) *hope and expectation* that the client can and will, with God's help, change himself and his life for the better.

RESPECT

The Christian counsellor's respect for his client is based on the Christian understanding of man, which affirms that every person created and loved by God is worthy of help and has the capacity to change and grow more mature. Many counsellors have the idea that man is able to solve his own problems without divine help. They see human beings as basically good and sufficient in themselves, and so able to meet any problem situation with the advice and support of other human beings. The Christian counsellor disagrees with this idea, because it separates man from God. It is true that many people have resources and strengths which they do not fully use. Most people do not live in the fullest way possible as human beings. They do not try to understand how their minds, bodies, and emotions work, or try to change their lives. The Christian counsellor recognizes this, and he also recognizes the many ways in which human beings can help and support each other. However, he does not evaluate people and situations in the same way as the counsellor who sees no place for God in any situation.

The Christian counsellor *begins* with God: he sees spiritual as well as emotional and other factors in each problem situation. And he bases his ideas of the meaning of acceptance in counselling on this same foundation. He accepts people on the basis that he and the client share a common human life, that the counsellor is not superior to the client and must never look down on anyone as useless or beyond help. He sees the client as a fellow human being with the possibilities of growing or not growing. He tries to understand the client's situation and feelings because he himself is a person in need.

But the Christian counsellor accepts others not only because of their common humanity, but because he believes that God loves and accepts everyone in Jesus Christ, whoever they are, and whatever they have done. Because God accepts everyone, and has shown this for all time in His love in Jesus Christ, the Christian counsellor cannot refuse to accept any person. When Paul advised the Roman Christians to 'accept one another as Christ has accepted you' (Rom. 15.7) he was writing to Christian congregations, but his words can be applied to all people everywhere.

If the client is a Christian, then the counsellor can make this acceptance very clear, because both he and the client understand that they are accepted in Christ, and have received this acceptance for themselves. They have both experienced 'God's glorious generosity which has made us welcome in the everlasting love he bears towards the Son' (Eph. 1.3–8, Phillips). This common 'welcome' becomes the foundation or basis on which they explore each situation together.

If the client is not a Christian, then the counsellor 'accepts' him or her as a person loved and welcomed by God, and as a brother or sister for whom Christ died (Rom. 14.15). The Christian counsellor recognizes himself as a sinner helping another sinner, or, as the Asian Christian leader, D. T. Niles, puts it: 'As one beggar telling another beggar where to find bread.' Even if the client does not respond to God's welcome in Christ, this does not stop the counsellor from accepting him: rather it adds something extra to the help he can give. Acceptance offered by the Christian counsellor may be the first step in helping the client to experience the deeper acceptance which God offers. Real acceptance by others is not a common experience; it often comes as a new discovery when a person feels and knows himself accepted by someone in such a way that the two of them can talk freely together, and reveal their feelings and problems without fear of being rejected.

The Christian counsellor recognizes that his ability to accept another person in this way results from his own acceptance by God. He is able to reflect and practise that which he himself experiences in his relationship with God, whose acceptance and welcome are without any limits. In Christian counselling, 'acceptance' is based, not merely on the common experience of sharing human life together, but on the spiritual reality that God has accepted mankind in Jesus Christ.

HONESTY AND SINCERITY

The Christian counsellor does not 'pretend' to be interested in the client when he is really not concerned at all. He does not 'pretend' that he is perfect himself and can therefore look down on and condemn the client. The counsellor tries to be honest with the client in understanding and evaluating the failures, weaknesses, and also the positive strengths he sees in each situation. He also tries to be honest about his own weaknesses and failures. He does not pretend that he himself has no problems. He offers help as one needy person to another, and also as one who believes that there is an answer to his needs and problems and to those of the person he is trying to help.

This need for honesty in counselling raises the question of 'judging' others. Does 'acceptance' of people mean that there can be no judging of them? Can acceptance and judgement go together, or not? One writer has said that there can be no place for judgement in counselling: 'It is clear, from a Christian point of view, that no one has the right to judge another human being; the command, "judge not", is incontrovertible, particularly since it was given a dynamic by Jesus's own life.' He meant that this was the basis of Jesus's approach to people, and that it must be binding on all Christian counsellors.

Does this mean, then, that a Christian counsellor must never judge another person's conduct or way of thinking, even if that conduct is harmful to the client himself or to other people? Is that what Jesus meant when he said 'Judge not that you be not judged' (Matt. 7.1)? If so, what should a Christian counsellor think of other Scripture verses which speak of the need to 'reprove', 'advise', 'warn', 'correct' (see 1 Thess. 5.14; Tit. 2.15; Eph. 5.11; 1 Tim. 5.20)? None of these actions are possible without some sort of 'judging' on the part of the person offering help. We must remember that in Matthew 7.1 Jesus was speaking to those among his hearers – the religious leaders – who condemned the sins of others, but were hypocritical and self-righteous about their own sins. In the GNB this verse is translated: 'stop judging by external standards, but judge by true standards'. The Amplified Bible translates it as 'be honest in your judgement and do not decide at a glance, superficially and by appearances; but judge fairly and righteously'. This is a true understanding of the positive aspect of judgement. What Jesus was opposing was the wrong sort of judging, or judging on the wrong foundation.

The word 'judging' has several meanings. In the sense of 'unfair criticism' or 'condemnation' it has no place in Christian counselling. Judging from a desire for revenge or 'pay-back', or because the counsellor thinks of himself as superior to the client, is always wrong. But judging in the sense of carefully and thoughtfully 'evaluating', 'deciding', 'discriminating' between right and wrong, or between different possible actions, is an essential and necessary part of effective counselling. If the counsellor does not try to evaluate the client's situation in this sense, then he is failing to be honest, and failing to use the ability which God has given him. Without some evaluation and assessment, he cannot hope to clarify the situation or give any effective help.

The counsellor must therefore be prepared to evaluate the situation in a fair and positive way. He should not criticize unfairly or condemn the client just because he disapproves of what the client has done, or has a personal feeling against him. If this evaluation is done with love and concern, the counsellor may feel that he must criticize some of the client's ideas and actions. But he will do this, not in a harsh way, but in a way which builds up rather than breaking down. His criticism will be constructive, not destructive, and so will help the client to reach a deeper understanding and evaluation of his own situation and actions.

Self-evaluation and self-judgement by the person or group in need is always more effective than any evaluation by the counsellor as an outside person. It is the foundation upon which they can begin to reshape their life and attitudes. But many people find it difficult to reach this goal of self-evaluation without help from an experienced and concerned counsellor who is prepared to be honest in evaluating the situation. And only by speaking the truth in an attitude of love and concern (see Eph. 4.15) can the counsellor help people to see their situation as it truly is.

Jesus Himself assumed that Christians would find it necessary to judge others, and He explained how positive judgement is to be given: not in a hasty way without understanding, not without first putting our own lives straight. We must never judge a person to be hopeless. Jesus Himself has shown that God does not regard any person as hopeless (see John 7.24).

So we see that acceptance and evaluation are possible at the same time. In some situations the counsellor can give no *approval* to the client's actions; he must not pass them over as if they did not matter. But the important thing is to give the evaluation in such a way that it really helps the client to understand the situation and evaluate it for himself.

HOPE AND EXPECTATION

The writer Malcolm Brown explains this idea as follows: 'We accept the whole person, which includes his ability to grow into maturity. Our acceptance is not only related to the way our client is behaving now, but shows an expectation that his behaviour can improve. To leave out the idea of expectation in our acceptance of the client shows a failure to treat him as a whole person (and thus is not really acceptance at all). All people have the power to develop, a power that is capable of making a response within the counselling relationship.'

Thus expectation in counselling means seeing the client as a 'responsible' person who has the God-given ability to respond and to work positively towards his own maturity. It means rightly expecting and encouraging him to use that ability. This attitude reflects God's attitude to man. God accepts us freely: this is our great privilege. But He also expects us to act in certain ways towards Him and others as a result of this acceptance: this is man's responsibility. Acceptance is not an end in itself. It is more like the beginning of a new way, by which a person can develop and mature in the way God intends.

The great model of true acceptance of others is seen in Jesus, whose approach to people clearly showed respect, honesty, and hopeful expectation. We have already noted the difference between Jesus's attitude towards Zaccheus and that of other people, as described in Luke 19.1–10 (p. 37). The people's attitude included anger (as a collector of taxes, Zaccheus took more than his due), fear (Zaccheus represented and worked for the Roman government which had the power to punish and imprison), hatred and scorn (they felt Zaccheus had betrayed his own people), and rejection (the total result of their anger, fear, hatred, and scorn). As a result of this, Zaccheus felt lonely and isolated, an outcast from his own people. He expected and received condemnation as a 'sinner' from the respectable people and the religious leaders. It was quite natural for the people to have these attitudes to Zaccheus, and the treatment he received from them was partly his own fault. In many societies anyone whose action conflicts with accepted patterns of behaviour is treated as Zaccheus was. The people aimed to show Zaccheus that he was rejected and would remain so unless he came back into line with their expectations. But in fact their attitude stood in the way of a better relationship with him, and until he met Jesus, Zaccheus was a selfish, bitter, and lonely man who at the same time was eagerly searching for a better way.

Unlike other people, Jesus approached Zaccheus with friendliness and concern. His initiative ('Come down, I am going to your place to eat!') showed the divine love in action. In asking to share a meal with Zaccheus, Jesus showed His desire to share and understand the ideas and feelings of this outcast man. Jesus showed that He *respected* Zaccheus as a person, and wanted to help him straighten out his life; and that encouraged Zaccheus to make a new start. Jesus, as the Counsellor, did not offer any spoken evaluation of Zaccheus's life; but His attitude of love and concern encouraged Zaccheus to evaluate himself. Restoration followed as Zaccheus tried to make amends for his previous actions and attitudes, and began to live in a new and more responsible way. Jesus's 'acceptance' of Zaccheus did not, however, mean that He supported his unjust business methods or his selfish approach to life. It did mean that He wanted to help Zaccheus, even though, according to the ideas of his own people, he did not deserve any help or encouragement. Thus an attitude of respect and hopeful expectation resulted in an honest relationship in which positive evaluation and amendment was possible. (We should also note that by offering acceptance and friendship to Zaccheus, whom the people regarded as their enemy, Jesus was risking rejection and misunderstanding for Himself.)

Another example of 'acceptance' by Jesus is found in the incident of the woman taken in adultery (see John 8.1–11). According to the law, the woman deserved to be punished. But the religious leaders who brought her to Jesus were not really concerned to uphold the law or protect the morals of society. They wanted to discredit Jesus by trapping Him into making a false statement, and were using the woman as a bait. She was not the real target of their attack, and their attitude clearly showed their lack of true concern for her. They also wanted to show themselves off as righteous, by comparing their own respectability and virtue with the unfortunate woman's sin. Jesus uncovered this desire when He demanded that the sinless and perfect ones among them should throw the first stone in punishment of the woman. He recognized the true intentions of her accusers, and met their questions by prompting them to evaluate their own lives.

Some people have asked whether, by showing concern and respect for the woman, Jesus was not in fact undermining the law against adultery. Was His attitude of forgiveness not a threat to the whole moral system under which Jewish society lived at that time? Certainly this seemed to be so to the religious leaders of the time. They regarded Jesus's attitude towards sinners and outcasts as too easy-going, and even dangerous. His words, 'I do not condemn you', seemed to mean that He was not concerned about the moral failure of this woman and of others who ignored the demands of the law. They thought He did not care whether a person lived a good life or not.

But Jesus's next words to the woman: 'Go, and sin no more', showed that this was not the case. His attitude of forgiveness for her past and present 'sin' and failure carried with it a challenge and demand for a new style of living in the future. An 'accepted' person who refuses the responsibility of trying to grow and change is failing to understand the meaning of forgiveness and acceptance. As Counsellor, Jesus showed clearly the demands which acceptance involves.

In those two examples, the people concerned (Zaccheus and the woman taken in adultery) did show themselves ready to accept the acceptance offered by Jesus, and to try and fulfil His hope and expectation for them. But this does not always happen. True acceptance is costly for both counsellor and client. It is costly for the counsellor because it involves entering fully into the client's life situation. It means continuing to respect the client even though other people may condemn and reject him. It may also involve befriending and respecting people who think of themselves as unworthy of any help and support.

True acceptance can also be costly to the client: and honest evaluation of the situation is often a painful process because it challenges people to change their way of life, and lays on them the responsibility of growing towards greater maturity. Sometimes it produces conflict and anger between counsellor and client, and can lead to the possibility of a broken relationship between them. The danger of this happening will only be avoided if the counsellor takes care to rid himself of certain wrong and negative attitudes towards the client, and towards the counselling situation as a whole.

NEGATIVE ATTITUDES

'Negative' attitudes are those which prevent good acceptance and understanding of others. It is quite possible for a counsellor to be genuinely interested in the client, and truly desire to help him overcome his problems, but at the same time to have wrong attitudes which may prevent him from doing so. Even if these attitudes are not expressed in words, the client will almost certainly sense or feel them. Some examples of these negative or destructive attitudes are:

Superiority: e.g. 'What do you think you are doing? You really should have known better than to act like that. Why don't you use your common sense a bit more?' (Many people do act foolishly and fail to think before they do and say things. But they will not respond positively to a counsellor with a superior attitude.)

Superficiality: e.g. 'Oh, not Agnes again! What has she done this time? She's a real trouble-maker, and doesn't deserve any more help!' (This may be true, but the counsellor is only looking at the problem from the outside. The real question he must ask is '*Why* is Agnes such a trouble-maker?')

Scorn or contempt for the client: e.g. 'What's wrong with this fellow, so weak and easily tempted! Why can't he stand on his own feet, instead of all the time running to me for help with his problems?' (But it is just because he *is* weak that he needs the counsellor's help if he is to stand against temptation. 1 Cor. 10.13 may be helpful here.)

Lack of sympathy: e.g. 'How can people act like this and yet claim to be Christians? Their faith is like the top spread of a sandwich, and doesn't really mean much.' (True, this is a common problem. Many Christians do not live up to what they say they believe. Again, this is why they need counselling – the counsellor's task is to help them to deepen their faith and realize the meaning of being Christian. And what about the counsellor's own actions? Can he expect his clients to do better than he – or than Paul claimed to do, according to Rom. 7.18, 19?)

Over-severity: 'This husband really needs to be told-off and put straight. A good stern warning will straighten him out. So let him listen to this – and do what I say!' (In some situations straight talk may be necessary, but with many clients it will frighten or upset them, and so do more harm than good.)

Impatience: 'In trouble again? How many times do you have to be told before you take any notice? You're only getting what you deserve!' (The counsellor's main task is not to condemn or suggest punishment, but to help the client find direction and meaning in life. He must be careful not to take an aggressive or bullying tone.)

Selfishness: 'Why can't people come at a better time? I have to get ready to go out. I told them when I would be available – why can't people stick to what's been arranged?' (People can indeed be a nuisance to a busy counsellor. But those in greatest trouble may find it difficult to think of anything but their own problem. If the counsellor puts his own convenience first he will get off to a bad start, as clients will sense his impatience.)

Priggishness (false pride or false shame): e.g. 'What a rotten business this is! It's a disgrace to the Church. What will people think? – and the bishop's coming to visit us next week too!' (If the counsellor is shocked or ashamed, and shows that he cares more about the opinion of outsiders than about helping those in trouble, then the client too will feel ashamed and despised, and will probably be unwilling to share his problem any further.)

These are just a few of the attitudes that can hinder effective counselling. Of course there are others. Each counsellor needs to take an honest look at his own attitudes, and work to rid himself of those which are most likely to spoil his relationship with clients and prevent him from helping them.

AWARENESS AND UNDERSTANDING

No counselling is possible without a true understanding of the people and problems involved in the situation. This means getting a clear idea about two things: (1) What are the *facts* of the problem, i.e. what has happened or is happening; and (2) What do the people involved in the situation *think and feel* about it. It means trying to *understand* and *feel* the situation in the same way as those needing help.

Sometimes a pastor can understand the situation quite quickly. He can see what is troubling the client. But unless he can sympathize and share *people's feelings*, it may be difficult for him to offer help in an acceptable way. Here are two examples:

Example 14: Mrs Imalo, a shy and rather deaf member of a Church Council, felt that one or two of the leaders were controlling all the decisions made for the congregation, and that the advice and ideas of many people, including herself, were being rejected. So she felt that her contribution was not needed, and decided to withdraw from the council. The pastor, however, felt that Mrs Imalo was mistaken, and that the leaders really did try to encourage everyone to share in decision-making. He thought the truth was that Mrs Imalo herself was too shy to contribute much in the meetings. He knew she was deaf, and did not always hear what was said. He also knew she was sensitive about her deafness and would not acknowledge it to others.

So there were two views of the situation. In counselling Mrs Imalo, it was important for the pastor to understand *how* and *why* she felt as she did, i.e. to see things from her point of view as well as his own. He did not agree with her, but if he had started by telling her so she would probably have refused any counselling help. By *understanding and sympathizing* with her interpretation of the situation, though not agreeing with it, he was in a good position to help her. Eventually she admitted her difficulty, and she got over her shyness.

Example 15: Bob, aged 45, was a pilot working for a big international airline. He was unmarried, and not a church-goer, but he went to a pastor for help because he was convinced he was being bewitched by two women who lived in the flat next to his in London. He said their voices followed him on his flights to Africa, and he felt that they knew and controlled his thoughts and actions. So he was asking for a priestly blessing, a Christian incantation to shield him from the spirits of the women. He also asked permission to sleep in the church, i.e. on consecrated ground, and when he was allowed to do so, said next morning that messengers from the two women had come disguised as nightwatchmen to check up on him. In fact there were no such nightwatchmen. The pastor concluded that Bob was suffering from loneliness and mental strain (he was overdue for leave) and that there was no witchcraft. But if he had told Bob this, Bob would not have believed it. So the pastor prayed with him and gave him a blessing, and also a copy of John's Gospel, with a booklet to guide him through reading it. The next day Bob said that the Gospel had helped him more than anything, and he found that it quietened the voices. However, the pastor felt that Bob was not fit to fly his aircraft with over a hundred people on board that night, though he would not himself withdraw from the flight. So the pastor contacted the airline chief, who agreed that Bob should be grounded, and perhaps should have a medical check-up – but the pastor insisted that he personally must tell Bob what he had done, since he had broken confidence. At first Bob was very angry, but later admitted that he was glad to be taken off duty.

This example shows how a client can be unaware of his real problem, and how important it is for a counsellor to *enter into a client's thoughts and feelings* if he is to give the help that is really needed.

But how is a counsellor to gain the necessary understanding of a situation and of another person's feelings? There are four chief lines of approach which will contribute towards such understanding:

(a) The counsellor must remember the importance of *listening* as well as talking.

(b) He must follow some of the different ways of *responding* to a client.

(c) He must recognize and *sympathize* with the feelings which may lie behind what a client is actually saying.

(d) He must cultivate and show attitudes that will *encourage* the client to feel confidence in the counsellor's ability to help and give guidance if necessary, and to be frank and open in discussing the situation.   •

TALKING AND LISTENING

Understanding can only occur if the client is *encouraged and allowed to talk*, and the counsellor is prepared to *listen*. To be effective, counselling must be a two-way communication. There is an important difference between counselling and preaching. In preaching, one person proclaims while others listen. Whoever gives the word or message has prepared beforehand what to say, and there is normally no opportunity for any discussion, agreement, or disagreement from the listeners. So preaching is a *one-way* communication.

Some ministers think that the only difference between preaching and counselling is that preaching is done in the church building, while counselling is done in the minister's study or the client's home. They think of pastoral counselling as just another form of one-way communication, in which the minister talks and advises and the person in need listens, absorbs, and then obeys what is said. But that is not true counselling, which must be a *two-way* communication in which *both* counsellor and client speak, and *both* listen. It must be a *sharing* process, in which the client is encouraged to talk freely, and the counsellor is prepared to listen attentively. This is especially important in the early stages of any counselling relationship.

Talking is important and essential to counselling for several reasons. First, it helps people to get their ideas and thinking straight. Talking and discussion help to sort out good ideas from poor ideas. Ideas are sifted (as corn is sifted by the wind or by a winnowing machine), and clarified as they are put into words. Secondly, talking helps to bring release from bad feelings and emotions which people store up or hold back within themselves. When people pour out or 'air' their feelings they often see things differently and begin to feel better. Talking can be like a safety-valve on a pump or machine, it lets out the pressure which builds up in people's lives. And again, talking helps people to gain self-confidence, and a sense of identity. The Revival Movement in East Africa, for example, has been cited as providing an opportunity for many lay people to discover that talking and 'self-expression' lead to spiritual health.

But why do some people feel that they need to talk about their problems to a counsellor? Why do they not turn to their family or their friends? Usually there are good reasons for this. For example, they may have no close relatives or friends with whom they can share their feelings. Or they may be afraid to worry or upset those who are close to them; or they may think the response will be anger or ridicule. They may also be afraid of gossip, which might distort the real situation. Some, too, may find it difficult to talk freely with the people around them if those people are deeply involved in the problem themselves. Or they may know that those around them will want to give advice without really listening or understanding the situation.

But if talking is to be effective, *listening* is absolutely essential. The value – indeed the vital necessity – of attentive listening has long been recognized, and is being re-emphasized by those engaged in counselling today.

As long ago as 2450 BC, one of the advisers of the Egyptian king wrote to his son, who was to follow him in the work: 'If you are one to whom petitions are made, be calm as you listen to the petitioner's speech. Do not rebuff him before he has said that for which he came. It is not necessary that everything should happen as he wants it, but a good hearing is a soothing of the heart.' And Proverbs 18.13 describes as 'folly and shame' the failing, common to many counsellors, of giving the answer to a problem *before* they have heard and understood it properly.

True listening involves much more than just hearing the client's words. It means attending also to his actions and feelings. A client's words will help the counsellor to understand the facts of the situation

'Counselling must be a two-way communication . . . there is an important difference between counselling and preaching' (p. 104).

A pastor visiting isolated 'parishioners' in north-western Canada, and a missionary priest calling on a Lepcha family in a Himalayan village, are both building up people's confidence by listening carefully and responding. What must pastors *avoid* doing in such situations?

as the client understands them. But his actions sometimes give a clearer picture of the truth. If a person fiddles with something, looks at the floor, smokes continually, laughs in a strained way, etc., these actions may show that he is nervous, or unsure of himself, or perhaps holding back the truth. Facial expressions, gestures, hesitation, or long pauses can also reveal something of what a person is really feeling. Such emotions as anger, hatred, fear, jealousy or a sense of rejection may be reflected in his tone of voice or the way he looks.

This sort of listening is sometimes called 'disciplined' or 'depth' listening, or 'listening with a third ear'. The counsellor listens and thinks deeply about what he hears and sees, reflecting on it and turning it over in his mind. Many ministers and pastors, however, find counselling difficult because they have been trained to talk, to preach, and to lead rather than to concentrate on listening to another person. Dietrich Bonhoeffer wrote: 'Many people are looking for an ear that will listen. They do not find it among Christians, because Christians are talking when they should be listening. He who no longer listens to his brother will soon no longer be listening to God either. One who cannot listen long and patiently will presently be talking beside the point, and never really speaking to others, even though he is not conscious of this.'

WAYS OF RESPONDING

The purpose of careful listening is to understand the problems of those who need help. But true listening does not mean saying nothing. Sometimes there will be silence between counsellor and client; sometimes the client will be talking freely. Then the counsellor must try to *respond* to what the client is saying, so as to encourage him to share his worries. Here are some of the different sorts of response which can be helpful.

A *reflective response* means giving back to the speaker an image or picture of his own ideas, as if he were looking into a mirror. When we look at a mirror we see perhaps that our face needs washing or our hair needs combing, but until we looked we did not fully realize these things about our appearance. When a counsellor reflects back to the client the idea the client was trying to express, this shows the client that what he is saying is understood. It can also help the client to see the problem in a new way. He may see that what seemed a very big problem is not so big as it first appeared to him, or that what seemed a small problem is really very important. A reflective response will not always reduce the size of the problem, but it can help to clarify the situation.

Example 16: John's wife, Mavis, came to talk about a problem she had at home. Fred, her elder brother, was always arguing with John and causing trouble. But Mavis couldn't tell him not to visit them, because he was senior to her, and she must respect him and try to help him. She explained what was happening:

Mavis: When John and Fred fight and argue, I get so upset. I feel sad and cross with both of them. But I am afraid of what will happen if I try to stop them.
Counsellor: You feel all mixed up inside, and confused about what to do with it?
(This sort of response encourages a person to talk more about the situation.)
Mavis (goes on)*:* Yes I do feel confused. I don't know why they argue all the time. I try to please them both because I really do care for them and love them. But they seem to use what I do for them as the reason for fighting.
By reflecting her ideas and words, the counsellor helped Mavis to describe the problem, without asking direct questions that might upset her more.

In the early stages of counselling, especially, a reflective response can help counsellor and client to explore the problem together. But the counsellor should not merely repeat what the client has said. He should try and 'focus' on the most significant points, and so encourage the client to clarify the situation further.

A probing or questioning response will help when the counsellor needs more information in order to understand the situation, or to 'open out' the discussion, perhaps because the client goes on about one aspect of the problem only.
Samples: 'Could you tell me a little more about that time?' – 'Yes I understand you. What happened then?' – 'So how did you feel when your uncle said that?'

These direct responses are best made when a good relationship has already been established. However, some counsellors do not like to use too many probing questions, because it makes them feel like a policeman investigating a crime, and because too many direct questions, such as 'why', 'when', 'how', etc., can make some clients feel uncomfortable. Also, in some cultural situations it is not considered polite to ask direct questions, so this sort of response would not be helpful.

An understanding or supporting response is used to reassure the client that the counsellor understands the situation, and is concerned to give help.
Samples: 'I can see how difficult it was for you when that happened.' – 'Yes, I understand, of course, quite so.' – 'Many people feel like that sometimes. You should not worry too much that your feelings are all mixed up.'

An interpretive response is used when the counsellor wants to give his own understanding of the situation, or make sure that his interpretation is correct. He can also use it to summarize what has been said, or to help the client understand what is happening.

Samples: 'The way you've described it, what seems to be happening is . . .' – 'What you did makes you feel guilty, is that it?' – 'You seem to be suggesting that the fault lies with your brother, is that right?'

As the counselling situation develops, the counsellor may want to use other sorts of response:

An evaluating response gives the counsellor's own opinion about the client's ideas or actions, or about the situation generally.

Samples: 'Yes, that would seem to be a good way to go about things.' – 'That's one important point you should think about. Perhaps you could also consider it this way. . . .'

This sort of response is useful, too, when the counsellor wants to express or emphasize the idea of *expectation*.

Sample: 'I understand how you feel, and why you broke that car window, but perhaps there is a better way to show your brother how upset you are about what he did.'

An action response is rather similar: here the counsellor encourages the client to consider what he can *do* towards solving the problem, or prompts him to behave in a certain way.

Samples: 'Now you will want to decide what you should do.' – 'Do you think it would help if you . . .?' – 'Others have found help in this sort of situation by . . .' – 'Let us think out and write down some ways of tackling this problem.'

An action response should only be used *after* a period of listening and clarification, when the counsellor is sure he fully understands the situation and the client's feelings. To suggest any sort of action before the client is ready for this is once again to fall into the trap we saw in Proverbs 18.13.

We may ask *when* these various responses should be used. But there can be no set rules, because each counselling situation is different. Sometimes a nod of the head, a smile, or a handshake can say more than many words. Sometimes silence is good, as it allows both counsellor and client to think more about what has been said. The chief thing to remember is that the purpose of any response is to *clarify* the situation, so as to give the greatest possible help to the person in need. If a response does that, then it is effective, whether or not it belongs to any standard list of 'good' responses.

PEOPLE'S FEELINGS

The counsellor should not think of his clients as if they were like an empty jar, or a blackboard, simply needing to be 'filled-in' with the answer to the problem. They are already full of their own ideas, feelings, and traditions, which influence their approach to people. And the counsellor too has feelings, ideas, and ways of relating to people that affect the way in which he tries to help others. So it is important for us to try and understand some of the *possible* feelings which the counsellor and client may have. (Note the word 'may', and think about the following ideas as 'possible' feelings. Not everyone will have all these feelings; they are examples, not rules.)

THE CLIENT

In the 'pre-counselling' situation, that is, before any counselling begins, the client already has certain experiences and beliefs, strengths and weaknesses of character, faith or lack of faith, skills in certain types of work, educational ability, and ways of doing things in that sort of situation. And besides having this general 'world-view' as a background to his problem, the client will also have particular feelings about the problem itself.

As we have already seen (p. 72), every client comes to the counsellor because:

(a) he has a problem;

(b) the problem causes him pain, so he wants to do something about it;

(c) his own attempts to solve it have not been successful;

(d) he thinks and hopes the counsellor can help him.

But besides these *positive* feelings about seeking help, he may also have *negative* feelings which make him confused and afraid about it. He is 'ambivalent' or mixed-up in his desire for help (see p. 67). Some examples of such negative feelings or anxieties are:

Resentment or anger about having to seek help at all,

Shame or fear of admitting his problem to another person,

Shyness or uncertainty about how the counsellor will receive him,

Unwillingness to face up to the possible pain of having the counsellor probe into his life,

Unwillingness to take action or accept new responsibilities that may be needed to straighten out the problem situation.

Sometimes these negative feelings are stronger than the pain of the problem, and may stop a person from seeking help. Many other experiences in life are similar to this. For example, we realize we should go to the doctor when we are unwell, but fear of what the doctor may find holds us back. When we have a bad toothache, we often prefer to suffer the pain rather than face the dentist's chair. We only overcome our fear and go and get the tooth pulled out when the pain gets really bad. Or when we have applied for a new job, and wait alongside other applicants for an interview, we feel so anxious that we wish the interview could be postponed; only our need for the job keeps us there and prompts us to go through the interview experience.

For many people this happens when they come to counselling. Some get no benefit because their negative feelings are stronger than their desire for help. Only if their problem is very painful or troublesome will they overcome their negative feelings and accept the help they need.

In this sort of situation the counsellor's attitudes can either strengthen the client's positive desire to seek help, or add to his negative fear and his inclination to reject any help offered. By an attitude of concern, friendliness, respect, openness, and humility, the counsellor can overcome some of the ambivalent feelings which the client may have.

THE COUNSELLOR

Like the client, the counsellor comes to the counselling situation with ideas and experience of his own, some training for his work, faith, attitudes to people, ideas about the purpose of his counselling, and some skills in helping people. And he too has particular feelings about the counselling relationship itself. Usually he has a real desire to help and accept the client. But he also may have some of the following negative feelings which can weaken his effectiveness:

Anxiety about the result of his work (Will I be able to handle this situation? Is this problem too big for me? What will happen if I make a mess of things?)

Fear that he will not be able to handle the client, and will end up by being used and controlled by him. If, say, a high-school teacher with a better standard of education than his own comes for counselling, he will wonder, 'Can I handle this person, or will he be too clever for me?' Or if a client is a political leader or a rich contributor to Church funds, he will wonder whether he can evaluate such a person's life without offending him or losing his respect.

A desire for unworthy satisfaction: One danger which every counsellor faces is the temptation to 'identify' with any wrong things the client has done, and which he, the counsellor, has wanted to do but has never dared. Or he may enjoy a feeling of self-righteousness when he hears of the client's unsatisfactory behaviour. Here are some examples.

Example 17: Pastor Frank was counselling a man and his wife who had a marriage problem. The wife had been sleeping with her husband's brother. She explained how her brother-in-law made magic against her, and kept tempting her until she finally gave in. In clarifying the situation, the pastor kept asking for more details; what sort of love magic was used? What did the wife and brother-in-law actually do? When and where did they sleep together? That is, he asked many unnecessary questions, because he had an unworthy desire to hear more about the sexual relationship. The situation was really quite clear, and he was merely satisfying his own curiosity.

Example 18: Dr Omar, a consultant psychiatrist, had been treating patients day after day for thirty-five years, until the time came for him to retire. But he could not face the idea of idleness, and the lack of people coming to him for help. Without his patients he felt useless, and himself became mentally sick, so that eventually he was admitted to the same hospital where he had sent his patients. The psychiatrist needed his patients even more than they needed him! The same thing can quite easily happen to a pastor.

In the story of the Pharisee and the publican in Luke 18.9–14, the Pharisee gained a lot of unworthy satisfaction by comparing himself with the publican. The same temptation to self-righteousness faces many pastors, as they compare their lives with those of the weaker members of the Church.

The counsellor needs to be aware of these possible feelings. A healthy self-understanding will help him to recognize possible negative ones and to try to overcome them. Obviously, the interaction of the feelings and attitudes of counsellor and client will influence the effectiveness of the counselling, and indeed will sometimes determine whether or not the counselling relationship starts at all. Counselling is never easy work, and the counsellor must continually review his ways of approaching people and his attitudes towards his relationship with them. His ability to help them will depend on how he thinks about and acts towards them.

To summarize the points made in this chapter, we can say that the counsellor's responsibility is to try to establish relationships with his clients which are healing, strengthening, and honest, through which he can help them to achieve maturity in all their personal and other relationships. His aim must be to be completely *for* the client, rather than for himself.

STUDY SUGGESTIONS

WORD STUDY

1. What are the meanings of each of the following terms in counselling?
   (a) judgement   (b) a reflective response   (c) expectation
   (d) disciplined listening
   Give an example in each case.

2. What is 'ambivalence' in (a) the client (b) the counsellor?

REVIEW OF CONTENT

3. In what ways is the Christian understanding of 'acceptance' different from many other ideas about acceptance?

4. Why is it important for the counsellor to have an 'aim'?

5. In what four chief ways can a pastor gain the necessary understanding of the client's situation and feelings?

6. What is the relationship between the work of preaching and the work of counselling? In what ways are preaching and counselling (a) similar, and (b) different?

7. Describe three of the possible sorts of feelings clients may have in a pre-counselling situation.

8. Briefly explain the idea of 'unworthy satisfaction' in the work of counselling.

BIBLE STUDY

9. What meaning does each of the following passages have for the work of a Christian counsellor today?
(a) 1 Thess. 5.14   (b) Eph. 5.11   (c) 1 Tim. 5.20.

10. Read Mark 10.17–22. This is another story of Jesus as a counsellor showing acceptance of someone. In what chief ways does this example differ from the examples of Zaccheus and the woman taken in adultery?

11. Read Mark 1 and 2. For each of the following passages which describe how Jesus met people and entered into relationships with them, say briefly:
(a) What happened in the story or incident;
(b) What attitudes Jesus showed to the people concerned.
Mark 1.21–28; 1.29–31; 1.32–39; 1.40–45; 2.13–17.

12. Read the Epistles of Peter and James. Give three references from these writings which tell of God's acceptance of mankind in Jesus Christ.

APPLICATION, OPINION, AND RESEARCH

13. At the beginning of this chapter it was suggested that you should write out what your own personal aim would be in offering counsel to people. Now that you have studied the chapter, in what ways, if any, would you want to change your completion of the sentence: 'When I counsel another person, my aim is . . .'?

14. Is it possible to respect a person you do not like? Is it possible to offer good counsel to a person who irritates you and makes you angry? Give reasons for your answers and discuss your ideas and experience of this with another person.

15. Read the passage quoted on p. 107, lines 15–17. To what extent, if any, are these words true for your own situation?
16. Can a pastor 'accept' a person and still discipline that person for breaking the rules of the Church? Give examples to support your answer.
17. How would you reply to someone who said 'This idea of "acceptance" destroys a minister's authority in the eyes of the people'?
18. On pp. 101, 102 some 'negative' attitudes are described. Give examples of some other negative attitudes which can hinder a counsellor from helping people.

SPECIAL EXERCISE IN LISTENING

Work with another person, calling yourselves A and B. A asks B briefly to give his opinion on some subject, perhaps a recent news item or something in which he is interested. A listens to B's story, but does not comment except to ask clarifying questions. After three or four minutes, A repeats back to B what he understands B's ideas and thoughts to be. B checks them for accuracy, and comments on A's listening ability. Then repeat the exercise this time with A giving the opinion, and B listening, etc.

SPECIAL EXERCISE ON RESPONSES

Read again Examples 3 and 4 (pp. 72–76). What sort of response was given by the counsellor in each case – reflective? active? probing? Discuss the situations with a friend or fellow-student, and say how effective you think the responses were. Do you think any other responses would have been more effective? If so, give an example.

7

The Practice of Counselling

The skills of listening and understanding, and the attitudes required for counselling, can be studied in theory, but they have to be practised and applied in real life situations. Some pastors (especially when they are new to the job) become tense and worried when the time comes to put their desire to help into action. 'Where do I start?' they ask. 'What can I say?' And even when they do get started, they may suddenly wonder, 'Where am I going in this relationship?' Even when they have studied the theory of counselling, some pastors still feel afraid and unsure of themselves when actually called on to help others. How then can a pastor build up the confidence to overcome these feelings of fear and uncertainty?

It is natural to feel some uncertainty when you are beginning a helping relationship with another person. But the experience of helping people gradually builds up confidence in this ministry. The important thing is to *learn* from our experiences, both our failures and our successes. It is useful, therefore, for pastors to check their own performance in counselling, asking themselves 'What method did I use? Was it as effective as it could be?' Talking over one's experiences with others involved in the ministry of counselling is also a good way to learn and to improve one's skills – remembering always the importance of maintaining the confidentiality of clients' affairs. (More detailed notes on evaluating one's counselling ministry will be found in the Epilogue, pp. 273–281.

Even before gaining experience, however, confidence can be built up on a foundation of knowledge of the *process* of counselling, and the *methods* appropriate for different situations.

COUNSELLING AS A PROCESS

Each counselling situation is a 'process', that is, it develops through *several stages* until the relationship between counsellor and client has served its purpose.

The whole process taken together forms one relationship between counsellor and client, and the various stages are interdependent, that is, they fit together, and it is not helpful to consider any one part of the relationship without reference to the whole. That would be like trying to examine a watch or clock by separating all the parts and asking which of these parts is the watch, or which part is the most important.

The answer is that *all* the parts are of importance. No one part will work by itself. All together form the watch and all contribute to its effective working. A counselling relationship is rather similar. All its different stages – its beginning, its middle, and its ending – are important, and together they make up the whole relationship. However, just as a watchmaker can separate or 'isolate' one or another part for closer examination, so we can divide up the counselling process, and isolate its different stages. We do this in order to understand more clearly what is necessary at each particular stage, and to gain a better understanding of what is involved in the whole relationship, and some idea of where it is heading.

At the same time, we must remember that the different stages do belong together, and that in actual counselling situations the stages do not come in any set order. Often the process seems to jump from one stage to another, and then return to earlier stages. So while it may be possible to map out the most frequently occurring pattern, this should not be taken as a rule to be followed on every occasion. We need to remember this as we examine the counselling relationship, and consider the main stages that occur in most counselling situations.

Usually the counselling process has *five* main stages. For the counsellor, these are:

(a) Making contact with those who need help;
(b) Getting introduced to the client and the problem situation;
(c) Focusing on the main problem and clarifying the situation;
(d) Working towards possible solutions of the problem;
(e) Ending the counselling relationship.

MAKING CONTACT

A pastor often has to take the initiative in making contact with those who need help. Contact can occur in many different ways. In some situations, of course, people will come to the pastor seeking for help. At other times the pastor himself must seek and find those who need him. It is no use his saying all the time, 'Come to me with your problems', and expecting people to make the first move. Often they will be too shy or too frightened. So the pastor must move out of his study or house to find and meet people in their living situations. We find a model for this in the ministry of Jesus (Luke 19.10).

There are many opportunities for a pastor to make contact with people which can lead on to counselling; for example:

After church services, when the word of God has been preached with sensitivity, some people may want to discuss some of the things they have heard in relation to their own lives and problems.

Hospitality and friendship are good ways of showing that you are easy to approach and ready to help anyone who may need it.

Visiting people in their homes. This should be carefully planned or you may come to people when they are busy, or when, for some reason, they do not want to talk.

Chance or informal meetings with people on the road, at the market, sharing in some community project, etc.

A regular interview time, or by specific appointments which are arranged beforehand.

Through introduction by another member of the congregation. Church members can be encouraged to bring needy friends to the pastor's attention, so long as this is not done in an interfering way.

Group discussions, in church or elsewhere, on such subjects as marriage, bereavement, etc., can encourage individuals to share their problems.

From this variety of possibilities, we can see that the opportunity for counselling can occur at almost any time, and the pastor should be able to recognize such opportunities when they occur.

In seeking to make contact with people, however, pastors often make two sorts of mistake.

1. They *wait too long before making a move* to help people. They hold back until the problem has become very big and complicated before they try to help, hoping that things will sort themselves out. This may indeed happen, but usually it is best to offer help before the problem becomes too big. As in medical practice, 'prevention is better than cure' – it is better to prevent sickness and disease before it starts, rather than wait until people get sick, and then try to make them better. Often, of course, the pastor is not aware of people's problems until they are brought to his notice, and can only come into the situation at that particular point. However, if he sees a problem developing between people, or in an individual's life, then he should try to help as soon as possible.

2. Pastors are *not always very sensitive* to the feelings of those they try to help. People's moods and feelings vary very much, and it is vitally important to try and sense how someone feels, and approach them at a time when they are ready to listen, or to speak of their problem. For example, it is difficult to talk quietly to a person who is full of anger and bitterness which makes him shout or become violent, or to anyone when they are drunk. When people are full of grief and sorrow, or are feeling very low, they may not want to hear more words. There is 'a time to speak', and 'a time to be silent' (Eccles. 3.7). Words of help spoken *at the right time* will be of great help to those who are ready to hear them. But words spoken *at the wrong time* may even cause more harm (see Prov. 25.11, 12; 29.20).

117

So when is the right time to speak? There can be no rule. As we have said, it is a matter of being sensitive to people's moods and feelings. The pastor needs to keep his eyes and ears open whenever he is with people, making 'look and listen' his watchwords. He also needs to ask the Holy Spirit to guide him when to speak and when to be silent. Usually if people come to the pastor of their own free choice, they are ready to open their hearts and also to listen. But often the pastor has to 'feel' his way into the situation, and do what he thinks is best. Sometimes he will feel that his words came just at the best time and were effective. At other times he may feel he should not have spoken when he did, or that other words would have been more helpful. Here again, the Christian counsellor needs the help of the Holy Spirit. And here too it is possible to learn from experience, and ask yourself *why* your words were helpful, or not helpful, with a particular client in a particular situation. (See also p. 280.)

Once contact has been made, what then?

GETTING INTRODUCED

The important things at the introductory stage are: (1) helping the client to feel at ease, especially when meeting for the first time; and (2) getting the 'feel' of the situation, so that both you and the client gain confidence that you will be able to share the problem. This is described as a sense of 'rapport' between two people, that is, being 'at one' and thus free to share thoughts and problems with one another. This feeling of mutual confidence is needed all through the counselling relationship, but it is especially important in the early stages.

Some counsellors feel that they can help rapport to develop by sharing some familiar pleasure with the client, such as having some food, or drinking tea or coffee together, or listening to a sports report or some music on the radio. It is important here to choose some pleasure that is culturally acceptable in the situation (and, of course, something that is acceptable to the Church). Care is needed too, because once you start eating or drinking together, it is easy to get 'sidetracked' into general conversation, and forget about the client's need. Many clients, too, find it easier to discuss their problems in a more formal and 'clinical' atmosphere, rather like that in a doctor's surgery.

Once confidence has developed, the counsellor encourages the client to explain the situation, and himself concentrates on listening and watching so as to gain an understanding of the person and the problem.

CLARIFYING THE PROBLEM

Gradually the introductory stage merges into the exploratory stage, where a counsellor tries to understand the situation from the client's point of view, and to build up a mental picture of the problem and its context. This stage of counselling has been compared to drawing a map before you start a journey. Imagine a person travelling through a jungle, or any unknown area. Unless he has a map, or at least a clear mental picture of the route, he is liable to get lost. He needs to know, at least roughly, what his position is and the direction he must take in order to reach his destination.

Similarly, it helps both counsellor and client if they construct in their minds some sort of map or outline of the situation, showing the people around the client (his family, friends, fellow workers, etc.), and the important factors in his life (his work, house, beliefs, assets, etc.). This will make it easier to understand the events that have led to the problem situation. This is called *'clarifying'*, and at this stage the counsellor will probably use various sorts of responses (see pp. 107–109), especially the reflective and questioning types. He may also give a short summary or interpretative statement from time to time, such as 'Let me see if I understand you', or 'It seems to me that', or 'What you are saying then, is, . . .', or 'This then is the problem, is it?' This encourages the client to let the counsellor know whether or not he is on the right path or 'wavelength'.

All this also helps the client to explore the problem anew for himself, and perhaps see it in a more complete way.

Sometimes there is one main problem to be isolated and dealt with; but often the problem is more complicated, and may seem to have many different branches. Then the counsellor has to try to discover what the *basic* problem is: the main 'trunk', rather than the less important branches. Sometimes, however, all the branches must be sorted out before any headway can be made towards an overall solution. In cases like this, and especially when the situation is a complicated one, the counsellor needs to allow himself time after the consultation to write down all the details which the client has told him. Even in simple cases it is vital when you next meet the client to be able to refer to his problem correctly. If you forget anything, the client will at once lose confidence and think you are not interested. And if you have a number of clients, you risk confusing one person's problem with someone else's. Of course the notebook you use for recording such details must be kept locked up in a 'confidential' drawer or cupboard, and must not be shown to anyone else.

'"Clarifying" helps the client to explore the problem for himself and perhaps see it in a more complete way' (p. 119) – just as focusing his microscope on a blood specimen helps a Nigerian researcher to see what disease a patient has. What can a microscope *not* show about a sick person's condition, which a pastor might discover?

'PRESENTING' PROBLEMS

Sometimes a client begins his explanation with a 'presenting' problem, that is, a problem which is real in itself, but which is not the true problem which is causing him deep concern and worry.

Example 19: William asked his pastor to help him understand some of the difficult verses in the Bible. He said he was finding it hard to keep up with his fellow students at high school. But after speaking for a short time about the Bible, he said: 'I wonder if I could talk to you about another problem too – with my girlfriend. . . .' Then he began to unfold the problem that was *really* bothering him.

Another way of 'presenting' a problem is when a client says he wants help for someone else. He describes the problem situation, and asks for advice that he can pass on to his friend. Sometimes, of course, such a request may be genuine, and must be accepted as such. Often, however, this is the way in which a shy person will seek help for a problem of his own. He will then apply the counsellor's advice to his own situation. The problem is his but this approach saves him from the fear and shame of revealing himself to the counsellor.

Indeed, in some cultural situations it is difficult or even impossible for people to make a direct request for help. They have a feeling of uncovering their inner self, or 'self-exposure', when face-to-face with an authority figure such as a pastor. To ease this feeling, they use a roundabout way of approaching the problem.

Example 20: One Sunday, Pastor Benson preached about friendship between boys and girls, and tried to give a Christian understanding of this subject. The next day he met Mark, one of the young people in the congregation, who spoke for a short time about school activities, and then asked: 'I wonder if I could come and talk to you sometime – ask you some questions about the things you said in your sermon yesterday?'

Pastor: 'Yes, of course you can. Perhaps we could talk a bit more now?'
Mark: I don't want to bother you too much and you are probably very busy.
Pastor: Well, I'm happy to help if I can. Perhaps we could talk now as we walk along.
Mark: Well, it's not about me really. My brother is in trouble with this girl – he has been seeing her a lot and would like to marry her. But he is already promised to a girl from our home village, so he doesn't know what to do. I want to advise him, but don't know what to say. I wonder what you would suggest?
Pastor: Your brother is really worried about this?
Mark: Oh yes, but I don't think he will talk to anyone about it. He is very shy and doesn't want others to know about it.

Pastor: You don't think he would come and talk to me, so that we could work out something?

Mark: No, no – he wouldn't come. He's on shift work – very tied up. That's why I thought perhaps you could explain some things to me and I could tell him.

Pastor (sensing that this may be a roundabout beginning): What sort of things do you mean?

Mark then began to ask some of the questions he had. The pastor was not sure whether the problem really belonged to Mark or to his brother, but was alert to the possibility that Mark might be using this way to get help for himself.

For what reasons do people use an indirect approach or offer a presenting problem to the counsellor? Some possible reasons are:

(a) In some cultures it is not the custom to present a problem in a direct way.

(b) The client may feel ashamed of the situation or afraid of the counsellor, and want to ease into the counselling relationship gradually, rather than jumping straight in.

(c) The client may be testing the counsellor, to see what sort of response he will give. If the counsellor condemns and speaks harshly, the client may decide not to consult him further. But if the counsellor's attitude is interested and accepting, the client will be encouraged to talk about the real problem.

(d) A client may be unaware what his chief problem is, and this makes him feel anxious, or angry, upset, and mixed-up. He needs help to find the real problem. So he starts by listing a whole lot of things that are causing him concern.

(e) The client may not know how to explain his real problem, and thinks that if he starts with something else, it may be possible to move on to the real problem later.

It is essential for the counsellor to accept the client's approach, even though he may sense that the real problem has not yet appeared, or has only been touched on lightly. The counsellor must always work at the client's pace rather than his own. The work of counselling is not like conducting a quiz or investigation. It is more a matter of exploring a problem together.

Also the counsellor must beware of treating a problem as 'only a presenting problem', and forgetting about it as he waits for the real one to come out. He should listen carefully and patiently, and evaluate each problem raised to see whether it is the real problem in the situation or not. He should treat each problem seriously unless he is sure the client is not being truthful or genuine in seeking help. And even when the client is obviously inventing a story, it is important to discover *why* he is doing so, because that may have something to do with what is really worrying him.

Sometimes the counsellor can help the client to be open and truthful by telling of someone else in a similar situation whose problem was successfully solved. This gives the client confidence by making him feel that he is not the only one to have such a problem.

Sometimes too, the counsellor may need to meet any other people who are involved in the situation. There is a real danger of reaching a false solution as a result of hearing only one side of the story. Especially when the problem involves a group, it is important to let everyone have their say. Only when the situation has been fully clarified, and the real problem uncovered, can the counsellor lead on to the stage of examining possible solutions.

WORKING TOWARDS POSSIBLE SOLUTIONS

As the situation becomes clear, and counsellor and client understand it better (the empty spaces on the map are being filled in), possible ways of dealing with the problem begin to appear. Here are some questions to note at this stage:

(a) Has the problem occurred before? Think about any *unsuccessful* ways which were used to try to deal with it, and consider *why they were unsuccessful.*

(b) Is there anything the client needs to *do* and *can* do that would help to solve the problem? Does he need, for example, to adjust to a new situation? – to forgive and be reconciled to another person? – to confess some wrong action? honestly to face up to attitudes or actions of his own which are causing the problem? – to find ways of relieving his worry and anxiety? – to find the courage to cut into the root of the problem, and start a new way of relating to other people?

(c) Is the client likely to grow into a more mature person as a result of this experience? What spiritual resources can you offer that may help him to do so? – prayer? – Bible study? – fellowship with other Christians? (We discuss this subject more fully in chapter 8.)

(d) Does the client need continuing help and encouragement if he is to put possible solutions into action, instead of just talking about them? Does he need to be assured that if a possible solution is tried but fails, that need not be the end of the matter – you will always be ready to look at the situation with him again, and help him find some other solution.

Some pastors become worried and feel they are useless if they cannot give a clear answer or suggest an immediate solution for every problem. This may result from their own mistaken understanding of a pastor as one who must have an answer for every problem in order to maintain his status in the eyes of the people. Or it may come from his reaction to the mistaken expectations of other people, who often think of the pastor as an 'answer man', especially where spiritual problems are concerned. They are accustomed to hearing strong words from the pulpit, and expect the same when they come to the pastor for counsel. Too often, both pastors and people have the mistaken idea that a counsellor is rather like a mechanic who mends a bicycle or repairs a motor car. The customer tells the mechanic what seems to be wrong with the machine, the mechanic fits the necessary spare parts, and all is in working order again. So they think that once the counsellor knows what the problem is, he should be able to 'repair' the situation at once, or clearly show the client how to do so.

But counselling is not like that. People are not like machines; it is not just a matter of finding what is wrong and fitting a spare part. Often there is no easy answer to a person's problem. The 'mending' process may be long and difficult. It may be something which the counsellor cannot do, and it will be up to the client to carry out the repair himself. Counselling is much more like the practice of medicine. Sometimes when people are ill the cure is fairly easy to find: the symptoms are clear and the remedy is well-known. But sometimes the cause of a person's sickness is difficult to diagnose. Then the doctor must try different medicines, and the patient must help, too, by carrying out the doctor's suggestions, before the cure is discovered and the patient becomes well again.

So even when there is no easy answer to a client's difficulties, a counsellor should not feel that his work is a failure. Not every client can be helped, and in many situations little or no help can be given. But whatever the outcome of the counselling, whether it is 'successful' or not, the counsellor must continue to accept the client and be ready to stand by him.

ENDING THE COUNSELLING

Sometimes the counselling relationship can end quite naturally, for example in situations where the client's chief need was for information, as in educational counselling. Once this is given, the client's need for help is over. The same thing can happen in situations where the client is mature and able to react in responsible ways to solve his problems. Once he fully understands and accepts the action he should take to solve his problem, all the counsellor has to do is to assure him of continuing interest and support if he should need it.

In all cases the counsellor should *encourage* the client to stand on his own feet. But it can give people confidence in helping themselves if they know that the counsellor is available should the situation become too difficult for them to handle. And sometimes a counsellor must be ready to stand by people over a long period, for example when they are experiencing sorrow following a bereavement, or in prolonged sickness, or in the break-up of a family through divorce and separation, or following the loss of a job, or when a person is struggling to overcome a long-standing habit such as drunkeness.

There is, however, a danger that a client may become over-dependent on a counsellor. Some pastors are even tempted to make people dependent on them for continuing help, when their real need is to become free from 'pastoral control' and walk by themselves. (This is another sort of 'unworthy satisfaction' a pastor should avoid!)

The aim of all Christian counselling is to introduce or help the client to turn to mature dependence on Christ for help in times of difficulty. This means focusing on the needs of the client, not those of the counsellor. So the counsellor must always keep the client's needs uppermost in his mind, and decide in each situation which will best help him to achieve maturity in Christ: to end the counselling help, or to continue it for a longer period.

Finally, in thinking about the various phases or stages in the counselling process, we need to remember:

(a) The stages may not come in any set order. They may overlap; they may all happen in one brief counselling time; or they may be spread over a longer period of several meetings with the client.

(b) The counsellor cannot solve the problem by himself. He and the client must work *together* to achieve a solution.

(c) The counsellor should not treat the stages of the counselling process as *rules*, or try to make his methods conform to them exactly.

(d) These 'stages' are best used simply as guidelines, when trying to answer such questions as: Where are we going in this counselling situation? – What do I do next? – Have I jumped to a solution too quickly, without fully clarifying the situation? – Am I pushing the client too hard, or perhaps not pushing him enough? – Is this the best way to help this client to become a more mature person, able to stand on his own feet?

SOME METHODS OF COUNSELLING

Because the counsellor has to relate his work to many different situations or contexts, he needs to use a number of different methods of counselling. Some pastors tend always to follow the same method; they feel safe and comfortable with people when using a method they are accustomed to, and find it difficult to use other methods effectively. Most pastors, however, find it best to use a variety of methods, and perhaps to combine different methods according to the situation.

In choosing which method to use, the counsellor must take note of the following factors:

(a) The *sort of person* needing help;

(b) The *sort of problem* being faced;

(c) The *sort of counsellor* best fitted to help; sometimes a close friend or relative whom the client respects very much is better able to help than a trained and more 'official' pastoral counsellor of whom the client may feel frightened or shy;

(d) The *sort of situation* or context in which the problem has happened or is happening.

Like the various stages in the counselling process, different counselling methods may overlap, or may need to be combined in a different order according to the situation. Here we shall consider the three basic methods most commonly used: *directive*, *non-directive*, and *identifying*, and also the *flexible* approach in which the counsellor may use a combination of these methods.

DIRECTIVE METHOD: THE AUTHORITATIVE APPROACH

This method has been used for centuries, especially in areas where the counsellor is traditionally recognized as an authority figure. In this method:

1. The client brings the problem to the counsellor, or the counsellor goes to give help.

2. The counsellor is expected to provide the answer. The problem may be clarified by the counsellor and the client talking together, but the answer is something which the counsellor will bring into the situation.

3. The client acts (or should act) upon the answer given.

In this method the main stages can be described as follows (with the chief role of the counsellor shown in italics): (a) problem revealed, (b) problem clarified, (c) *answer provided*, (d) action taken on answer given.

As we can see, it is the counsellor who has the most active role as problem-solver.

Example 21 (directive method): Context: Pastor Kilami works in the Highlands area of Papua New Guinea, where the Church has been established for about twenty-five years. Polygamy is widely practised, and the Church accepts polygamists as full members. One day Anna, a regular Church member, came to visit the pastor.

Pastor: Good morning, what can I do to help you?

Anna: I have a problem I would like to talk to you about, and get some help.

Pastor: What is worrying you?

Anna: Well, my husband has taken a second wife. But I am the first wife, so I feel he should give me more respect than this new wife. I have done

126

everything for him, looking after the pigs, the gardens, and so on for many years. But now he has neglected me for many days.

Pastor: What do you mean when you say 'neglected'?

Anna: He has left me alone, and not visited me at all.

Pastor: So you are not living with your husband, then?

Anna: No, I am staying with my eldest daughter about two miles away.

Pastor: Why did you leave your husband's house?

Anna: Because I hate seeing him with another woman. It makes me mad and sad. She seems to own everything I have given him, and I am just pushed around.

Pastor: What are your feelings towards the second wife?

Anna: I am a Christian, and I have no ill feelings, but I do get mad when I see her with my husband.

Pastor: Do you think your husband neglects you because you have left him?

Anna: No, not at all. He treated me unfairly even when I was first with him. And now he has married this second woman, I am just a slave. He never comes to church any more either. He just stays with her.

Pastor: What do you expect him to do for you now?

Anna: I don't expect anything. All I want is his love and concern. I am the first wife, and according to our custom the first wife has power over the others.

Pastor: So in fact you do have some ill feelings towards this second wife. Does she feel that way towards you?

Anna: I don't know. I think she feels all right towards me.

Pastor: Then shouldn't you try to love them both? I think perhaps you should visit them regularly, and even go back to your husband's home. If you stay away you will only be unhappy.

Anna: Well I don't know. (Pause.) Do you really think I should go back to my husband and stay with him?

Pastor: Well, you have said you still want his love, so I think perhaps you should try. Remember that marriage means husbands and wives should live together. That is what God wants. Sharing your life together is the whole purpose of marriage. Also God wants you to forgive others, even when they seem to behave wrongly towards you. You need to ask God to forgive the bad feelings you have towards your husband and towards his second wife. Then God's forgiveness will help you to be forgiving yourself, and to feel at one with your husband. God will surely give you His grace and His help if you turn to Him in prayer.

Anna: I know that is true. But what about my husband? What if he hits me because I ran away.

Pastor: Well, that will be hard for you. But you love your husband, and you should try to do what is right. Remember how Jesus forgave those who were angry with him and hurt him; and how he taught that if we have anything against anyone we should forgive them. Sometimes we feel that others don't want us when it is not really so. I think you should go to your husband and try to tell him quietly about your feelings towards him, and about your problem with this other wife. I know that will be difficult for you, but if you pray to God He will help you to do it. (Pause.) So ask God to help you, but then go back to your husband and live with him and the other wife. You may even be able to help them to live a good Christian life.

Anna: I will try, thank you, I will try to do what you say.

Anna went away then, but returned some weeks later and told Pastor Kilami that the three of them were living happily together again. The husband came back to the Church, and the second wife, who was also a Church member, confirmed that they were living in a much happier way than before.

Pastor Kilami explained his method of counselling as follows: Mostly I give direct advice, and encourage people to more mature thinking. I use this method because Christianity is new here. The people are slow in their thinking, and slow to change because of their traditional background. Often they just cannot help themselves or even see what they ought to do. Therefore I have to tell them, and make a road for them. Later, when they understand better, then they can help themselves. But now they are like children when these problems come. They need someone to guide them along.'

To people brought up in an authority-structured society, the role of the pastor as directive counsellor is not only accepted, but also *expected*. They expect to be freed from the problems of life by following the wise directions of those in authority – in Anna's case the pastor.

We should note that the example of Pastor Kilami and Anna comes from a relatively under-developed area, and is intended chiefly to show the role of the pastor as an authority figure. In other areas the attitude of the Church towards polygamy could be very different. In some places, the task of the first wife might be to regain not only her husband's care and affection, but her place as sole wife, so long as careful provision was made for the welfare and livelihood of the second wife. There are also situations where a first wife might *want* her husband to take other wives in order to help her with the work of the gardens, or with the children. The problem then might be one of conflict between traditional marriage customs in the area and the rules of the Church about Christian marriage (see pp. 177–187).

The following are some situations where the directive method of counselling can be especially effective:

(a) Where the client has tried to solve the problem for himself, but has failed, and is willing to accept the wisdom and authority of the counsellor as likely to be more successful;

(b) Where the client needs factual information, e.g. concerning employment, a career for himself or some other member of his family, legal matters, etc.;

(c) Where danger threatens, e.g. the client is liable to be violent and may harm others, or may even commit suicide; or is afraid of violence from someone else;

(d) Where the client needs a confronting word to help point out the seriousness of the situation (see Example 11, p. 87, and compare also the direct style of Nathan with King David in 2 Samuel 11 and 12);

(e) Where the client is so confused that he cannot see the possibility of any solution;

(f) With children and mentally disturbed people.

NON-DIRECTIVE METHOD: THE 'REFLECTIVE' APPROACH

This method is often called the 'client-centred approach', because the responsibility for solving the problem belongs to the client, not the counsellor. This method assumes that people are basically good and strong in themselves, and capable of finding solutions to their own problems. The counsellor's job is to help the client come to a solution by working with him to clarify the situation. This is done by concentrating on the client's inward feelings, rather than just noting the outward facts. The counsellor will use several sorts of response, but reflective responses will be especially helpful. As the client's own attitudes are reflected back to him in an atmosphere of acceptance, he begins to develop a new understanding and awareness of what is wrong, and how he may be able to overcome his difficulties.

In this method, which is based on the idea of individual responsibility:

1. The client comes with a problem.

2. By listening, reflecting, clarifying, etc., the counsellor helps the client to gain a deeper understanding of the problem, but

3. The counsellor does *not* attempt to give an answer.

4. The client comes to a personal solution based on the new understanding gained through the counsellor's clarifying work.

5. The counsellor helps the client to assess and build on his own resources and strengths.

6. The client decides what action to take in the situation, and acts upon his decision.

As we can see, in this method the main stages are (with the role of the counsellor in italics): (a) problem revealed, (b) *problem clarified*, (c) possible answers to problem considered, (d) answer chosen and action taken.

The chief role of the counsellor in this method is that of a 'sounding board' or *clarifier* of the situation, and not one who actively provides a solution to the problem. He may perhaps suggest some possible answers, but he encourages the client to make his own personal and responsible decision, and choose the course of action to be taken.

Example 22 (non-directive method): Context: Pastor Jude is in charge of a city congregation in Nigeria. Returning home one afternoon he met Dora, a Church member, aged about thirty.

Pastor: Good afternoon, Dora. How are you?

Dora: I am just going to the doctor. I've been ill for a while.

Pastor: Yes, you don't look too good. And we've missed you in church.

Dora: Well, I've been off work for three weeks now and missed church too because of my sickness. So I must see if the doctor can help me.

Pastor: Yes, I'm sure you are wise to see him.

Dora: Well, I don't know. I was never like this before, and I don't know what is making me ill. Perhaps part of it is worry about my boyfriend.

Pastor: Your boyfriend?

Dora: Yes – you know how he goes to the pub after work. Sometimes he doesn't come home until midnight and disturbs my sleep.

Pastor: He makes a noise and disturbs you?

Dora: Yes, especially when I have fallen asleep after staying up and expecting him home sooner. Every night he comes home drunk, and complains about the food being cold. Or if it's not the food, he argues about something else. I just can't understand what he wants or what's going on.

Pastor: You feel very unsettled?

Dora: Yes, I am. Living with a man like him is very difficult. But I really can't live alone. So we've been in the flat for a couple of months now. Usually we both go to church but I felt ashamed when one of the ladies in the choir asked if he was my boyfriend. I told her yes, but I feel this question about my life was very awkward.

Pastor: So the way you are living now seems wrong to you, does it? It makes you feel ashamed and upset?

Dora: Yes, that's just the trouble. And he's upset too. (Pause.) But I can't see why he doesn't do something about it. He should behave better. I told him if he doesn't want to come home in the evening he ought to leave me alone. We can't go on staying together and still go to church. He should know better. I asked him if he really wanted to stay with me and get married. He said yes, but he still doesn't seem really clear about it.

Pastor: Are you beginning to feel he doesn't really want you?

Dora: I think so. Perhaps it's my own fault. We met each other at church, and I never thought we'd end up living this way.

Pastor: You mean he doesn't really understand what is involved in being a Christian? When you try to speak to him about it he doesn't want to answer?

Dora: That's exactly what I mean. But I don't know if I have the courage to let him go. The doctor said that part of my trouble is worry, and I really think he is right.

Pastor: You mean you've been feeling bad because you have a bad conscience, and the doctor thinks it's necessary for your health that you leave your boyfriend?

Dora: I think so. And I think I'd better follow his advice. You know, this conversation has helped me see things more clearly.

Pastor: Well, that's a good beginning. It seems you really have to make up your mind. Does this man love you enough to make a Christian marriage with you, or should you leave him and find help in your friends?

Dora: Yes, I suppose so. (Pause.) Could we talk again about all this?

Pastor: Yes, of course.

Dora: Thank you very much, you have helped me a lot.

Note the 'reflective' sort of responses Pastor Jude gave in order to help Dora clarify the situation for herself. It was only at the end that he described in detail two possible courses of action that were open to her.

Pastors can use both the directive and the non-directive methods to sustain, guide, feed, teach, and encourage people to live responsibly. But the Christian way is also a moral way, with certain guidelines (for example, the Ten Commandments) on how to try and live in accordance with God's will. The pastor has the authority to make these guidelines clear, and help people to follow them.

So the directive approach is often suitable when people need guidance and the pastor has to lead them towards a solution. There is always a danger, however, that he will force or drag people along, rather than leading them in a gentle way and encouraging them to be responsible for their own thinking and actions.

The non-directive approach is particularly valuable when the pastor sees that people are capable of taking responsibility for steering their own lives, and are ready for further growth and greater maturity. The danger here is that a pastor may use this method with clients who are not ready for it. Lacking any clear word of help, the client then becomes even more confused and lost, because his own understanding and resources are not strong enough to cope with any new responsibility. This can often happen where the cultural tradition is an authoritarian one, so that people are accustomed to depending on leaders for guidance and encouragement.

Many counsellors, therefore, prefer to vary their approach according to need. They use ideas from both the directive and the non-directive methods. This is sometimes called an 'eclectic' approach. It means choosing or selecting whatever seems the most effective from other methods, and using this in a combined approach suitable to the particular situation. One such eclectic approach is known as the 'identification' method.

IDENTIFICATION METHOD: A SHARING APPROACH

This combines elements from both directive and non-directive methods. It also adds the further idea of *sharing* between counsellor and client, i.e. the sharing of similar problems, conflicts, and possible solutions. In identification counselling:

1. The client brings the problem and shares it with the counsellor.
2. The counsellor helps to clarify the problem, and *tells of his own similar experience* of conflict or trouble.
3. The counsellor *shares* the solution he has found in his own experience.
4. The counsellor and the client *together* consider possible ways of solving the problem.
5. The client comes to a decision and acts in the light of this sharing.

The main stages of this method, therefore, are as follows (with the role of the counsellor in italics) (a) problem revealed, (b) problem clarified, (c) *similar problem or conflict shared*, (d) *counsellor's own solution shared*, (e) choice made and action taken.

The chief role of the counsellor in this method is seen as that of a *sharer*, one who has been actively involved in a similar situation, and can thus *identify* with the client in seeking a solution to the present problem.

Example 23 (identification method): Context: Pastor Barnabas had become very friendly with David, an expatriate engineer who had married a local school-teacher, and they shared some common interests. One day, when David was visiting Pastor Barnabas he became very quiet, and there was silence for a time. Then David began to speak.

David: I wonder whether I could talk to you about something that has been bothering me?

Pastor: If you would like to, yes, of course.

David: It isn't much really – you may just laugh at me.

Pastor: I promise I won't laugh. Let's hear about it.

David: Well, you know my wife, Leila. We're not getting on very well these days, and I'm a bit worried about it.

Pastor: Can you tell me what you are worried about?

David: Well, you know how it is. When we were first married everything was great. It didn't seem to matter that this was her home country and I was from overseas. We worked out a really good relationship together. She was good with my friends too, but all that seems to have changed.

Pastor: How do you mean 'changed'?

David: Well, she seemed happy when I invited people to our home. She liked to cook for them and be friendly. We were really happy, even though some

132

people have said we were unwise to marry. Well, she's pregnant now, and . . .

Pastor: That has caused problems, has it?

David: In a sort of way, yes. We still want to be together, but she doesn't seem so interested in me. She's tired all the time.

Pastor: That probably comes from being pregnant. But I still don't quite see what you are unhappy about.

David: Well, you see, she doesn't want me to sleep with her any more. She gets cranky about it. Then I get cross too, and we finish up having an argument.

Pastor: Have you tried to talk to her about this together, and find out why she doesn't want it?

David: Yes, I've tried. But she gets very shy and won't say much – just something about her background being different to mine. I don't see what that has to do with it – it seems crazy to me, just because she's pregnant.

Pastor: You didn't expect this when you got married?

David: Well, we talked about it a bit – wondered how we'd get on together, and some of the problems we might find. But it all seems different now.

Pastor: How does Leila herself feel about it?

David: She doesn't seem to want me. She thinks we shouldn't sleep together at all while she's pregnant.

Pastor: And that really bothers you?

David: Well, I do find it pretty hard.

Pastor: I can well understand that.

David: But there's more to it too – there's this girl at work, you see, who's very keen to be friends with me.

Pastor: And you like her too?

David: Well, yes, I do. And – well, the other day she said something to me, and I had to get out of there quickly, because she was obviously ready to start something. But now I can't stop thinking about it. I'm just afraid I'll get caught out if I don't watch myself.

Pastor: Does Leila know about this?

David: Oh no, I couldn't tell her. She'd just accuse me of playing about with other girls. I'm not, and I don't want to, but I'm afraid I will if things don't improve. So what can I do? I thought you might be able to help me, or perhaps both of us – I just feel rotten about the whole business.

Pastor: I don't know if this will help you much, David, but I do understand how you feel. And I think a lot of men feel the same way sometimes. Anyway, I know I do, and it can be really tough. My wife makes me mad sometimes when she's tired, and I think she just doesn't want me. I guess it would be easy to play around with someone else, especially when we've had a row at home about something. We have our arguments too!

David: What do you do about it?

Pastor: Well, when we first tried to talk about it, it just seemed to make things worse. We didn't seem to understand each other at all – at least that's how I saw it. But gradually we made some headway and found we could talk about it more. We just had to struggle along, and finally managed to get on top of it. But it was really hard going at first.

David: At least your wife would talk – but Leila doesn't want to talk at all.

Pastor: Have you ever wondered *why* she doesn't want to talk?

David: I guess she may be afraid I might laugh at her ideas – this stupid tradition of not sleeping together when you are pregnant.

Pastor: Perhaps it only seems stupid because the idea is strange to you. A woman does feel different, you know, when she's going to have a child. Things like sleeping together take on a different meaning. That's why it was always the custom among our people for a man to let his wife sleep alone during pregnancy. Of course it was easier in the old days, when a man had several wives, but I expect Leila finds it difficult to change her ideas about it. So perhaps you'll both have to work harder at this part of your marriage.

David: What do you mean?

Pastor: You'll have to accept the fact that coming from different backgrounds you look at things in different ways, and so you have to try to understand each other's ideas better.

David: Well, I'd certainly like to try. (Pause.) Did you really mean that – about feeling the same way yourself?

Pastor: Yes, of course, why do you ask?

David: Oh, you as a pastor – I never thought – it surprised me a bit.

Pastor: Well, what do you think you can do about your own situation?

David: I'll think about it some more, and try and talk to Leila again. You've helped me to understand her side of things a bit better. This talk is just what I needed.

In this example Pastor Barnabas had helped David just by being ready to share his own weakness and conflict with him, as a man and a friend; and also by sharing his ideas as someone coming from a different cultural background. But David was also a Christian and a member of Pastor Barnabas's congregation, so Barnabas ended by suggesting that David might read Heb. 4.14–16. He told David that he himself had found these verses helpful because they reminded him that Jesus Himself was tempted and can sympathize with our weakness, and so we can always be confident of His grace and help when we are tempted ourselves. David said he would certainly try, and went home in a much more hopeful frame of mind.

We must recognize however, that the idea of identification or sharing in counselling is difficult for some people – both counsellors and clients – to accept. They think that the counsellor should not get too close to the client, or reveal his own weaknesses. They believe he should concentrate on the client only, and not on himself. In some cultural situations, too, the idea of sharing common experiences of strengths and weaknesses, and working together towards a solution, may seem very strange. The following comments were made by pastors who found it hard to accept the idea of sharing:

(a) 'If I reveal my weaknesses and share them with others, people will have no confidence in me. They don't expect the pastor to be the same as they are. They expect and want him to be different – otherwise why is he a pastor?'

(b) 'Sharing my problems means admitting my own weakness, and that could make people refuse to accept any answer I could give. How can a pastor really help people unless they think he has the answers? Also, to admit to problems would cause me a loss of status, and this could destroy my own sense of confidence and security in my work.'

In some cultural situations the idea of 'self-exposure' conflicts with the accepted ways of relating to others. Any shame or embarrassment causes a person to 'lose face', and 'face' is very important. To prevent this, and 'save face', the problem of failure in a person's life has to be approached in a very roundabout way. In these areas, most pastoral counsellors would have to use a very directive approach, in which there is no sharing, and the pastor himself remains 'hidden' and protected from any self-revelation. Where this happens, communication is in danger of becoming 'one-way' – that is, a *monologue* from counsellor to client.

The counsellor can also hide himself from scrutiny in a non-directive method of counselling, and again communication can become a monologue, but this time the other way round: from client to counsellor. The client does all the talking, while the counsellor listens, occasionally reflecting and encouraging, but without revealing anything of himself.

Identification counselling, on the other hand, is based on *dialogue*, a two-way communication and sharing. One pastor described how and why he changed from being a non-sharing to a sharing counsellor:

'In the past I talked to troubled people who revealed something of themselves, but who also wanted to know about me. Where did I stand? Did I have any problems? The accepted way of counselling I had been taught was that the pastor should "hedge" and not reveal himself. But I think now that such a response is wrong. A dialogue in which the pastor as well as the troubled person enters the conversation is much more productive of maturity and growth.'

That pastor had recognized a basic aim of identifying counselling, which is to help all those involved in the situation to *grow*. This encourages a 'growth-producing' relationship in which they learn to trust each other with their thoughts and experiences, knowing that these will be valued and respected. For a pastor to identify with others does mean admitting weakness as a person. But this does not mean weakness as a counsellor. People's confidence in his ability to help them will depend chiefly on their understanding of the meaning of the gospel for their lives, and of who they are as Christians. The problem of sharing has to be related, not only to the pastor's accepted status as a leader in the Church, but also to his status – and the status of his clients – as fellow-believers in Jesus Christ.

Any true and reflective Christian leader who is ministering to others must take his place as a person alongside other people, sharing in their problems in an involved and caring way. The counsellor needs to show that he himself has problems, and so can understand and share the burdens of others; he too is weak but he has been made strong in Christ. L. Richards, an experienced counsellor and youth leader, has written:

'To help others, we have to live with them as expressed in the sentence "We are sinners, but we are also justified and accepted sinners." This is not a truth taught just by words, but a truth which must be experienced. The experience is one which comes when one person hears another admit to his struggles as well as his victories; his rebellions as well as his knowledge of God's guidance. We are in Christ, yet we know we fall short of what He wants us to be. But we are in Him and becoming more like Him. (See Rom. 6.4.) When we understand this we do not have to hide the fact that we are sinners. We know He loves us, and therefore we have confidence in His love and accept our shortcomings.

'The Christian who accepts himself like this is free to be honest with God. And if we can be honest with God, then we should be able to be honest with others. Only as they see us as we are, human and needy, yet becoming new people through the power of God's spirit, will they understand the gospel and the great gifts God has given us in Christ.'

In summarizing this idea of identification and sharing in the work of pastoral counselling, we have to consider three questions:

1. In thinking about people's confidence, is the pastor trying to lead them to have confidence in *his* ability and strength, or is he leading them, through his example, to have confidence in God? Can a pastor lead others to put their trust in Christ, if he does not admit that he is in need himself and yet constantly finds that God meets his need?

2. Is 'self-exposure' useful for pastoral counsellors, or is it too dangerous? It means that the counsellor who offers help has to expose his own 'human-ness', and his similarity to those he is helping. If he is to show people his weakness, must he not also show them that Christ is his hope and strength? In 2 Corinthians 1.3–8, Paul seems to suggest that in the sharing of weaknesses and needs, others can see the power and love of Christ, and new possibilities for living in Him.

3. Can a leader who presents himself as unfailingly strong really minister effectively to others? Does he not seem so different that they

despair when they see him, because he seems so strong while they are so weak? Is it perhaps the leader who shows himself as he really is, with all his weakness and need, who most inspires and helps people when he also shows them the strength he has found in the gospel? Paul saw himself as the chief of sinners (1 Tim. 1.15). He did not hesitate to reveal his weakness and his problems, but he did not hesitate, either, to praise God for His help (Phil. 4.13). As Richards concluded: 'Only the self-revealing person can serve as a living example of the grace and power of God. The person who opens his life to others, giving and accepting the love that forgives and trusts and covers many sins, is the person who can really help others.' Only if there is this personal involvement and identification, can a true *spiritual* ministry take place. Perhaps, too, only if the pastor is willing to share with others as he expects them to share with him, will he himself continue to *grow* in maturity and wisdom as helper and enabler of others.

So we see that the counsellor has to be flexible in his approach. He has to consider in each case whether the client belongs to a traditional authority-based culture, or is able to make a more individualistic approach to problems. Any counselling method is 'correct' which effectively achieves the aim of helping the client to develop towards maturity, and to experience the abundant life that is available in Jesus Christ. This is more important than following a particular counselling text-book.

COMBINING METHODS: THE FLEXIBLE APPROACH

We have already given some consideration to the counselling of and by groups (see pp. 58, 82 and 83). The following example of group counselling shows how aspects of the directive, non-directive, and identification methods can be combined.

Example 24 (flexible approach): This situation was an urban one, but the problem was conflict between two different tribal groups within one Christian congregation (we shall call them group A and group B). Philemon, the pastor involved in the situation, had family connections with both groups. This how he described it:

Late one evening some members of the congregation called me to intervene in a noisy fight between two different clan groups. I hesitated to rush in, so I told them to go back and I would be with them in five minutes. After a quiet time with the Lord for guidance, I came to where the people were arguing and fighting. I could sense that things were serious, because they were really talking 'hot'. So I walked slowly among them and sat down at a place which I felt was the centre, where I could be seen by the two angry crowds of people.

They carried on with their exchange of insulting words, but I could hear

137

'Any counselling method is "correct" which helps the client to develop towards maturity . . . in Jesus' (p. 137).

By sharing his own doubts and fears with a woman who felt she was losing her faith in a time of crisis, a pastor so encouraged her that she took the opportunity to renew her own baptismal vows when she brought her baby to be christened. What can a pastor himself gain from such sharing?

people whispering to their friends: 'Hush, stop talking! Can't you see the pastor is sitting there and waiting to speak?' This had no effect, and the talking became louder and angrier. I just sat on patiently, saying nothing and making no attempt to stop the noise. I listened carefully, as I did not know what was the cause of the trouble. Gradually the problem became clear without my having to ask anyone. A man in group A was married to a woman whose father belonged to group B. During the husband's absence from home his own father had said insulting words to the woman, his daughter-in-law, and had made immoral suggestions to her. This had created ill-feeling between the two family groups. Realizing the difficulty of the problem, I did not jump in at once with any counselling, but waited for the people to settle down. When I could hear that people in both groups were just repeating the same words over and over again, I intervened, asking 'Have you finished?' There was a pause on both sides.

Pastor: Have you any more words to say to each other?

Group A leader: No, pastor.

Group B leader: No pastor.

Pastor: Have you really said all you want to say, or will there be more insulting words later when I have gone.

Both leaders: No, we've said all we want to say.

Pastor: I'm not here to stop you talking, like a policeman, so if you have more words, say them now, so that all of us can hear them.

Both leaders: No, pastor, we have said all there is to be said. We have no more words burning in us.

Pastor: So it's all right with both groups, is it, if I say something now? (A long pause, then both leaders said that it was all right for me to speak.)

Pastor: I come here as your pastor, but also as a member of both your family groups. I belong to you, group A, because my grandmother came from your area. I also belong to you, group B, because my grandfather is one of you. So I'm not a stranger to you. But I am ashamed of you, my own people, because you cannot solve your problems peacefully, but try to solve them by fighting and hurting each other. Perhaps some of you don't want me to talk to you. But I'm a fellow member of both sides, and as your pastor I have a right to talk. (Another long pause, but no questions or any response.)

Pastor: Well, what do you want to do, now that your relationship is broken through fighting and insulting each other? (Yet another long pause. The women in both groups started to cry, and told the men, especially the group leaders, that it was they who had caused the trouble by their bad attitudes. When quietness was restored, I intervened again.)

Pastor (to group A leader): Have you any betelnut? (The local equivalent of drinking tea, etc., as a means of social fellowship.)

Group leader: Yes, I have.

Pastor (to group B leader): Have you any betelnut?

Group B leader: Yes, I have.

Pastor: Do you wish to be friends again and finish this fighting. (After another pause, both leaders said 'Yes' – with tears, so I knew that it was a real 'Yes'.)

Pastor: Share the betelnut among yourselves and be reunited. I want you leaders of the two groups to step out and as Christians show everyone that you have really forgiven each other. (The leaders paused, then walked towards each other. They shook hands and hugged each other, still rather tearful. This was followed by hand-shaking all round, and more sharing of betelnut.)

Pastor: Can we pray now as brothers and sisters?

Both groups: Yes, we can.

Pastor: In our prayer let us open our hearts and ask God to guide us. You have all shared together and shown that you do not hate each other any more. But let us commit ourselves to the Lord. (I then asked group leaders and members to lead in prayer, and when they had done this I finished with a prayer myself.)

STUDY SUGGESTIONS

WORD STUDY

1. Explain the difference between the 'process' of counselling and the 'method' of counselling.
2. What is the difference between 'monologue' and 'dialogue'?
3. What do you understand by the 'context' of counselling?
4. Which of the following words would you use in describing the 'identification' approach to counselling?
   sharing knowing ignoring shaming listening helping
   guiding rebuking partnership revealing

REVIEW OF CONTENT

5. What are the five main stages in the counselling process?
6. At what stage in the *process* of counselling is a client likely to offer a 'presenting' problem? Give an example of such a problem from your own situation.
7. List some of the ways in which a counsellor can 'clarify' a situation.
8. (a) Name three different methods used in counselling, and briefly describe what happens in each.
   (b) What factors must the counsellor take note of in deciding which method to use?
9. Describe a relationship which could be called a 'growth-producing' relationship.
10. (a) In what sort of situation is it specially important for a counsellor to be 'flexible' in his approach?

(b) In what sort of situation can it be more helpful if he is authoritative?

BIBLE STUDY

11. Proverbs 25.11–12 and 29.20 emphasize the importance of speaking the right words at the right time. What teaching about the use of words is given in each of the following passages?
(a) Matt. 12.36–37 (b) Eph. 4.29 (c) James 3.1–12.
12. Read the following passages and say in each case whether it describes: (i) a situation where Jesus used the directive approach to people, (ii) a situation where He used the non-directive approach, or (iii) a situation where He identified himself with them.
(a) Mark 1.21–28 (b) Mark 10.17–22 (c) John 4.7–15
(d) John 8.1–11 (e) Luke 10.25–37 (f) Luke 19.1–10
13. Explain briefly in your own words Paul's teaching on the subject of identification, as expressed in each of the following passages:
(a) Rom. 13.3–5 (b) Rom. 14.13–19 (c) 1 Cor. 9.22
(d) Gal.6.1–5 (e) Phil. 2.1–7.

APPLICATION, OPINION, AND RESEARCH

14. On p. 122 we listed some reasons why clients sometimes use an indirect approach or offer a presenting problem to the counsellor. What further reasons for doing so can you add from your own experience?
15. Describe two problem situations from your own experience, or that of your family, in which the non-directive type of counselling would have been particularly helpful.
16. Try to evaluate the counselling given in each of the examples given in this chapter, nos 21, 22, 23, and 24. You may find it helpful to consider the following questions about each example:
(a) How effective was the counselling offered?
(b What weak points were there?
(c) What more could have been done to help the people concerned to grow towards deeper maturity?
In what ways, if any, do you think Pastor Philemon might have been able to improve on the counselling done by Pastor Kilami and Pastor Barnabas?
17. If you have experience as a counsellor, try to evaluate your own way of working. Which of the three basic methods discussed in this chapter do you use most – i.e., directive, non-directive, or identifying? Which method do you feel most at ease with, and why?

8

Spiritual Resources in Counselling

Before we study the spiritual resources available to the pastoral counsellor, we may usefully ask: 'Is there anything distinctive or special about *Christian* pastoral counselling, and if so, what is it? Or is our pastoral counselling just the same as the counselling done by those who do not claim to be Christians?' Before continuing with this chapter, think about this question and if possible discuss it with others, and write down your conclusions.

In many ways, Christian pastoral counselling *is* like any other counselling. Many of the ideas and principles are the same, e.g. the need for sincere acceptance, disciplined listening, identification, etc. The broad aim of helping people is basic to all counselling. When a Christian counsellor tries to help people he uses methods which all counsellors accept, whether they are Christians or not. And pastors can learn many good things from counsellors who do not share the Christian beliefs about God and man.

However, there are also important *differences* between Christian pastoral counselling and other counselling. Some pastors do not realize this. They think of their counselling work as exactly like that done by any psychologist or social worker. Some even feel that because they are not trained in psychology or social science they ought not to undertake counselling at all. They think it should be left to 'specialist' workers who are better trained for it than themselves. If a pastor tries to counsel people, they think, he is being like a 'quack' doctor who falsely claims to have a medical degree.

There is some truth behind this feeling. Most pastoral workers are not trained psychologists or social workers, and should not pretend that they are. There are many problems too deep and complicated for an untrained person to handle safely. Pastors should be ready to recognize these, and always refer them to someone (a doctor, psychiatrist, or perhaps a lawyer) who has the necessary training and expertise to deal with them. But a pastoral counsellor does have a *special* contribution to make, because he can offer religious and spiritual resources to people who need them, and these are not usually offered by counsellors who are not practising Christians.

We have already studied in detail the distinctive ideas about God and man on which pastoral counselling is built. At this point it will be helpful to summarize these beliefs as follows:

(a) God as Creator, actively cares for His world and all people in it.

(b) Man can only be truly known in his relationship to God.

(c) In Jesus Christ, God provides the way of freedom from all that destroys the true meaning of life.

(d) The Holy Spirit is active and present in the world, ready to make the divine power and resources available to those who truly seek God's help.

(e) The Church is part of God's plan for the world, and provides a caring, serving fellowship in which people may find the true meaning of knowing God in their lives.

Christian pastors who understand these ideas, and turn to spiritual resources in their counselling ministry, are drawing upon a source of help which the Church has used for many years, and which opens out many possibilities for people in need. Four of the main spiritual resources are:

The Scriptures;

Prayer;

The sacraments;

The fellowship of the Church.

The effective use of these, and indeed of any spiritual resources, depends on our basic belief in the role and activity of the Holy Spirit in the counselling situation. So we start by considering what this means for counsellor and client.

THE WORK OF THE HOLY SPIRIT

Daniel Day Williams, in *The Minister and the Care of Souls*, wrote: 'To bring salvation to the human spirit is the goal of all Christian ministry and pastoral care.' This means that the scope of pastoral care is very wide, and to achieve that goal the pastor must link himself with the Holy Spirit of God. He cannot hope to reach it by his own effort alone.

The Holy Spirit is the 'life-giving' power, the divine creative activity which flows into the lives of believers, reconciling men and women to God and to each other, making them into new people. The Holy Spirit is the means of God's presence in His world, actively at work among us, promoting what is good, and bringing enlightenment and faith (see John 16.4–11).

THE CONSEQUENCES OF BELIEF IN THE SPIRIT

The Holy Spirit is present at all times, directing our understanding towards Jesus Christ, and making it possible for us to straighten out our lives in the light of what we see in Him. The Spirit is especially present when a person is struggling with problems, and trying to discover the basic meaning of life. However, this does not mean that

143

every conclusion we reach and every decision we take is the result of divine guidance.

The Holy Spirit is present and working in each counselling situation, even when neither counsellor nor client is aware of this. Again, however, this does not mean that all the advice given and choices made are prompted by the Spirit.

The presence of the Spirit does not do away with the task of the counsellor, nor the client's responsibility to work for a solution to the problem situation. The Holy Spirit chooses to work through the efforts of men and women, but He is not controlled by them. Sometimes He will work in a situation where all human effort has brought no effective result. But He doesn't *force* people to accept His help. Sometimes the action taken as a result of counselling is entirely human in origin, and may even be contrary to God's will.

For the counsellor, belief in the Holy Spirit has the following consequences:

(a) The counsellor sees God, rather than himself, as the real counsellor in the situation. One writer has said: 'The spiritually secure pastor knows that the life of the client is actually in the hands of God, not in his own. The Holy Spirit, and not he himself, is the counsellor.'

(b) The counsellor can move into the situation in confidence that this work of the Spirit is going on, knowing that God is more concerned for the client than he himself can ever be. He need not think that he alone is responsible for the client or for the outcome of his counselling. Even if he feels unable to give any effective help, the client is still in God's care. The Christian counsellor feels a great responsibility, but because of his belief in the Spirit he sees this responsibility in a new way.

(c) Instead of being overwhelmed by feelings of discouragement and frustration, or even failure, in a difficult situation, the Christian counsellor can humbly and confidently turn to the Spirit as a source of guidance and strength. This makes a great difference to the way in which he approaches each counselling situation.

(d) At the same time, the counsellor has to recognize that this divine presence and activity can itself be frustrated or even nullified unless he himself is willing to open his eyes and his mind and his heart to what the Spirit is saying and doing. Human insensitivity and misunderstanding and selfishness can all too easily block out the light of the Spirit's guidance. So the counsellor cannot automatically lay claim to a divine '*imprimatur*', or seal of approval, for everything that happens in the counselling process.

THE 'RESOURCES' OF THE SPIRIT IN COUNSELLING

In earlier chapters we referred only to *two* 'persons' as being involved in any counselling situation: the counsellor and the client. But now we have seen that there is always a *third* person present, who is more powerful than either of the other two, who 'stands in the middle between them'. Every counselling situation consists of (a) the counsellor, (b) the divine presence, and (c) the client. Jesus said, 'When two or three are gathered in my name, there am I in the midst of them' (Matt. 18.20); and 'I will pray to the Father and he will give you another counsellor, to be with you for ever' (John 14.16). As Bishop John V. Taylor has said, the Holy Spirit is the 'invisible go-between' who sparks off between counsellor and client (if they will let Him) a current of communication, and makes them aware of each other, activating them from inside. And it is from this communication and lively awareness that the 'I-Thou' relationship essential to effective counselling derives (see p. 51).

Those who do not believe find it difficult, if not impossible, to understand the meaning of the divine presence. The true counsellor, that is the Holy Spirit, is always there in the situation. But without faith, as Jesus told His disciples, we are unable to recognize Him or to receive the light and power of His help and guidance (John 14.17).

The presence of the Holy Spirit makes the spiritual resources we have listed very important for the Christian counsellor. The Church has always used what it calls 'the means of grace' to help people in their problems. As we have seen, these include the hearing and reading of the Scriptures, prayer, the sacraments, and sharing in the fellowship of the Church, and it is through these most especially that the Holy Spirit guides and strengthens people. There are two points we should note here:

1. The activity of the Holy Spirit is not limited to these resources. Some pastors think that the Holy Spirit will only be active in the situation if the Scriptures are read or prayer is offered. This is not true. The Holy Spirit does bring blessing and help to people by these means, but is in no way bound or restricted by them. As Lord and Giver of Life, the Holy Spirit is free to work when and how and where and through whatever agency He will.

2. Similarly, for the counsellor, using these traditional spiritual resources does not mean that other resources and techniques are not valuable and effective. The counsellor should use all the effective methods and resources available. He should not under-estimate the importance of traditional resources, though he should not treat them as a 'cure-all' for every problem. The Christian counsellor will humbly recognize that God is just as much Lord of the new resources discovered by doctors and scientists in His world today. So long as the Christian counsellor is truly open and sensitive to the Holy Spirit's direction, he is free to use whatever resource or method seems most helpful in any situation.

USING THE BIBLE

The Bible is an important tool in counselling. It not only provides a true understanding of people's basic needs, but also gives the answer to these needs. So the Bible becomes a living word, reaching out to people in their present problem situations – 'living' through the presence and activity of the Holy Spirit who brings illumination and meaning to the written page. As we read, meditate upon, and apply this written word to our lives today, so God's presence and activity become real to us. The Scriptures themselves provide the evidence of their importance in counselling. For example:

(a) They bring light to our human situation (Ps. 119.105).

(b) They show us the mind of God, and encourage us to bring our own thoughts into line with His (Isa. 55.6–9).

(c) They show us the way to believe in Jesus Christ, and find new life in Him (John 20.30, 31).

(d) They offer us encouragement, comfort, and hope in times of distress and difficulty (Rom. 15.4).

(e) They offer correction, instruction, and true teaching, and show us the right way to live (2 Tim. 3.15–17).

(f) They enter deeply into our inner lives, and help us to recognize and understand our own inward thoughts and desires (Heb. 4.12).

However, in spite of these claims made by the Scriptures themselves, many pastors fail to use the Bible as an effective resource in their counselling work, and some do not use it at all. There are various reasons for this. Some pastors regard the Bible as out of date because it was written so long ago, and think it has little relevance for people's lives today. Many have not learnt how to use it properly, and so prefer to work without it. Some pastors are afraid that people will think of the Bible as a sort of 'fetish', or as a book with magical powers that can provide an instant 'cure' for any problem situation. And some do not want to see the Bible used like a heavy stick, to beat people into submission through blindly following its teachings. There are wrong ways as well as right ways of using the Bible, and great care is needed if it is to be used effectively.

The following examples show some ways in which two different pastors used the Scriptures in trying to help people. When you have studied them carefully, try to evaluate the way the pastor used the Bible in each case. Do you think the help offered was likely to be effective? If not, what do you think was wrong? How might the Scriptures have been used to better effect?

Example 25: Andrew was very much troubled by sexual desires and thoughts which tempted him to speak and behave in unacceptable ways. He went to his pastor with this problem, hoping to get help and guidance. The pastor listened carefully, and then advised Andrew how he could control his thoughts and behaviour, and defeat these strong desires. He gave Andrew a copy of the Scriptures, and suggested he should read certain verses when the temptations came to him. He also advised Andrew to place the Bible under his pillow when he went to bed: 'If you do this,' he said, 'it will drive away your evil thoughts and dreams and help you to sleep properly without these tempting thoughts coming to you all the time.' Andrew promised that he would follow this advice, and said he felt sure it would help him to overcome his problem.

Example 26: Rafi was not a member of the Church, but he visited Pastor Francis, seeking help over his problem of drinking, and of fighting with his wife when he was drunk. After talking for a short time, Rafi began to tell the pastor about his drinking habits.

Rafi: I can't blame my wife for getting angry with me – you can see that my life is in a mess because of this.

Pastor: Have you thought *why* you drink so much?

Rafi: I don't know. I just seem to follow my friends. I'm afraid they will despise me if I say no. And I feel mean if I don't buy drinks for them. So I just do it to keep in with the others.

Pastor: Well, that is a problem. You know the Bible says that the fear of man is a snare (Prov. 29.25). You will never be strong unless you stop minding what people think.

Rafi: I suppose you are right. I hate all this fighting at home, and really want to stop, but it is so difficult.

Pastor: God will help you if you really want to stop it. His word says: 'Call on me in time of trouble and I will save you' (Ps. 50.15).

Rafi: And it isn't only the drinking my wife complains about, either. When I was drunk the other night, I got into a poker game, and didn't go home until I had lost all my money.

Pastor: Yes, one thing leads to another: first drunkenness – and now gambling as well. That isn't good. The Bible tells us clearly that both these things are wrong. When St Paul wrote to the Christians at Corinth he said, 'Neither the immoral . . . nor the greedy, nor drunkards . . . will inherit the kingdom of God' (1 Cor. 6.9, 10). And again in Proverbs we read: 'He who follows worthless pursuits will have plenty of poverty. . . . He who hastens to be rich will not go unpunished' (Prov. 28.19, 20).

Rafi: Yes I know. That's why I came to you for some help.

Pastor: Well, it seems that first of all you need to think carefully about your way of living, and make a real decision to change your wrong ways. Then ask the Lord for His forgiveness. Listen to Isa. 55.6, 7: 'Seek the Lord while he is near. Let the wicked forsake his way and the unrighteous man his thoughts, and let him return to the Lord, and he will abundantly pardon.'

Rafi: Yes, I know you are right. I'll try to remember those verses, and maybe

I'll manage to do better in future. Perhaps I could come and talk to you about it again some time?

USING SCRIPTURE EFFECTIVELY

To be effective, the Bible must be used properly, and this is something every pastoral counsellor has to learn. Paul's advice to Timothy is still true for pastoral workers today: 'Concentrate on being a workman . . . who knows how to use the word of truth to the best advantage' (2 Tim. 3.15, Phillips). This skill is not necessarily gained by studying the Bible in a theological college; nor does it come just because we have mastered all the facts about the authorship, date of writing, and historical background to the Scriptures. The knowledge needed for pastoral work is different from the knowledge that enables us to pass an exam in biblical criticism or exegesis.

We have likened the Scriptures to a tool in the counsellor's hand, and as with any tool, it is only through actual practice that we become skilful in using it. Just as a carpenter needs practice before he knows which saw or which screwdriver to use for a particular job, so a pastor must know *which* Scriptures to use, and *when* to use them, and this is not always taught in courses on the Bible. Many pastors do know a lot *about* the Bible, but are still unsure about *how to use it* in a pastoral situation. For that, we have to know the *content* of the Scriptures themselves well enough to be able to apply their message to the actual situations in which needy people find themselves.

Besides the pastor's knowledge, effective use of the Bible depends chiefly on two other factors:

1. *The counsellor's own attitude to the Bible:* What sort of attitude should it be? Here are some suggestions:

He must firmly believe that the teachings of the Bible are true and relevant for people's lives today.

He should be building his own life on these teachings.

He should be continually 'practising' – i.e. learning from the Scriptures himself, as well as using them to help others.

He should be memorizing suitable passages of Scripture, so as to know exactly what he is offering to others.

Many people find memorizing Scripture very helpful. Those who use the Bible most effectively in helping others are those who have equipped themselves with a good 'store' of Bible passages which speak to many different human problems. Too many counsellors, however, do not know the Bible well enough to use it with any confidence. They vaguely remember a passage, but then have to search for it: 'Let me see – is it in Matthew? James? Romans? – Where?' and this confuses the client. Like a soldier who needs his weapons ready to hand, a pastoral worker needs to have the Scriptures ready on his tongue. This readiness is not something which can be achieved just before you visit a sick person, or prepare to counsel someone. The most effective preparation takes place quietly and continually, in the pastor's own reading and meditating on the meaning of the Bible for his life and the life of his people.

2. *The way the counsellor uses the Bible:* Scripture must be used in a *loving* way to help the client to think about his problem in relationship to God. It must bring light into the situation, not make it darker or more difficult.

Scripture can only be used effectively when the counsellor has really tried to understand the problem. Usually this understanding is necessary before any Bible teaching can be applied directly. Only then will the pastor be able to decide which particular passage or passages of Scripture to choose, and how best to apply or explain them.

Each counsellor must decide when is the best time to introduce Scripture. Some pastors like to begin the counselling with a short general Bible reading (and usually with a prayer). They feel this helps the client to recognize the presence of God in the situation. Others prefer to wait until they have some understanding of the client's need, and in some situations may decide not to use Scripture at all. But as we have said, Scripture is usually most effective when the pastor relates it to his own understanding of the situation. It can then bring light or hope or encouragement, or a challenge that is directly relevant to the person involved.

Any Scripture used should of course be relevant to the problem: that is, the words should be clear, and their meaning for the problem situation plain to see. Difficult or obscure verses which are hard to understand are likely to confuse rather than to help.

This does not mean that the Scripture must relate *exactly* to the client's problem. It may be impossible to find a passage from books written 2,000 years ago that deals directly with a particular problem of today. But nearly always some verses can be found that will bring light and help to the client. Thus, when a client is depressed and feels guilty because he has acted wrongly towards someone there may be no verse which refers to that particular wrong action. But there are plenty of well-known passages about forgiveness, restoration, and the power of Christ to help in times of need (e.g. 1 John 1.9, 10; Heb. 4.14–16); and such passages as Ps. 23; Rom. 8.35–39; or Matt. 11.28–30 can be used in many different situations to bring new hope and life to distressed people.

Here also we need to recognize the work of the Holy Spirit, who speaks to people through the Scriptures in ways we do not always understand. The counsellor's part is to select the passage which to him seems the most useful for a particular situation. With some clients he may want to explain it briefly; but he will always trust to the Holy Spirit to give it meaning and power to speak to the client's need.

The passage chosen can be read either by the counsellor or the client. Many people find new meaning when they read the Bible for themselves. They hear their own voices, and discover, perhaps for the first time, that they are personally involved with the Scripture. With those who are shy, or who cannot read, the counsellor will read the passage himself, a verse at a time, and then ask the client to repeat the words after him. Some clients are helped if the pastor 'personalizes' the passage, that is, puts the client's name into it. For example, with John 3.16: 'God so loved Albert that he gave his only son . . .' – or '. . . if Albert believes . . . , etc.' This can be done with many of the passages which promise God's help, e.g. Ps. 23; 1 John 1.7–9.

If the counsellor expects to see the client a second time, it can be helpful to ask him to read and think about certain verses as a sort of homework, and then discuss them during the next visit. Some counsellors like to write out Scripture verses and give them to clients to think about, especially those who are sick or housebound, or who have no Bible of their own.

Some clients may need to have the selected passage explained to them. This is especially important in any discussion of specific spiritual problems, or matters of false teaching, when it is essential to gain a deeper understanding of the true meaning. The *amount* of explanation needed will depend on how much the client already knows, and on the counsellor's own understanding of the situation. It is important not to confuse the client with detail about the historical or literary background which the pastor learnt at college but which is not relevant to the client's situation. But it is also very important not to 'talk down' to clients as if they were children. Some clients may even have studied the Scriptures more deeply than the pastor has!

The Scripture passage or passages used should be brief, rather than too long. Often when people are in trouble, they can only concentrate on one idea at a time, so that too many verses together may confuse them. This is especially so with people who are sick, or distressed through grief. A few easy verses will help them more than a long complicated passage.

All these suggestions will only be effective if the counsellor really knows and depends on the Scriptures for himself. And this familiarity with them depends on the amount of time he spends reading and meditating on their meaning for human lives. The pastors who claim that the Bible is not much use in counselling are usually those who do not really know what the Bible says. A counsellor who neglects to use the Bible himself will never be able to use it effectively in helping others.

HELPFUL SCRIPTURE REFERENCES

There are many ways of equipping yourself with a store of suitable Bible passages to use in particular situations. Some Bibles list verses to read in times of sorrow, rejoicing, despair, fear, anger, etc., but many pastoral counsellors prefer to make up their own collection. At the end of this Guide we give a list of such passages, simply as a starting point (p. 283). Helpful verses are suggested for a number of different problem situations. You could extend the list by adding other problem situations you have experienced, and any Bible passages you have found helpful. Keep on adding to the list as you gain more experience, until you have passages for a wide range of situations.

USING PRAYER

Prayer is especially important in the ministry of counselling because it is man's chief way of keeping close to God. As with the use of Scripture, we give some examples of how prayer can be used, and suggest that you study and evaluate the helpfulness or otherwise of the method used in each situation.

Example 27: Little Dorothea, the child of a local Church leader in a Malaysian village, became very sick. The father took the child to the nearest medical centre for treatment, and then went to Pastor Henry and asked him to pray for the child's healing. They prayed together, and Henry comforted the man and his family in their distress. Henry encouraged them to pray together at home too, for the child's recovery.

However, Dorothea did not improve, so the father asked a village healer to pray to the spirits for help. He paid a sum of money to the healer, who performed a ritual and said some prayers for the child. The father still continued to meet with Pastor Henry and pray with him for God's help, and the pastor encouraged him to keep on doing this. The pastor did not know that the man had gone to the village healer. However, this was a fairly common practice among the people, who always tried to get help from any possible source, so Henry would not have been greatly surprised.

Eventually Dorothea recovered, and the family were very happy. The father said he believed that the child's healing was due to *all* the prayers that had been offered, and that help had come both from the spirits and from God.

Example 28: Pastor Bunapa always uses prayer in counselling. One evening he was called to see a married couple who were so often fighting that their children and other relatives were very unhappy and disturbed. He came to the house, where many of the family were gathered, and sat down with the couple, Jolo and Vera. Everyone was obviously upset, but they talked about general things for a short time and shared some food together. Then, after a short silence, Bunapa asked everyone present to pray, and asked God for His help in their difficult situation. This was his prayer: 'Lord God, you are the great God and you know everything we do and say. You know when we do good things and when we do wrong things. You know what our lives are like in our families and among our friends. We need your help now because we cannot see our way clearly. Show us the way to live, because we are very weak without you and our faith is not strong. Help us to have a stronger faith in your love for us. Thank you for giving us your son Jesus Christ. Guide us as we talk together now about this problem which is facing this family, and help us to do what is best. Amen.'

Later, someone asked Pastor Bunapa why he prayed in this way *before* starting the counselling. He replied that he did so for several reasons: because the people expected him to do so, because he wanted to remind them that God knows all about every situation, because people are weak and need God's help all the time, and because he wanted God to guide the counselling situation right from the beginning. He wanted to put the whole problem into God's hands.

For a third example read again the description of Pastor Philemon's counselling in a dispute between two different clan groups (Example 24, p. 137). Note the way in which Pastor Philemon used the resource of prayer. *Before* he went into the situation he prayed for God's guidance to deal with the situation. Then he went to meet the people involved and worked through the situation towards an acceptable solution. Finally, when the dispute was ended, he asked those involved to pray together. He also prayed for God's help to be with them in their lives.

As you evaluate each of these three examples, ask yourself: 'Is this a good way to use prayer? Was it the sort of prayer most likely to be helpful in that particular situation?

WHY USE PRAYER IN COUNSELLING?

We do not pray in order to attract God's attention, nor to persuade Him to change His mind about our problems. God is already interested in us, and we cannot force His attention just by saying extra prayers. But there are many ways in which prayer can help both counsellor and client:

1. Prayer opens up our living situation and enables us to draw on the deep resources of God's strength and wisdom.

2. Prayer brings us into touch with the mind of God, so that we begin to see the problem in a new and clearer way. It also enables us to draw upon more than our own wisdom to meet the problem.

3. Prayer reminds us that our own understanding and strength is

limited, and that we can find the true meaning of life and of all our relationships in the teachings and example of Jesus Christ.

4. Prayer helps us to find and experience God's forgiveness and His sustaining love in the midst of our failures and problems.

HOW AND WHEN TO USE PRAYER

A pastor's use of prayer in counselling depends on his own understanding of the purposes of prayer, and of the situation in which he is working.

As with the Scriptures, some counsellors prefer to use prayer at the start of the counselling. Others prefer to wait until they understand the situation, and then use prayer to bring clarity and strength into the problem area. Others rarely use prayer during the actual counselling situation: they pray alone beforehand, and continue to pray for themselves and for those involved in the situation after the counselling help has been given.

The following guidelines may be helpful in thinking about how we can use prayer in our counselling.

1. There are no *rules* about this. Each counsellor must act according to the situation as he sees it. If he feels that prayer would be helpful, or if the client asks for it, he can go ahead on that basis.

2. However, there are some situations in which prayer is specially helpful: in times of mourning or sorrow; with old people, especially those who cannot easily move about; with sick people; with people who are distressed; with people preparing for some special occasion in their lives, such as marriage, baptism, confirmation, etc.; in times of joy and thanksgiving after a problem situation has been resolved and relationships restored.

3. Prayer should *not* be used to cover up poor listening, or to hide a poor relationship between counsellor and client. Sometimes a counsellor fails to understand a situation properly, either through lack of careful listening or because he is too impatient. There is then a temptation to sum up a situation, offer a quick solution, and then as it were shift the responsibility on to God by 'sealing' the counselling with a prayer. This is *not* likely to meet the client's real need.

4. Prayer can be a help in clarifying the situation by opening the way for the divine resources and wisdom to begin operating. This does not mean that the counsellor and client work out the solution and then ask God to bless their good work! It means working *with* the divine wisdom and presence all through the counselling situation.

5. Many people *expect* the pastor to pray, and this is good. However, he must beware of treating prayer as a sort of magic ritual, or as a tool which can be used to solve any problem and get people out of trouble.

WHAT SORT OF PRAYERS SHOULD WE USE?

The prayers should be kept short and simple, so that the client and any other people present can easily understand and themselves 'participate' in the prayer. The following are some hints (*not* rules) to be kept in mind when prayer is used in counselling:

(a) Thank God for His presence and concern for everyone at all times, and especially for those in need in the present situation.

(b) Recognize before God the real needs of those being helped – their feelings, doubts, and fears; and thank God for His understanding of these.

(c)   Emphasize God's resources and promises, which are available to everyone who trusts themselves to Him.

(d) Use words which are easy to understand, rather than 'technical' terms, and use words which relate directly to the client's problem.

(e) Talk about the problem itself, using people's names to remind them that God is present and active in the situation and ready to listen when they open their hearts and minds to Him.

If appropriate, also invite the client and any others present to join with you in saying a familiar prayer, such as the Lord's Prayer or the Grace. This can be specially helpful at the close of the counselling.

FELLOWSHIP IN THE CHURCH

We have seen how a pastor can rightly use the counselling situation to bring new Christians into the Church, and encourage lapsed or weak ones to renew their commitment to Christ. In this way he helps them to accept the 'inestimable benefit' of belonging to God and experiencing His grace and power in their lives. The pastor can also help people to fulfil their need for 'belonging' (see p. 39), and give them comfort and strength, by encouraging them to accept the fellowship of other Christians.

As we saw, people in trouble find help in the knowledge that they are not alone, that others have come through the same sort of experience. An old English proverb says: 'A trouble shared is a trouble halved', and of course this is true of everyone, not only Christians. But Christians have a special reason for helping those in trouble (see Matt. 10.42).

Christian fellowship also means more than just telling people that others have troubles too. It means actually *sharing* the trouble: helping and supporting those in need, not just with words of sympathy, but in a practical way. Paul told the Galatians: 'Bear one another's burdens' – saying that in this way they would 'fulfil the law of Christ' (Gal. 6.2). Clearly, fellowship of this sort is not something the pastor can provide by himself. Here most of all he needs to be able to call on a 'helping team'. Christian fellowship as a resource for helping those in need is the responsibility of the whole congregation – the whole 'household of the faith' as St Paul called it (Gal. 6.10). This fellowship, or comradeship, is part of the ministry of *every* Christian, a ministry of love and active concern in which every member of the Church has a contribution to make.

The New Testament provides us with a clear pattern of the Church as a caring community in which individuals, families, and household groups, while keeping their many differences and personalities, all belong together in one fellowship, because all are joined to Jesus Christ in the communion of the Holy Spirit.

(a) As the 'body of Christ' (1 Cor. 12.27) this fellowship carries on His work in the wider community within which it is set. As Christ was sent into the world by the Father, so the body of Christ continues His loving service to the world (see John 20.21, 22).

(b) In this service everyone in the fellowship has a part to play, and everyone is called to use the gifts God has given. 'There are varieties of gifts, but the same Spirit; . . . varieties of service, but the same Lord . . . varieties of working, but the same God who inspires them all . . . for the common good' (see 1 Cor. 12.4–7).

(c) The whole fellowship is enlivened and given the strength and energy for this work by the power of the Holy Spirit. It is not just a social club formed by its members for their own pleasure and benefit, but a loving fellowship formed by God. As such its work must be done in unity of purpose and action. As such it is able to offer the divine resources of love, faith, forgiveness, and strength to troubled people (2 Cor. 1.22, 23; 3.3–6; Gal. 5.22—6.2).

(d) Within this fellowship the pastor is both a member of the team and its appointed leader. His task is not so much that of a supreme commander without whose presence or permission nothing can be done, but rather that of a team captain and coach combined. His job is to offer encouragement, advice, and training, so that the whole team may be actively involved in the work of caring for others, with 'each part working properly' (Eph. 4.15, 16).

WHAT SORT OF FELLOWSHIP?

In what practical ways, then, can a pastor expect Church members to support his counselling with care and fellowship? Jesus Himself described some of these ways in the teaching He gave His disciples shortly before His death. (Read carefully Matt. 25.31–46.)

(a) *'The king will say . . . I was hungry and you gave me food . . . thirsty and you gave me drink.'* Sometimes actual food and drink may be the form of 'fellowship' needed. This may be because a person is very poor (e.g. if they have lost their job, or their crops have been destroyed by pests, or fire, etc.) so that a gift of food for them or their children is the best way to help them. Or perhaps they are lonely or depressed, so that what they need is an invitation to share a meal, or come regularly for a drink and a chat.

But there are other forms of 'hunger' and 'thirst', e.g. the hunger of an overworked mother with many children for occasional rest and quiet, or the thirst of a boy with a special talent or interest for the opportunity to develop it. In such cases, fellowship may take the form of, say, an offer to 'baby-sit' for a few hours, or to seek out some book on the boy's special subject when next you visit the city library.

(b) *'I was a stranger and you welcomed me.'* Many people find it difficult to make new friends when they move house. Others are shy, and even in their home neighbourhood do not like talking to strangers. Very often, too, people tend to treat those from another area with suspicion or even hostility. Many who come to a pastor for help, do so because they are not able to settle down in a new place, or a new job. Those who come to the city feel frightened of the traffic, and are confused by the crowds and the noise. Those who come to the country feel lost without the bustle and the many amenities of town life. In these situations 'fellowship' means the offer of a friendly welcome by neighbours or workmates and Church members who tell the strangers where to find what they need, and make them feel at home (see Example 9, p. 86).

(c) *'I was naked and you clothed me.'* Providing necessities for those less fortunate than ourselves is a very practical way of helping them. But sometimes the loan of money, or perhaps the offer of a job so that people can earn enough to pay for what they need, can be more helpful than an outright gift. Sensitivity is required in the 'givers' if those in need are to be encouraged, rather than made to feel under an obligation. To lend can be better than to give, since lending does not deprive people of the dignity of paying back the loan in due course. (See below under 'dangers', pp. 162, 163, and also p. 125, lines 4–8.)

(d) *'I was sick and you visited me.'* Helping the sick is one of the most important ways of offering fellowship, whether they are sick in body or mind, or in spirit, such as the recently bereaved. This may mean simply visiting them at home or in hospital, or it may mean offering to do for them what they cannot do for themselves because of their sickness, e.g. nursing them, or looking after their families or their animals or their gardens. In this case, also, those who offer help must be understanding and sensitive. The pastor may find it useful to consult with the doctor or hospital treating the sick person before suggesting to Church members what sort of help they should offer. (See chapters 10 and 11 for detailed discussion of ways of helping the sick and the bereaved.)

(e) *'I was in prison and you came to me.'* In most countries today there are strict rules limiting the visits which those who are serving prison sentences may receive. But there are other ways of 'coming' to prisoners – and to their families, who may suddenly be left without support. When people leave prison, too, they often need help in adjusting to ordinary life again. Indeed, the supportive and undemanding fellowship of individuals can make all the difference when people are waiting for some change in their lives, or working towards some decision which may alter the way they live. And being deprived of physical liberty as punishment for breaking the law is not the only form of 'imprisonment' that people can suffer.

THE NEED FOR SENSITIVITY AND SELECTIVITY

We have already seen that people in trouble or need tend to 'turn in upon themselves'. Though they may yearn for the help and comradeship of others, they cannot bring themselves to admit or accept the fact.

A pastor therefore needs to be very *sensitive* in encouraging Church members to sustain someone with their fellowship in a particular situation. He will encourage all Christians to be alert to the needs of others. But in counselling he will usually try to enlist the help of people whom he knows to have experienced similar difficulties, or who share the client's particular interests.

Most Christians will remember how Paul told the Church leaders from Ephesus about Jesus's teaching that 'it is more blessed to give than to receive' (Acts 20.35, AV). We often assume that these words mean that God approves of ('blesses') 'givers' more than He approves of 'receivers'. According to modern translators, however, what Jesus really said was that 'there is more happiness in giving than in receiving' (TEV). We have to remember that there can be no giving without someone to do the receiving. When we offer fellowship to someone in need, we are not the only ones to confer a favour – those who receive are enabling us to enjoy the happiness of being 'givers'. So the 'giving' is shared. Sometimes, indeed, a pastor may find that what a client most needs is not to receive help at all, but to be asked to *give* help and fellowship to others in the congregation or the community. This, more than anything, can sometimes help them to feel that they really belong to the fellowship of the Church.

THE SACRAMENTS IN COUNSELLING

So far we have been discussing the informal fellowship which Christians in groups enjoy together. This caring love of Christians for one another can be seen as a reflection of God's love for all people. But even more important for most Christians is the direct experience of

157

God's sustaining love and grace which they gain through the sacraments of the Church.

The teaching and practice of different Churches regarding the sacraments varies widely, and readers should relate the notes which follow to the situation in the Church to which they belong. But most Churches would agree that through the sacraments Christians are incorporated in Christ, and through Him are united to one another. And in all Churches Baptism and the Lord's Supper are recognized as the two 'gospel' sacraments instituted by Christ Himself.

BAPTISM

Most pastors would probably not regard baptism as an actual 'resource' in the context of counselling, though a client who is not a Christian may decide, as a result of counselling, to become a candidate for baptism and Church membership. However, a Christian can sometimes be helped in coming to a solution of the problem situation by renewing his or her baptismal vows. Or such renewal may 'seal' a person's decision to *act* in the situation and begin a new life of commitment to Christ.

THE LORD'S SUPPER

Different Churches give different names to the sacrament of the Lord's Supper, calling it the 'Eucharist', the 'Holy Communion', or the 'Mass', instead. These names reflect different ways of interpreting the biblical accounts of the meal Jesus took with His disciples before His betrayal, and of the beliefs and practices of the early Church. To some extent, they also, perhaps, reflect different ways in which pastoral counsellors will see the sacraments as a spiritual resource in their counselling.

Churches differ, chiefly, about the exact nature of Christ's presence in the Supper, and the exact relationship between the outward elements and the spiritual gifts they convey. But in making this their central act of worship, all Churches agree about the essential truths it sets forth. All see it as the 'visible reminder of the historic fact of Christ's death in the past . . . the promise and assurance of the final gathering together of all Christ's people with Him in the future' – and in the present: 'the reality of fellowship in which all believers are made "one bread, one body"'. In His fellowship and through this service, sinful Christians are reconciled to God, delivered from sin and sorrow, and given grace and strength to live a new life in Christ. So we can clearly see the importance, in the counselling situation, of the fellowship which people experience in the sacrament of the Lord's Supper.

The exact ways in which the counsellor uses this 'resource', and the

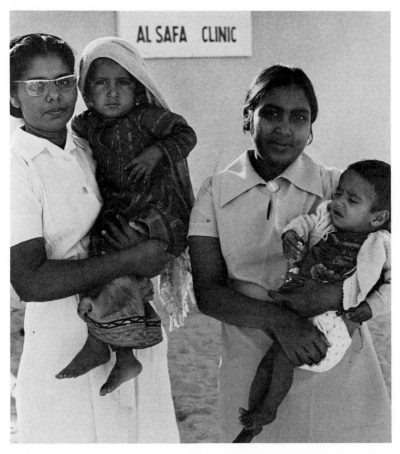

'People in trouble tend to turn in upon themselves. Sometimes what they most need is to *give* help and fellowship' (p. 157).

When a young Pakistani wife lost her first baby and was told she could have no more children, it was in helping at a clinic for sick orphans that she was able to give and receive the fellowship she needed in order to readjust to life. What other benefits can result from this sort of fellowship?

circumstances in which he encourages and prepares clients to do so, must clearly depend not only on the teaching, but also on the practice of his Church. In some Churches and some areas the Lord's Supper is celebrated only rarely. In others it is a daily observance. In some Churches every detail of the service is laid down; in some there are firm rules about who can attend and partake in the service, how they must prepare themselves for it, etc. In some Churches members who are known to have broken the rules of the Church are forbidden to receive the sacrament (i.e. they are 'excommunicated') as a matter of discipline, until they have amended their lives, perhaps after formal confession and absolution. In others such members are encouraged to come to Communion, as a special opportunity for opening themselves to receive from God the grace and strength they need in order to amend their lives or find a solution to their problems.

Pastoral counsellors can rightly encourage clients to seek help in the fellowship of the Lord's Supper only within the 'order' of their own Church situation, seeking always, of course, for the guidance of the Holy Spirit.

Occasionally it is the pastor himself who needs the grace mediated through the Lord's Supper, in order to counsel a particular client effectively. This was so in the following example, where counsellor and client together were helped to overcome not only the client's main problem, but a further problem which had arisen between them.

Example 29: Anita, a young and attractive secretary, went to the parish minister, Jethro, for counsel. As a practising Christian, she was worried about her relationship with Walter, a married man working in the same office. Jethro advised Anita to ask for transfer to another department, and encouraged her to come more regularly to Church and to make her Communion more often. Soon she was able to assure him that she was not seeing Walter any more. But after some weeks she came to Jethro again, because she now had the problem of loneliness and depression, and of feeling unwanted. Jethro suggested she should help his wife with some of the Church activities, and because she was grateful to him, Anita offered to do extra typing for the Church office. She began working regularly with Jethro, and he often asked her to help him in the evenings too, when his wife was out at meetings. Before long Anita realized it was the story of Walter all over again. Jethro kept paying her embarrassing compliments, and clearly they were getting too fond of each other. She made excuses to stay away, but Jethro came to find her, and told her she must be more regular. This time, coming to Church, and especially taking Communion from Jethro's hands, only made her feel more guilty. Anita felt the fault was partly Jethro's, but he seemed unaware of what was happening, and she didn't know what to do. Jethro's counselling method had been very 'authoritarian', and she didn't know how to tell him she thought they were doing wrong. If only she could talk to him as if they were just a man and a woman, instead of counsellor and client!

Anita prayed that somehow God would give her courage to speak – and soon her prayer was answered. The Archdeacon was to visit the parish and celebrate Holy Communion at a special service for Church workers. At this service Jethro received Communion from the Archdeacon along with his helpers. Kneeling in fellowship with Jethro at the Lord's table, Anita knew for sure that they were equal in their need for grace and forgiveness. Through the sacrament, Christ gave her the courage to speak to Jethro as a sister to a brother. She told him why she would not be helping him in the Church office any more. At first Jethro was angry. But then he admitted that Anita was right, and that to go on seeing each other would be a continuing temptation for them both. There was no other Anglican church near, so Anita decided to join the local Methodist congregation instead. Again Jethro was angry, but in the end he saw the wisdom of her decision.

This example of Pastor Jethro and Anita illustrates the importance of the sacraments in the counselling situation. It also illustrates one of the dangers which counsellors have to avoid, that of becoming personally 'involved' with those whom they are trying to help.

PENANCE (CONFESSION AND ABSOLUTION)

We have left sacramental Confession and Absolution to the last. Like the other 'traditional' sacraments, Confirmation, Extreme Unction, Ordination, and Matrimony (which would only rarely be relevant in the context of counselling) not all Churches recognize or practice it as a sacrament. However, Private Penance, with a formal confession of sin to an ordained minister, can sometimes be very effective in liberating people from a burden of guilt or anxiety. Also, people are sometimes more ready to 'confess' what is troubling them, when they know that the seal of confession places the minister under an absolute obligation not to reveal anything said; and the formal words of absolution assure them of Christ's own promise of forgiveness (see Matt. 18.18 and John 20.23). And even though the minister may question the penitent at some length, and suggest ways of avoiding future temptation, the solemnity of the sacramental procedure helps to reduce some of the dangers involved in a situation like that of Jethro and Anita. In Roman Catholic and other Churches where formal Confession is regularly used, pastoral counsellors will find this resource of particular value. In most Protestant Churches, however, the idea that God's forgiveness is to be mediated through an ordained minister is not acceptable.

Even without the 'seal' of secrecy imposed on the minister who hears sacramental confessions, pastors must *always* be careful to maintain strict *confidentiality*. A pastor is not free to tell anyone, not even his fellow clergy, what the client has told him in confidence – that is, unless the client is willing that he should do so. If he gossips, even to his own wife, he will lose the trust of those he wishes to help. Similarly, all Church members must be ready to offer fellowship to anyone in need, without asking too many questions.

COUNSELLING AND EVANGELISM

Finally, in all this discussion about the resources to be used in counselling, one vital question has not been considered, and that is the relationship between counselling and evangelism. Should counselling itself be used as a 'resource' – as an opportunity and means of bringing new Christians into the Church?

Some Church leaders believe that counselling provides a special opportunity for evangelism. They think that pastors should actively try to convert any non-Christians who may come to them for counselling, and encourage seekers and lukewarm Christians to commit their lives more fully to the service of Christ and the fellowship of the Church. Others believe that evangelism should not be brought into the counselling situation at all.

It is true that there are a number of dangers which pastors need to avoid if they wish to include evangelism as part of their aim in counselling. If too much emphasis is laid upon the need for evangelism, their counselling may become less effective.

SOME DANGERS TO BE AVOIDED

The reasons for *opposing* the use of counselling as a means for evangelism can be summarized as follows:

(a) The counsellor who aims at converting people is taking an unfair advantage of them at a time when they are especially vulnerable.

(b) There is a danger that people may 'decide for Christ' as a way of pleasing the counsellor, rather than because they feel a positive call to do so. This can happen very easily in an 'authoritarian' society, where a pastor has much influence over people's lives.

(c) There is a danger that people may regard conversion or a special commitment as an easy 'surface way' of bargaining with God or 'bribing' Him to help them, or even as a 'magical' way of solving their problems. True counselling has to go deeper than a surface answer like this. 'God is not mocked' by any such self-regarding or superficial methods of counselling. 'Whatever a man sows he will also reap.' Only 'he who sows to the Spirit will from the Spirit reap eternal life' (Gal. 6.7, 8).

(d) There is a danger that people may think that *all* problems are 'spiritual' in nature. But this is not so. Many problems are not solved by using spiritual resources alone. Many Christians who have a living relationship with Jesus, also have problems in their relationships with others, and experience difficulties which are related to their emotional, psychological, and intellectual needs. These have to be treated as such, and often have to be solved in a practical way, and not just by 'leaving it up to God'.

(e) There is a danger that the pastor may begin to evaluate his counselling by the number of clients whom he converts, or who make a special commitment. He may become more concerned with winning people for Christ, rather than with helping them to overcome their problems. If that happens, he may even begin to treat people as 'things' rather than 'persons'.

(f) Where counselling is seen chiefly as a means of evangelism and conversion there is a danger that the content of the counselling may become very limited. In some Churches the word 'counsellor' is used to describe those who are trained to receive the people who respond at big evangelistic rallies and meetings. This sort of 'counselling' is usually limited to explaining certain Bible verses to those who respond, helping them to clarify or strengthen their decision to follow Christ, and encouraging them to join a congregation. It offers no special help to those who are in need or in any kind of trouble. As we have seen, true pastoral counselling involves much more than this.

(g) There is a danger that by seeking for conversion, the counsellor may impose his own standards and values on the client. This is not helpful in counselling, and it is not even helpful in evangelism, because people should always have freedom to decide and make up their own minds as to what their response will be.

Nevertheless, the work of helping people to make a commitment to Christ is of fundamental importance, whether the commitment results from an appeal by an evangelist, from talking quietly with a concerned friend, or from experiencing the power of God to sustain and help in times of need. So it is important for a pastor to know how to give this help when a real need for it arises in the course of counselling.

HOW TO COMBINE EVANGELISM WITH COUNSELLING

There are many valid definitions of evangelism. Two definitions which are helpful in the context of counselling are:

1. Evangelism is the work of presenting Jesus Christ to men and women, so that they have an opportunity to say 'yes' or 'no' to Him;

2. Evangelism is the work of presenting Jesus Christ in the power of the Holy Spirit, so that men and women may put their trust in Him, and serve Him in the fellowship of the Church and in their daily lives.

These definitions do not say anything about *methods* of evangelism. The heart of evangelism is helping a person to come face to face with the '*evangel*' or good news, that is, with Jesus Christ Himself, and to receive from Him the freedom He offers. This can be done in many ways without any undue force or pressure being applied to the person in need. In the counselling relationship it often happens that people come to a point in their lives where they see the new possibilities of freedom which Christ offers them. Helping them to accept that freedom is not forcing them to go against their own desire, provided the pastor makes sure that they really understand what they are doing. Some Christian counsellors seem to be afraid of dealing very deeply with spiritual problems or encouraging people to make any commitment. At one pastor's conference on pastoral care, the question was asked: 'What does pastoral counselling have to do with the salvation of souls?' Some counsellors seemed to think that there is no connection at all between these two ideas. They think that men and women can solve their problems through human help and wisdom alone, without the need for any divine help or good news.

Other pastors try to reduce *all* problems to spiritual factors, and this too is a wrong way to proceed. The truly effective counsellor tries to understand *all* the factors which are present in the situation, without ignoring any. And if a counsellor really believes that the teaching in such passages as Romans 3.23; John 10.10; or 2 Corinthians 5.17 is true, and that it is still relevant today, then he will show a person who is seeking forgiveness and restoration the way of freedom in Christ. He will challenge a person who has no real aim in life to follow Christ as Lord. He will show a person who is defeated by bad habits the power of Christ to give release from that problem.

Helping people to accept such freedom is the true meaning of evangelism, and is an important part of pastoral care. This is one of the facts which make Christian pastoral counselling different from other counselling – since its aim is to relate people to Jesus Christ, and thus bring them salvation.

Evangelism can be most effectively combined with counselling provided the pastor keeps the following points in mind:

1. The pastor should give the client a clear understanding of what is involved in committing oneself to Christ, and what trusting in Him and following Him is likely to mean in one's life. Any encouragement to do so should arise naturally as the counselling relationship develops.

2. The client's problems must always be fully explored and discussed in detail. The spiritual factors in the situation must also be fully explored, and full use must be made of the spiritual resources we have already discussed; but the counselling must not be limited to the spiritual factors in the situation.

3. Success in counselling is not measured by the number of clients who are 'converted', or persuaded to commit themselves to Christ.

Counselling is truly successful when the client is encouraged to experience the freedom Jesus offers, and enabled to deal with his problems in ways which help him to grow towards maturity as a human being and as a Christian.

4. Any attempt to help people to 'believe and live the gospel', should come as a natural outflow of the counselling itself, which should show that all life is related to God, and that the gospel is a basic fact which enters into every situation. In this way, the gospel call to repent, believe, and find freedom can develop at whatever point is most appropriate in the particular situation.

The following example shows a skilful combining of evangelism with pastoral care of the sick, in which the client was helped to find a new meaning in life.

Example 30: Pastor Jones was visiting Mrs Long, a middle-aged American woman who was in hospital recovering after an eye operation. He began by asking her how she was feeling.

Mrs Long: I'm doing fine, I guess, considering everything.

Pastor: That's a fine attitude, it's not always easy to be so brave about things.

Mrs Long: Perhaps not, but that's the way I feel about it.

Pastor: What has helped you to feel this way?

Mrs Long: Well, I just think what *could* have happened to me! I'm lucky to have come out of it as well as I did. Both of my eyes could have been injured, but as it is, only one was damaged. I am thankful for that.

Pastor: When you think what might have happened, you think you are fortunate to have come out of it as well as you did?

Mrs Long: That's right.

Pastor: Do you have a family of your own?

Mrs Long: Yes, I have three children. I miss them very much, but I'm not too worried about them. My mother is taking care of them, so I can just concentrate on getting well, and be with them again soon.

Pastor: It's good that you have a dependable person to look after them. I'm sure they must miss you too. What about your husband, has he been in to see you?

Mrs Long: My husband is in prison.

Pastor: Oh, I see – that probably means you have had extra responsibilities at home?

Mrs Long: I hope this won't sound bad to you, but actually things have been better for me without my husband around. Some of my friends think I am dreadful to say that. But they don't know the trouble and misery I have had with him. They don't know how badly he treated me and the family.

Pastor: Now that he's gone, you feel better off?

Mrs Long: That's right. Now I can do things with my children which he would never let me do. I can take them places and buy them things that I never could before.

Pastor: I'm sure you are looking forward to that.

Mrs Long: Yes, I am.

Pastor: Tell me, is this your home town?

Mrs Long: No, I was brought up in New York and later I moved to California. Then, after I got married, we came here.

Pastor: I see, I didn't know that. I don't believe you are a member of our Church?

Mrs Long: No, I'm not a member of any Church.

Pastor: Have you ever thought about becoming a Christian?

Mrs Long: Yes, I have. I feel it's very important – something everyone should do. I certainly intend to join a Church sometime.

Pastor: Did you ever go to church in New York?

Mrs Long: Yes, I did go to church as a child. My mother and father are Baptists.

Pastor: Why do you think you never became an active Christian?

Mrs Long: I don't know. There have been times when I've felt there has been something inside me holding me back.

Pastor: What do you think that was?

Mrs Long: I don't exactly know, I can't exactly describe it. But I do feel I will really become a Christian some day.

Pastor: This thing that you say was holding you back. It reminds me of what we call 'original sin' – rebelling against God and thinking we can get along without Him in our lives. Is that the sort of thing you felt?

Mrs Long: I don't know. Perhaps. Maybe I didn't think I needed God.

Pastor: Has anyone ever talked to you before about becoming a Christian?

Mrs Long: Yes, but I never quite saw it the way you put it.

Pastor: I asked because you seem to know already about many of the things I am saying.

Mrs Long: Yes, I was brought up in Sunday School and Church.

Pastor: Then you probably know already that you can become a Christian right now. If you are willing to commit your life to Christ as your Lord, then He will become your Saviour. You can surrender your life to Him now. Of course this means that you'd surrender now the life that you live out for Him each day. If you can make this surrender of yourself to Him, then He will become your Saviour. How does this sound to you? Does it speak to you at all?

Mrs Long: Yes it does. I've heard these things before, but I never quite saw them as I do now.

Pastor: Why do you think you see them differently now?

Mrs Long: I don't know. All day today I've felt differently. Now you've come and talked to me about becoming a Christian. And it just seems to me that this is what I want to do.

Pastor: You really feel, then, that this is what you want to do now?
Mrs Long: Yes, it is.

In this example, the client had felt lost in her worry over her children, trouble over her husband, concern for her eye, and her desire to be working again. She was awakened to her need for some strength beyond herself, and found this new strength and meaning for her life in her acceptance of Jesus Christ. For her, this acceptance meant a willingness to admit her weakness and to trust in the strength that God would give her. In talking with Mrs Long, the pastor showed skill in understanding the deeper needs in her life. His 'reflective' approach helped her to sort out her own ideas and feelings, and eventually led her to the point where the challenge to commit herself to Christ and find a new meaning and strength in life made good sense to her. Her acceptance and commitment arose naturally from within the situation; Pastor James did not force it upon her in any unnatural way. The deeper meaning of this trust in Christ developed as the woman grew in her understanding of Christian commitment.

STUDY SUGGESTIONS

WORD STUDY

1. The words 'present' and 'presence' can be used about human beings, and also about God, Jesus, and the Holy Spirit. What difference in meaning, if any, do they have when we use them about God, Jesus, or the Holy Spirit on the one hand, as compared to when we use them about human beings on the other hand?
2. Give one definition of 'evangelism'.
3. Which *four* of the following words give the best meaning of 'commitment'?
   dedication   sharing   belief   obedience   opposition   service
   leadership   promise   support   indifference

REVIEW OF CONTENT

4. Describe:
   (a) two ways in which Christian pastoral counselling is the same as other counselling, and
   (b) two ways in which it is different.
5. What are the four chief spiritual resources which can be used in pastoral counselling?
6. What is involved in 'surrendering your life to Christ'?
7. For what six chief reasons is the Bible important for counselling?

8. For each of the passages below:
   (i) Describe the situation in which Jesus was making use of Scripture.
   (ii) How can His use of Scripture be a useful guide for people today?
   (a) Matthew 8.5–13   (b) Matt. 11.2–6   (c) Matt. 15.1–9.
   (d) Mark 2.23–28   (e) Mark 12.18–27   (f) Luke 4.1–13
   (g) Luke 11.37–52   (h) Luke 12.13–21.
9. Examine Paul's prayers in Ephesians 1.15–20 and 3.14–21. What do these prayers show us about his pastoral relationship with the people to whom he was writing?
10. What are the chief things you learn about prayer, from the following passages?
   Psalm 3.1–4   Psalm 18.6, 23, 24   Psalm 51.15–17
   Matthew 6.5–8   Matthew 7.7–11   John 11.41–44   Acts 9.36–42
   Philippians 1.3–5   Phil. 1.19, 20.

APPLICATION, OPINION, AND RESEARCH

11. 'The Holy Spirit is the real counsellor' in any pastoral relationship (see p. 144).
   (a) Do you agree with this statement? If so, what point is there, if any, in training people for counselling?
   (b) How would you answer someone who said: 'I don't need to receive any training for counselling. I rely on the Holy Spirit for guidance, and I follow His leading.'
12. Explain your own experience, as either counsellor or client, of using (a) the Bible, and (b) prayer, in the work of counselling. Are these spiritual resources used widely, in your experience? If so, how do you evaluate their effectiveness?
13. 'If God knows all about us, and is interested in us, and our prayers cannot force His attention upon us, well then, why should we pray?' How would you answer this question?
14. In what ways, if any, is Christian prayer which is offered to God the Father of our Lord Jesus Christ, different from prayers offered to tribal and ancestral spirits?
15. 'Prayer changes things' (see pp. 152, 153). What, if anything, does prayer change? Give examples to support your answer.
16. Describe briefly the teaching and practice of your Church in regard to confession and forgiveness. What are your personal feelings about the value of 'sacramental' confession and absolution?
17. 'In some Churches members who have broken the rules of the Church are "excommunicated" until they have amended their

lives. . . . In others they are encouraged to come to Communion . . . to receive from God the grace and strength they need in order to amend their lives' (p. 160).

Does your Church encourage those who have 'broken the rules' to come to Communion, or does it warn them to keep away? Try to discover what some fellow members of your congregation think and feel on this subject. What do you yourself feel about partaking of the Lord's Supper at times when you are experiencing any sense of guilt or shame?

18. 'Being deprived of physical liberty . . . is not the only sort of "imprisonment" people can suffer' (p. 157).

What other sorts of 'imprisonment' can you think of that people may be suffering today, and in what ways could Christians 'visit' them?

19. Describe from your own experience (or your imagination) two problem situations in which Christian fellowship could help a client, and what sort of fellowship could be offered.

20. Explain what pastoral counselling has to do with the salvation of souls.

21. Do you think the work of pastoral evangelism is effective today
    (a) in your Church as a whole (i.e. as a denomination), and
    (b) in your own ministry?
    If not, in what ways do you think it could be made more effective in each case?

22. Evaluate the relationship between Pastor Jones and Mrs Long in Example 30.
    (a) What type or types of counselling approach and response did Pastor Jones use?
    (b) How effective was his use of each of these types of coun-
    ·   selling?

23. 'There was no other Anglican church near, so Anita decided to join the local Methodist congregation instead' (p. 161). What is your opinion of Anita's decision to change from one denomination to another as a means of avoiding temptation? Give reasons for your answer.

24. Imagine you are counselling the people in each of the following situations, and decide it would be helpful to pray with or for those concerned. Then write down a short prayer of the sort you think would be most suitable in each case, and say at what stage of the counselling process you would use it.
    (a) You are visiting Norman in hospital, a member of the Church choir who is recovering from a minor operation.
    (b) Ellen Thomas, a new member of the congregation whom you don't know very well, has come to you in great distress because

her husband has a drinking problem, which is not only upsetting her and the children, but may cause him to lose his job.

(c) You are visiting Priscilla, an elderly woman whose sister has just been killed in a motor accident.

(d) Alan, a boy in his last year at school, has come for advice because his father, a Churchwarden, wants him to train as an engineer and then join the family business, but Alan himself feels he has a call to study medicine.

25. For each of the situations described in Q. 24, find a passage from Paul's Letter to the Philippians which might bring guidance, encouragement, or comfort to the people concerned.

PART III
SOME COMMON COUNSELLING SITUATIONS

In the following chapters we consider in a fairly general way subjects involving wider issues of personal and communal ethics as well as matters of immediate Christian concern. Many of these call for discussion at greater length than is possible in this Guide, and to understand them more fully, pastors will need to read further, both from the list provided on pp. xiii–xiv, and from whatever literature is available on these subjects as relating to the teaching of their own Church or their particular regional or local situation.

9
Marriage and Family Relationships

Very many of the problems about which people seek counselling help are associated in some way with marriage and family life. In 1912 J. H. Oldham, the first Editor of the *International Review of Missions*, conducted an inquiry among missionaries in many lands about their most urgent problems. Many of them mentioned the problem of marriage. One missionary in Africa wrote: 'Not only the most pressing but the most puzzling, insistent, and far-reaching of problems, is that of Christian marriage in the heathen world. It is ever present.'

Problems associated with marriage are perhaps less 'puzzling' today, because leaders and teachers in the Church now know more about traditional customs in many countries and cultures, and also the physical and psychological aspects of the sexual relationship are better understood. But they are still 'ever present'. This is as true in the so-called 'Christian' countries of the West as it is in areas where Christians are few among people of other religions.

THE CULTURAL CONTEXT

Marriage is one of the most important events in the lives of people in every culture. But marriage cannot just be 'fitted into' or extracted from the cultural situation, as if it stood by itself. Ideas and customs about marriage are part of the traditional structure of accepted activities and ideas which are the backbone of any society. For this reason it is difficult in one chapter to discuss every aspect of such a wide subject. There are so many sides to the question of marriage, and so many different marriage customs among different cultural groups, that to set out one overall approach to marriage would certainly miss out some important points in relation to any particular situation.

In many African societies, for example, the most important aspects of marriage are regarded as:

The *joining together of two families or clans*, rather than the joining of one man and one woman;

the *status and authority* which a married man enjoys but which a single man does not have;

the *gaining or sharing of land and goods* belonging to the two families or clans or tribes;

the *adding of new members* to the family or other group when children result from the marriage.

In most Western countries, on the other hand, quite different aspects of marriage may be regarded as most important, for example:

The *individual love* between the man and the woman, which does not depend on their families or any wider group;

the *companionship and sharing of interests* between husband and wife, even if no children result from the marriage;

the *separation of the married couple* from their parents or family group, and the setting-up of a new family unit;

the *social status* which a married woman enjoys, but which even in these days of 'women's lib' an unmarried woman often does not.

One thing, however, is common to all situations today: changing ways of living are affecting marriage customs and relationships everywhere. These changes vary from country to country. In some areas society is changing more rapidly and more deeply than in other areas, but the fact of change is experienced by everyone.

Marriage and family relationships are also affected by continuing social factors such as unemployment, migrant labour, prostitution, venereal disease, birth control, child care, and so on. But we cannot discuss all these matters in detail in this book. Pastoral counsellors need to read all they can on subjects relating to marriage and its place in society, especially books which deal with the particular situation in which the counsellors are working.

Despite the great variation in customs and ideas, however, there are some basic aspects of the subject, which pastoral counsellors need to understand if they are to be effective in helping people to overcome problems in their marriage and family life. In this chapter we shall discuss four of these basic aspects:

1. The importance of marriage in any particular society, and traditional patterns of marriage there;

2. The Christian understanding of marriage;

3. Some common problems relating to marriage and their causes;

4. Some ways of helping people to overcome these problems.

Examples will be given, mainly from Africa and the Pacific region. As with other case studies in this book, readers should use these examples as a starting point for thinking about marriage in their own country and cultural background. To help you to do so, it will be useful if you start by noting down the answers to the following questions as they relate to the particular marriage customs and attitudes of people in your own area.

1. What is regarded as the *chief purpose* of marriage? – for mutual help and companionship between a man and a woman? – to provide a man with sexual satisfaction? – to provide a secure home in which children are born and brought up? – a business arrangement between two family or other groups to ensure that farms are worked and sufficient food supplied? – or some other purpose?

2. What is the most common pattern of family life? – extended? – nuclear? Who is the boss in any family – the man? the woman? the children? or the relatives?

3. Is polygamy practised? by all? by a few? not at all?

4. Are arranged marriages the pattern (i.e. those planned by parents or relatives), or do young people choose their partners by themselves – or are both of these ways accepted?

5. Are 'mixed marriages' (i.e. marriages between people of different races, different tribes, or different religious beliefs) accepted or opposed?

6. What form of bride-wealth ('bride-price') or economic exchange is practised between families and groups? Is this custom strong or weak?

7. What preparation, if any, is given to betrothed couples about the meaning of marriage and the relationship between husband and wife, (a) among Christians, (b) among people of other religions?

8. Are sexual relations before marriage accepted and allowed or opposed? Does the teaching of the Church differ from traditional ideas on this point?

9. Is talk and discussion about sexual matters allowed, or is sex regarded as a 'taboo' or forbidden subject which cannot be discussed freely?

10. How does the Church treat members whose marriage has run into difficulties? What is the practice of your own Church regarding divorce? and regarding remarriage of those who have been divorced?

11. What is the position of women in society? Is marriage regarded as the only career for a girl, or is it accepted that some women should

be trained for a job and become financially independent? What is the custom regarding widows?

12. What are the problems which most frequently cause marriages to break up?

13. When people are experiencing problems in their marriages, where can they find help?

If possible, discuss your answers to these questions with someone from a different situation, and note any similarities and differences. This will form a good basis for thinking about marriage and its place in society.

'UNIVERSAL' FACTORS

We have seen that many variations in marriage customs exist, but there are some 'universal' factors which form the 'essence' of a valid marriage and so influence family relationships anywhere. They are worth noting, because it is in connection with these basic factors that many of the misunderstandings and problems relating to marriage arise. They are of several sorts:

There are *personal* factors, such as the role of those being married, and the influence of elders, parents, and guardians in consenting to a marriage or choosing the partners.

There are *economic and financial* factors, such as the exchange of gifts, the payment of some form of bride-wealth or bride-price, the making of marriage settlements, the financial arrangements for setting up a new home.

There are usually some questions of *ritual*, e.g. the traditional or customary wedding ceremonies celebrating the coming together of the bride and groom.

There are *legal and social* factors, such as the changes in legal status and responsibility, and in social standing, which follow upon marriage.

Many of the misunderstandings about marriage today result from social change which has caused the traditional principles in these matters to be weakened or ignored altogether. When this happens people become confused about the meaning of marriage and about their role within the marriage relationship.

To provide some examples of these basic factors as they apply in a particular area, we outline below the results of a study of traditional ideas and marriage customs in Papua New Guinea. In the past, when these ideas and customs were the rule, marriages may have been more stable than they are today, but that does not mean they conformed to Christian standards.

PERSONAL FACTORS

Marriage relationships in Papua New Guinea are strongly affected by *attitudes towards women*. Several different ideas influence people's attitudes to marriage. Perhaps the most important of these is the so-called 'garden' idea, especially as it relates to fertility and conception. According to this idea marriage is like a garden in which the man owns the land, plants his seed in it, and eventually reaps the harvest. The woman is the garden. She belongs to the man, receives his seed, and is responsible for its care and growth. The woman is expected to be a good garden and to bear good fruit. But the man's part in producing children is considered the most important, because without the seed, there will be no fruit. Any child born is the man's child, part of his life and spirit. The man plays the active role, the woman is a passive receiver of what he sows.

This garden idea is often accompanied by the superstition that women are 'impure'. Until medical researchers discovered the connection between the menstrual period and the ability to bear children, this was always thought to be a time of uncleanness (see Lev. 12.1–5; 15.19–24), and of danger to others, especially to unmarried men. This deep-seated fear of women means they have traditionally been excluded from most of the religious cults, kept in their place, and given their own special work. Medical science has brought a better understanding, and is helping to overcome such superstitious ideas and practices, but in some areas boys are still taught to believe that women are dangerous. Relationships between men and women are therefore marked by a basic enmity, which results in a lot of tension and conflict. In spite of this, however, there is much affection and comradeship between marriage partners. Repeated cruelty by the husband is not common, though wives will generally accept an occasional beating.

On the more personal and sexual side, there often seems to be very little trust between husband and wife. Jealousy tends to be strong, and any suspected sexual activity or close friendship with someone of the opposite sex is regarded very seriously. In adultery the woman is regarded as more guilty than the man. If the man is caught sowing seed in a garden which is not his own, he can pay some compensation to the rightful owner, and that puts the matter right. But if a woman allows a strange seed to be sown in her husband's garden, the whole harvest – that is, the family line – is regarded as spoiled.

The garden idea also leads to the mistaken idea that marriage without children is useless, so that any childless marriage is a cause of great sadness and shame (and the woman is always blamed for it, whatever the true cause may be). (See Gen. 16.1–6 and 1 Sam. 1.1–7.)

Methods of choosing a marriage partner vary in different parts of Papua New Guinea. In many places the young people have little freedom of choice. Where a bride-price has to be paid, the young man is usually dependent on his family for this, and those who pay will influence the choice of bride. But though the experience and wisdom of parents and relatives is everywhere regarded as more reliable than that of a young man or girl, much greater choice is allowed in some areas. There may be discussion between parents and the young people concerned, and in some places the young people can even refuse to accept their relatives' advice.

Attitudes to sexual relationships, too, vary in different tribal areas. Sex before marriage is permitted in some but strongly disapproved of in others, especially where ideas about female impurity are strong. In some places a good deal of sexual freedom is allowed as long as pregnancy does not occur. If a girl does become pregnant, the man is expected to marry her.

ECONOMIC FACTORS

There is always some form of marriage payment which cements together both the couple themselves and the two groups to which they belong. In some parts of Papua New Guinea there are very complicated and important bride-price systems, but elsewhere the custom is becoming less strong.

People of other cultural traditions often condemn the custom of bride-wealth or bride-price, saying it is a sort of purchase, so that the woman becomes the man's slave. There is some truth in this where the woman is regarded as an inferior. But it is also true that through marriage she becomes lost to her family or tribe, while the man's family or tribe gains a useful and valuable new member. So it seems only fair for the man's family to restore the balance by compensating those who lose her. Sometimes the payment is regarded as reimbursement for the cost of the woman's upbringing and perhaps her education. However, the payment is not always one-sided. Often there is also payment of dowry from the woman's family, and gifts continue to be exchanged between the two groups as long as the marriage lasts. Nowadays, too, the 'payment' has become a purely symbolic part of the ritual ceremony, such as the formal presentation of a hoe or other object. (In some other parts of the world dowry contributed by the woman's family is as important as any contribution from the man's side.)

In Papua New Guinea the whole clan or family has been responsible for any bride-payment, not just the bridegroom himself. But the help received usually has to be repaid by the bridegroom, e.g. by contributing toward the bride-payments of his younger relatives.

Those who support the continuance of traditional 'bride-price' systems rightly point to the fact that some form of financial 'marriage-settlement' is often made in so-called 'Christian' countries also. What is wrong about such customs, wherever they occur, is that they can easily lead to the mistaken idea that a woman is not only inferior to a man, but something to be bought and sold, an 'object' rather than a person whom God loves and values.

RITUAL FACTORS

We shall not discuss these here, because the ceremonies which mark any wedding in Papua New Guinea, as elsewhere, not only vary from place to place, but reflect or symbolize the personal, economic, and legal or social aspects of marriage which we are looking at under those separate headings.

LEGAL AND SOCIAL FACTORS

Most people in Papua New Guinea belong to small tribal groups organized on the basis of kinship, many of them without any hereditary leadership. Marriage is therefore more than just a relationship between two individuals. It is an important means of providing legal, social, and even political alliances between different tribes, clans, and families. This makes for strength and stability in the marriage tie.

Traditionally both monogamy and polygamy were practised, and a man's status was often judged by the number of wives he had and the alliances they brought about, as well as the wealth he possessed in the way of gardens, pigs, and children. Polygamy is still strong in some parts of the country, but monogamy is more usual now, partly as a result of Christian teaching, but also because today few men can afford to have many wives.

In most areas the husband and his relatives still have strong rights over the wife, who is completely taken over into her husband's family. In other areas the wife remains a member of her parents' family, and is not cut off from it by the new link with her husband's kin. Because of traditional attitudes to childlessness, however, divorce for this reason is common. Marriage and parenthood are regarded as the sign of full adult status, and in the past there were no recognized roles for unmarried people. Today, this is no longer always the case, and, in urban areas especially, the economic advantages of marriage may be more important than the desire for a large family. Social stability and the welfare of the family or clan as a whole, is still usually regarded as more important than feelings of mutual attraction.

These then have been the traditional factors affecting marriage relationships in Papua New Guinea. But changes are everywhere affecting the situation (see pp. 185, 186 and chapter 12).

THE CHRISTIAN UNDERSTANDING OF MARRIAGE

The Church teaches that marriage is important to Christians chiefly because it is part of God's plan. In the Scriptures, marriage is described as one of God's good gifts to men and women: something to be accepted from Him and used in the way He intends. The ideas and rules about marriage, divorce, and sexual relations vary in detail from one part of the Church to another, but the problems and difficulties which Christians experience in marriage and family life are much the same as those experienced by people of other religions and traditions. In some respects their Christian faith and Church membership may cause added problems. In other respects their faith, and the sympathy and support of fellow-Christians, can help them to overcome their difficulties. It will be useful, therefore, to note some of the more important points in the Christian understanding of marriage which are common to Church people of all denominations.

MARRIAGE AS PART OF GOD'S PLAN

(a) Marriage is part of God's creative plan for the world. It is not merely a cultural habit which has developed in various ways according to people's needs in each particular society. Christians sometimes define marriage as an 'order of creation', i.e. the way in which God intends that men and women should live together in love and rear their children. Human beings, like many others among God's creatures, are created as males and females, and according to Scripture the order of marriage was given to mankind before any break in the relationship with God. So the family stands as one of the foundations of human existence (Gen. 1.26, 27).

(b) God has appointed human beings to be responsible for the created world. Part of this responsibility is for men and women to use their sexuality in the way God intends, that is, in marriage. And the bearing and rearing of children involves more than just the physical activity which ensures the biological continuance of the human species. It is part of our God-given responsibility (Gen. 1.28). This does not mean that everyone must marry and have children. Different people carry out their responsibility in different ways, and for some the single state is the best (1 Cor. 7.1, 2, 5–8). This is especially so in today's developed societies, where the opportunities for service are increasingly varied.

(c) According to God's plan, marriage means that a man and a woman become 'united'. Through living together they are able to grow into a unity of mind and spirit as well as body. This partnership in unity is the foundation of the relationship between husband and wife, the foundation on which they build a new family. For this 'a man leaves his father and his mother' (Gen. 2.24) – and even more, a woman leaves the family in which she has been brought up, so that the two of

'According to God's plan marriage means that a man and a woman become united . . . this partnership in unity is the foundation on which they build a new family' (p. 178). 'Methods of choosing a partner vary . . . in many places the young people have little freedom of choice' (p. 175).

A baby brings added unity to a young Australian couple. At a Japanese wedding the 'match-maker' and his wife, rather than the parents, sit next to the bride and groom for the photograph. What customs can help a married couple to become united? What can hinder their unity?

179

them may 'cleave' to each other, and through their sexual relationship become 'one flesh'.

THE SEXUAL RELATIONSHIP

(d) The sexual relationship is a vital part of the marriage bond, and there need be no shame or guilt about it when we experience it in the way God intends. The first partners in marriage were 'naked and not ashamed' (Gen. 2.25). Our physical bodies are not to be despised as sinful, but to be honoured and used in ways which celebrate the gift of sex with joy and gratitude. For those who are in Christ, the body is the temple of the Holy Spirit, and something to be used for the glory of God (1 Cor. 6.19, 20).

(e) The sexual relationship is important not only for the purpose of child-bearing and satisfying people's sexual drives, but also for mutual enjoyment, companionship, and fun between husband and wife. Both Jesus, and Paul after Him, based their teaching about the marriage relationship on Genesis 2.24 (see Mark 10.2–12 and Eph. 5.25–30).

(f) Sin – that is, separation from God – affects the whole of human life, and sinful desires and attitudes very often spoil the marriage relationship. Selfish misuse of the gift of sex leads to quarrelling, jealousy, cruelty, fear, and adultery. The Scriptures contain many warnings against the wrong use of sex (see Exod. 20.7; Matt. 19.3–9; Col. 3.18, 19).

(g) This 'wrong use' includes sexual relationships outside marriage, and Christians are warned against 'fornication' as well as against adultery (see Eph. 5.3–10 and 1 Cor. 6.15–18 – 'immorality' in the RSV translates the Greek word *porneia*, which means sexual relationships that are not according to God's plan).

(h) Christian marriage is 'monogamous', i.e. a one-to-one relationship between husband and wife, for life. Many passages in the New Testament indicate that the marriage relationship should be between one man and one woman, excluding all others, e.g. 'the two shall become one' (Eph. 5.31; see also Matt. 5.27, 48; John 4.16–18; Rom. 12.1, 2; 1 Cor. 7.2, 3; 2 Cor. 11.2; Eph. 5.33). There is no record in the Gospels that Jesus gave specific teaching on the subject, but this may be because monogamy was the accepted custom of the Jews at that time, and was therefore taken for granted. In many countries today polygamy is an accepted part of the cultural system, and this raises big questions and problems for Christians. But Jesus's general attitude to the subject seems clear (see Mark 10.2–12), and the Church everywhere teaches us that monogamy is the ideal to which Christians should aspire. For further discussion of some of the problems which Christians face in situations where polygamy is an essential part of traditional marriage customs and social structures, readers are referred to chapter 9 of TEF Study Guide 9, '*Go . . . and make Disciples*'.

THE MARRIAGE RELATIONSHIP 'IN CHRIST'

(i) Writers in the Old Testament and the New Testament pointed to the marriage bond between husband and wife as a symbol of the deep relationship between God and His people Israel, and between Christ and His new people the Church. This shows that human marriage should reflect God's steadfast love and care for His creation, a love which is itself reflected in Christ's living and dying for the sake of the Church (see Isa. 54.4–8; 62.1–5; Jer.2.1; 31.31, 32; 2 Cor. 11.2; Eph. 5.25–27; Rev.21.2, 9–11).

(j) In many societies, the traditional marriage customs contain some elements which are contrary to Christian ideas. But the gospel promises 'newness'. The gospel does not necessarily destroy cultural and traditional marriage, but can purify it. Wherever the Church seeks to understand and accept all that is good in traditional marriage practices, while at the same time pointing to those that seem to conflict with Christian teaching, the marriage relationship can be made 'new' in Christ (see 2 Cor. 5.17).

(k) Every human society has its particular ways of marking or 'celebrating' the change of status that occurs when a man and a woman join each other in marriage, and so form a new link between their families, clans, or tribes. By these ceremonies the marriage is recognized as 'legal' and valid according to the custom or law of the tribe or nation. Among Christians, marriage is 'solemnized' at a special service, usually in church. The couple make their marriage vows in the presence of a minister or other qualified person and of witnesses, who join in praying for God's blessing on their future life together. But in both traditional and Christian marriage it is the public commitment of the man and woman to each other which makes the marriage valid and binding, not the words or actions of the minister. And it is the faith of the couple and their joint commitment of their lives to Christ which makes the marriage a Christian one, not the particular order of service, or the fact that it takes place in a church building.

(l) These various points emphasize the fact that Christian marriage and family life 'in the Lord' are part of the gospel of the Kingdom which God offers, through Christ, to all people. Because Christian marriages are 'in Christ' they share in the new life of the Kingdom. The advice and instruction about marriage given by New Testament writers is meant to help Christians to understand how their marriages are to be lived 'in Christ', and how they can experience this 'newness' in their marriage relationships.

Also, within Christian marriage thus made new in Christ, the biological act of sex is seen in a new way, not only as the physical means by which human beings (like many other forms of created life) obey God's command to 'be fruitful', but also as a symbol of God's continuing love and care for the world He has made. It is an act in which man and woman share in the creative activity of God. The love within marriage, too, is seen in a new way. As expressed in the relationship between husband and wife, it is to reflect God's love, sharing and compassion; and the relationships between parents and children are likewise to reflect His love, respect, care, and instruction (see Eph. 5.25—6.4; Col. 3.18, 19).

This does not mean that all Christian marriages will always show this 'newness' of the gospel. Because we are sinful, we often fail in our marriages and in our family living. Repentance and forgiveness are needed in every marriage and every family, as husband and wife learn to live with each other and with their children (Eph. 4.32). To help people to understand this is one of the chief tasks of the 'marriage and family guidance' counsellor.

SOME PROBLEMS AND CAUSES OF TROUBLE

SOME TYPICAL PROBLEMS

Here are four typical examples of the sort of marriage and family problems that counsellors find arising today. When you have studied them in the light of what we have noted above about traditional marriage customs, and about the meaning of Christian marriage, note down what you see as the underlying factors that have caused each problem to arise. At this stage, do not try to offer solutions to the problems; simply try to isolate what you see as the reasons for them: Do the reasons come from inside or outside the marriage? Are they 'cultural' reasons? – or the result of social change? – or misunderstanding of the real purpose of marriage? or are the reasons more personal to the individuals concerned?

Example 31: John and Kamala are students at a teacher training college in Northern India. They have become very friendly and spend a lot of time together. Others speak of them as each other's 'boyfriend' and 'girlfriend'. They come from different parts of the country and belong to different Churches. John is a Methodist and Kamala is a Lutheran. During their time in college they have come to feel that they are in love and want to marry. However, they each know that they are expected to marry people chosen for them by their parents, who think that each will be going back to teach and settle down and marry someone in their home area.

John is also urging Kamala to go further in their friendship and to have sexual intercourse with him. He says that this will be a sign of their love, and will seal their promises to each other. Kamala does not know what to think. She knows that her Church teaching is against sexual relationships before marriage, yet she feels that she really loves John and wants to live with him always. But how can she tell if this is true love or not? She is too shy to talk to her student friends about it, and no one has ever helped her to think about the real meaning of love and friendship. If she refuses to have intercourse with John, will she lose him? But what will her parents and family think if she decides to marry someone from a different Church and place? Will they welcome her back if she does?

Example 32: Anthony had not sought counsel, but his brother was so worried by the obvious unhappiness of Anthony and his wife that he asked pastor Jonas about the best way to help him. Jonas said he could not give advice until he had seen the problem for himself, so he went to visit Anthony.

Pastor (when Anthony opened the door): Hello, friend.

Anthony: Good morning, come in.

(They talked for a few moments about different things, then came a pause.)

Pastor: I have really come in case you would like to talk about this problem you seem to be having.

Anthony: I suppose you mean my fighting with my wife. Did my brother tell you? Why doesn't he mind his own business? Why does my family want to put their nose into my marriage?

Pastor: Well, he's worried about you, so I thought I should come and see you.

Anthony: Oh well – I do have a bit of a problem.

Pastor: Could you tell me something more about it?

Anthony (much quieter): Well, I seem to be very unhappy with my wife. We fight a lot. She is always threatening to leave me unless I treat her better. And then she runs off to her parents all the time, and says things about me.

Pastor: You argue a lot with her?

Anthony: Yes, she's always at me, and I'm tired of it!

Pastor: What do you argue about?

Anthony: Oh, she gets jealous whenever I talk to anyone else, or even look sideways at someone. She won't let me out of her sight. But that's not the main thing. It's my drinking. She says I waste money, and she doesn't get enough. That makes her really cross.

Pastor: She can't manage on the money you give her, is that it?

Anthony: Well, that's what she says. She treats me like a small boy, shouting at me, and telling that mother of hers.

Pastor: How do you feel when she does that?

Anthony: Feel? – Well, I get really mad. I don't spend so much. It's her own fault. If she used the money carefully, she wouldn't be short. Besides, I like to have a drink with my friends after work.

Pastor: So she thinks the money side of things is not fair? What do you think? Do you think the way you treat her and the children is fair?

Anthony: What do you mean, 'fair'? Of course it's fair. She's always growling. I need some money to spend as I want to, that's all. That's fair enough.

Pastor: Perhaps you should think of the family needs a bit more. Things are getting very expensive you know.

Anthony: Taking her side, are you? You think she's right and I am wrong?

Pastor: No, I didn't say that.

Anthony: Yes you did! (He gets angry again.) You're just the same as the others, everyone is on her side.

Pastor: I think perhaps you should try and see all around the problem.

Anthony: Well, I do. It's my business, and I'm not going to have her tell me what to do all the time. She acts as if she's the man and I'm the woman. She needs a good whack, and I reckon she'll get it if she goes on like this. Anyway, I have to go to work now, I can't talk any more.

Example 33: Mubita and Nasilele, a Zambian couple, have got married because Nasilele was going to have a baby. They had first met two years earlier, and went to see the pastor then because they hoped to get married later on, but already had a physical relationship. Both were members of the Youth Church, and were committed Christians, but were finding it very difficult to stand against the generally accepted ways of behaving in the city where they lived. When they went to visit friends and were invited to stay overnight, even among some Christians they were given one bed for them both. To follow true Christian principles would have taken great determination. Nasilele wanted to do so, but Mubita was less enthusiastic. They started using a method of contraception recommended by Nasilele's grandmother, which in fact was quite unreliable. Before long, Nasilele became pregnant, and they got married in a hurry. Now they are facing great problems of poverty. Mubita has had to take a job without completing his training as an engineer, so as to keep Nasilele and the child, although he had won a scholarship to the USA and hoped to take his degree before marrying. The scholarship is still open, but the decision he faces is a hard one: what will Nasilele do if he goes away and leaves her alone with the baby for three years?

Example 34: The following report in a New Guinea newspaper was headed: 'Break with Traditional Marriage'.

'Girls in the Eastern Highlands seem to be breaking traditional marriage customs. In one region about ninety per cent of first marriages do not last two years. The traditional custom was that marriages were arranged by the parents, and the girl was required to spend at least one year living with her prospective in-laws before the marriage took place. This is now causing problems, because while the girl is living with her future husband's parents, the husband-to-be is often away working in towns or other districts, as there is not enough work for educated people in the villages. So the girls may have to wait up to four years before their husbands return to claim them.

'Many girls refuse to accept this arrangement, and are starting to select husbands of their own choice, or becoming prostitutes in order to gain money to go to the big towns themselves. When this happens, the bridegrooms refuse to pay the bride-price unless they can be sure the marriage will be successful. Many arguments and quarrels are resulting from disputes over non-payment of bride-price for girls who were already promised.'

SOME TYPICAL CAUSES OF TROUBLE

Readers will probably have recognized that each of the problems we have described had its own particular reasons. But there also seem to be a number of basic factors which can cause trouble to arise in marriage and family relationships in many situations, quite apart from such personal factors as incompatibility, selfishness, insensitivity, etc. Most of these factors are the result of the very rapid social changes, with new ideas and ways of living, which have occurred almost everywhere, upsetting both the traditional and the Christian understanding of marriage.

(a) *The economic independence of young people* who take jobs is reducing their dependence on the family or clan group. But by leading to more 'nuclear' families it also deprives them of the financial and moral support of the extended family system which has been a stabilizing influence in the past.

(b) *A change in attitudes towards sex*, with constant reference to sex in radio and TV programmes, newspaper stories, and advertising, has resulted from the introduction of easy methods of contraception. This leads many young people to assume that sexual adventures before marriage, and promiscuity, are an essential part of growing up, while at the same time giving them an unrealistically 'romantic' idea of the sexual relationship.

(c) *The difference between the traditional ideas of the country, or modern secular ideologies, and Christian teaching about marriage* and about the relative status of men and women, is leading to confusion and conflict. Christian teaching has brought not only different ideas about the *purpose* of marriage, but different moral standards to be followed both inside and outside any personal relationship.

(d) *'Women's Lib' movements*, as well as Christian teaching and the spread of school education for girls, have brought great changes in the status of women, and the sorts of occupation they can follow in many countries. This has upset people's ideas of the respective roles of men and women, and led to many problems in marriage and family relationships.

(e) *A decline in the number of 'Church' marriages*, even amongst

Christians, means that many couples are starting out on their new life together with no opportunity to make any formal affirmation of their faith in Christ or solemn commitment of themselves to Him and to one another; so that there is no firm religious basis to their union.

In a 'Church' marriage the wedding normally takes place in a church building with a minister conducting the service, and usually a gathering of family and friends to act as 'witnesses' to the contract which the couple are making between them. There can be some problems with Church weddings, eg, for many Church weddings people are expected to have expensive new clothes and to hold a big party and feast for all their friends. Many people think all this is essential for a 'Christian' marriage, and regard any marriage entered into 'outside' the Church as not truly Christian.

But many young people today are too poor to afford new clothes or to entertain a large number of guests, so they choose to have a civil ceremony instead.

In any case, a Church wedding does not always lead to a Christian marriage. In Western countries especially, many couples get married in church who have no serious intention of keeping their marriage vows. They may separate, and even abandon their children, as soon as they get tired of each other. In other countries many Christian couples live together all their lives, and bring up their children with love and faithfulness without ever getting married at all.

So we see that the really important thing about a Christian marriage is not so much where the wedding ceremony takes place or how many people are invited to attend. The important thing is the faith in Jesus Christ of the couple being married and their firm intention to try and live together the sort of life God wills. This does not mean, however, that there is no importance at all in Church weddings. The fact that a marriage is 'solemnized' in a church should indicate that the couple understand at least something of the meaning of Christian marriage, and will try to live this out in their own situation. They have chosen to have their wedding in the place where God is worshipped, and where God's blessing, guidance, and help are so often sought and experienced. Even for people who profess to have no personal faith, the 'Church' has great significance, and a Church wedding helps many couples to recognize their need of God's help in their marriage. A Church wedding is a witness to the fact that this vitally important relationship between two people is part of God's plan for human life in His world.

(f) *A lack of clear Christian teaching and preparation for marriage.* The Hastings report on Christian marriage in Africa published in 1973 (see p. xii) refers to the widespread lack of instruction on the meaning of marriage, especially now that most schools are controlled by governments and not by the Churches:

'Today religious instruction in general has decreased. This has had its effect on those growing up and preparing for marriage. A vast number of children never go to school at all, and receive little religious instruction at any other time. This is particularly true with regard to instruction on the Christian understanding of marriage. In place after place this complaint was made very strongly: there is next to no Christian instruction given on the subject of sex and marriage in schools, confirmation classes, or sermons. Immediately prior to a Church wedding one or two instructions are normally given to those engaged. This is both late and too little, and of course does not apply at all to those who do not have their marriage solemnized in church.' This lack of instruction is compared to the large amount of instruction that was given in traditional society. The report points to a weakness in the Church's ministry which is found in most countries: 'In the past, African societies had very precise systems for providing sex and marital instruction. Many of these systems have largely broken down; where they still exist Christians often do not take part – have perhaps been forbidden to do so. The instruction given is anyway inadequate and partially unsuitable for young people in today's world. Many people nowadays, especially boys, are simply not receiving any coherent educational help in these matters – even if they attend a Church secondary school.'

Similarly, in a recent TV discussion programme in England a young girl complained that although most schools now provide clear instruction about the physical facts of sex, very few give any teaching about the emotional, psychological or moral aspects of boy-girl relationships.

(g) *The lack of adequate pastoral care.* In many countries pastoral workers are few, and those there are become overburdened and discouraged. Often, too, they lack proper training for this task, and need further instruction themselves before they can instruct others.

Another problem is that some Churches refuse to admit people to full Church membership, and deny them the sacraments, unless their marriages have been performed before a minister in the church building.

As far as the Church in Africa is concerned, it seems that many of the problems associated with Christian marriage are caused by outdated forms of Church administration, and the shortage of pastors with a full and up-to-date training in counselling.

OPPORTUNITIES FOR COUNSELLING

We have given so much space to the background of marriage and family problems because a knowledge and understanding of their causes is essential if effective help is to be given. But how is the ordinary pastor or parish minister to use this knowledge? Having learnt something of the background, how can he then actually help people with their problems, or better still, help to prevent some problems from arising. There are five chief ways in which he can do this:

1. by including general teaching on the subject in his sermons;

2. by organizing adult and youth group meetings and seminars from time to time to discuss particular problems and questions;

3. by giving 'premarital' counselling to prepare engaged couples or those about to become engaged for their future life together;

4. by making sure that every wedding service he conducts reflects the true meaning of Christian marriage, so that all those who participate clearly understand what they are doing;

5. by encouraging people who are experiencing problems in their marriage to come to him for counselling help.

SERMONS

Some pastors prefer to time their preaching about marriage and family life to coincide with special occasions, e.g. when there is to be a wedding or a baptism, or a confirmation service. Others like to plan a series of sermons on different problems that may arise. Whatever scheme is followed, it is essential to relate the teaching directly to the cultural traditions of the area. Sermons will only be effective, too, if they are based on Scripture texts that are directly relevant to the particular aspect of the subject under discussion. General 'moralizing' without theological or biblical foundation should be avoided!

Some Bible passages relating to various aspects of marriage are included in the general list of texts suitable for use in counselling, see p. 283. Of course these verses were written for people in East Mediterranean countries nearly 2,000 years ago. Pastors using them as a basis for sermons today need to interpret them in the light of present-day customs, and of new medical knowledge in such matters as family planning.

PREPARATION FOR MARRIAGE

DISCUSSION GROUPS AND SEMINARS

Questions about marriage and family life are very suitable for discussion either by regular congregational groups (e.g. men's or women's fellowships, confirmation classes for adult candidates, youth clubs, Mothers' Union, etc.), or in specially organized seminars, study weekends, etc. If he can, the pastor should enlist the help of married people in the congregation, either to lead the groups, or at least to share their own experience of working out common problems. For more formal groups the pastor may invite the help of specialists in social work, marriage guidance, family planning, etc.

When such groups first come together, however, it is best to start with fairly general topics, e.g. What is a Christian home? Should Christians demand a heavy bride-price or marriage settlement? Is marriage between Christians and non-Christians a good thing? What about families where father and mother are of different races or nationalities? Is the 'generation gap' between parents and children really inevitable? Can a woman be a wage earner and also an efficient housewife? What should be the respective roles of father and mother in bringing up their children? These are matters that affect and interest everyone, and sermons as well as discussions on such subjects can encourage people to sort out their own ideas and attitudes. But sermons and discussions will only be effective if pastors or other group leaders have thought and read about and discussed the subjects themselves.

PREMARITAL COUNSELLING

Many marriages fail because people get married without considering or understanding what this new relationship will mean for their lives. Traditional customs often included a long time of preparation, both for initiation at the coming of puberty and for marriage. But today this preparation is often neglected, and no teaching is given to guide young people in their lives. This problem has been recognized in many countries, and as long ago as 1958 the All Africa Conference of Churches recommended that: 'classes for marriage preparation should be offered by the Churches: both parties to the intended marriage should be encouraged to participate.' Some pastors do offer such teaching. But too many people come to their marriage today quite unprepared.

What does premarital counselling involve? It means meeting the people who are to be married and discussing some of the new experiences they will come up against in the marriage relationship. The following subjects will be relevant in those situations:

Marriage as a *permanent* relationship between two people (and thus one which affects their relationship with their families);

Marriage as an *exclusive* relationship between two people (and thus one which also affects their relationship with their friends);

Marriage as a *physical* relationship (and thus one which affects their attitudes to themselves and each other);

Marriage as a *creative* relationship (which will probably involve them both in entirely new relationships, with their children, but which may also involve them in the problem of childlessness);

Marriage as a *financial* relationship (which will involve them in a new situation of interdependence and sharing);
Marriage as a *legal* relationship (which will involve them in new responsibilities).

Clearly the details of premarital counselling (which may also involve discussing details of the wedding service) will depend on the particular situation. Discussion is usually more helpful than lectures or sermons. Group discussion with several engaged couples together can provide an opportunity to exchange ideas and opinions. But most helpful of all is the quiet discussion a pastor can have with an individual couple, about the problems of making a Christian marriage in a secular society or among people of another religion.

Some of the subjects listed above can only be discussed if the couple have sufficient education to understand them. Sometimes shyness and respect for the pastor as an authority figure may hinder discussion. Where this happens, some other person, perhaps a married teacher, can be trained to give this sort of counsel.

When should premarital counselling be given? In some areas most marriages are not performed in church, but follow traditional patterns. This need not prevent help being given to those who are to be married. But it means that the pastor must know and work in with local customs regarding marriage and the preparation for it. He will need to ask himself when is the best time and what is the most appropriate way to give help in this situation?

Sometimes this sort of premarital counselling may not be possible, e.g. when the marriage is 'arranged' and the couple themselves play little part in the preparations, or when people marry in a hurry because of pregnancy. But the need for counselling is often greater in such cases. How it is offered must depend on the initiative of the pastor and his ability to be creative and active in particular circumstances.

THE WEDDING CEREMONY

Whenever a pastor is asked to conduct a wedding service, he has an opportunity to show the meaning of Christian marriage and its relevance for people's daily lives.

THE CEREMONY

The wedding ceremony itself can help people understand that the success of a marriage does not depend on the amount of money spent on fine clothes and a big feast, but on the sincerity and commitment with which the couple enter on the marriage relationship.

To celebrate and enjoy the important events of life, such as marriage, is a natural and good thing, and celebration of any kind necessarily costs money. Many people feel that a 'big wedding' is worth while because of its significance to the couple, the family, and to society as a whole. We may remember that in biblical times – indeed as in many religions today – wedding celebrations lasted for several days, as a time of great joy and happiness. The supply of food and hospitality for the guests was very important – hence the host's anxiety when there was not enough wine at the wedding at Cana; but Jesus did not rebuke him for worrying about material things: He provided more wine! (John 2.1–11).

Too often, however, the natural desire to celebrate turns into a desire to 'show off', and to gain prestige by spending a lot of money – perhaps more than people can afford.

Insisting on big expensive weddings can have bad results, causing the marriage to be delayed or even postponed altogether. A certain African student had a customary marriage when he had saved enough to pay the bride-wealth, but then he had to save up again for another five years in order to have a church wedding. In some places people think the Church itself expects women who are married in church to wear long white Western-style dresses and the men to wear Western-style suits, even if these are not what people of the country usually wear for 'best'. Of course there is nothing wrong with wearing nice clothes for a wedding if people can afford them, and provided they do not make a church wedding seem 'foreign' to the situation in which it is being performed. But as we have already said, the true meaning and significance of a church wedding does not depend on what people wear, or whether it is a 'small' wedding or a 'big' one.

THE SERVICE

The order of service for a Christian wedding should be clear and easily understood by the couple themselves and by their families and friends sharing in the service. This means going through the service very carefully with the couple beforehand, and conducting it in a clear and open way. Some pastors 'drone' through the wedding service, with little communication between themselves and the people present. The service then becomes boring and difficult or even impossible to understand.

Not everyone who attends a church wedding knows the meaning of Christian marriage. For many of the guests, a wedding may be one of the very few times they ever enter a church. So the meaning of a marriage 'in Christ', and the way in which the gospel can bring new meaning to people's life together, should be clearly presented. In some Churches the order of service for marriage is fixed. If it is, the pastor should make sure that any address he gives shows clearly the meaning and relevance of Christian marriage, and that it will be understood by the congregation as well as by the couple themselves. If the order of service is not fixed, he can ask himself whether any changes should be made, so that those participating in the service will know what they are doing, and perhaps gain a clearer understanding of the Christian message.

An example of this was a wedding where most of the guests were from the higher ranks of society. The couple being married were strong Christians, whom the pastor knew well, so he was able to conduct the ceremony in a very personal and informal way, with both fun and Christian conviction. At the reception afterwards a young woman came up to him and said, 'I was married recently, in a registry office, because I've always been a convinced atheist. But this was such a wonderful wedding today that it made me really regret I am not a Christian and cannot have a marriage like that.'

TRADITIONAL MARRIAGE CEREMONIES

In situations where the overall Church or diocesan authorities allow it, some pastors adapt the wedding service to include symbols which are traditionally associated with marriage in the area concerned. For example, in New Britain bride and groom exchange lengths of local 'shell money', as a symbol of agreement and unity between the two families involved in the marriage. Or bride and groom are 'bound together' by a length of rope or leaves to signify their union. In other areas the two families share in drinking from a common cup, while elsewhere people prefer to use the European custom of exchanging rings. Many such symbols can be used to make a wedding service more meaningful. Besides being approved by the Church authorities, any such traditional forms should of course be discussed with the couple beforehand, and an explanation included in the service itself. This is specially important in situations where people are not accustomed to any joining of traditional and Christian practices.

In many countries 'customary' forms of marriage are legally valid and may even be the only form accepted by the government. That is to say, the only thing necessary to make a marriage valid according to the law is that it must be witnessed by the society in which it takes place. Where this is the case, Christians need to ask: can a customary marriage be a 'Christian marriage', and how can the customary form of marriage be related to Church weddings?

Any marriage can be called a 'Christian' marriage if the couple themselves are committed to Jesus Christ, and the form of marriage recognizes this commitment. Where customary marriage is the usual and legal form then the Church should recognize this and not oppose customary marriage as something wrong and illegal. A pastor should be aware of the law about marriage in his own country, and according to what his Church Council or diocesan committee permits, decide how best to overcome the lack of Christian content in any customary form. There are several ways of doing this, e.g.:

(a) Christian ideas and a Christian blessing can be inserted into the customary ceremony, with either the pastor or another representative of the Church sharing in the service wherever it is held:

(b) The customary service can be arranged to take place in the church building, with the Christian service before or after it.

(c) Those who have already been married in a customary form can be given a blessing either in church or at home, or in some other way recognized by the local community.

Whatever is done in this way does not make customary marriage into a legally valid marriage: it is already valid without any 'Christian' additions. The blessing of the pastor or the Church does not make the marriage 'legal'; it turns the marriage into one in which Christian ideals are an essential part.(Similarly it is not the blessing of the pastor or the Church which makes a 'church' marriage 'legal'. See p. 181 above.) In all cases, too, it is important to avoid the danger of an unsatisfactory syncretism of Christian and non-Christian elements.

REPAIRING AND RECONCILING

In most countries counselling for couples who are experiencing marriage problems is still urgently needed, even where the government or other secular agencies provide 'marriage guidance' services. The following comment on the African situation applies equally to many other areas:

'Traditional systems provided much help [for those already married]: when marriages were in trouble there were long discussions with parents and other senior relatives who were concerned to do justice to both sides. Such means can and should be used, but many people, particularly in urban situations, cannot easily turn today to older relatives for help and advice; moreover, traditional advice was offered according to the traditional ideas as to marriage roles, and today these are being questioned. The elders may simply not understand the pressures upon modern marriage and the expectations of the young, particularly young women.'

Any counselling given should be based on the principles we have discussed in earlier chapters. Many of the counselling problems already discussed in earlier chapters relate to marriage and family life.

THE PASTOR AS AN 'EXAMPLE'

Some pastors feel incompetent to proffer any advice about marriage

'Many marriages fail because people get married without understanding what the new relationship will mean. . . . The faith of the couple and their commitment to Christ make the marriage Christian, not the order of service or that it takes place in a church' (pp. 189 and 181).

The Church service at which a Jamaican girl will be given away by her father, and the civil ceremony for a French girl, are both 'white weddings' and are equally valid in law. What are the chief differences between them, and what effect if any will these differences have on whether the marriages 'succeed' or 'fail'?

194

problems because they are experiencing problems in their own married life. 'How can I speak to others,' they ask, 'when my own example of Christian marriage is not very good? Doesn't this destroy the value of anything I can say to other people?'

There are several points to think about in regard to this common feeling among pastors?

(a) If a pastor's own marriage is truly in need of repair, and the pastor knows this but does nothing about it, then his fear of being a hypocrite is justified. Criticism of a pastor's marriage is valid if he refuses to work at bringing it to the standard demanded of Christians.

(b) A pastor's feeling of being unable to counsel others is also justified if he knowingly and deliberately indulges in immoral behaviour, or behaviour which weakens anyone else's marriage relationship. 'Physician heal thyself' (Luke 4.23) is a fitting response to any pastor in this situation. By such actions a pastor destroys the credibility or 'truth' of anything he may say.

(c) If, however, the pastor is sincerely trying to live in the marriage relationship as God intends, then even if he has difficulties in his married life, he is in a very good position to speak to people in need of help. As a pastor, he has the opportunity to open out to people the possibilities of change and renewal which are part of the gospel. He does not have to be perfect in his own marriage before he can do this. If that was the condition of speaking to others, then no pastor could ever speak at all. He does not speak as one who is perfect, but as one who experiences some of the problems of marriage himself, and perhaps as one who has discovered the answer to some of these problems. This is the basis of 'identification counselling' (see p. 132), and this sort of counselling can be very effective.

(d) A pastor who is himself married will probably have experienced many of the problems facing his people, and so can speak from 'within' a situation rather than as an outsider. This does not mean that unmarried pastors cannot counsel effectively in marriage problems. The very good work of many unmarried pastoral workers, such as priests and sisters in the Roman Catholic Church, shows this. However, when conflict between marriage partners arises from difficulties in their physical relationship, they may be too shy to say so to a counsellor who is not married. In such cases even a married pastor may think it wise to suggest that they consult a doctor or specialist in marriage guidance or family planning. But he can certainly regard his own marriage not as a hindrance to counselling, but as an asset which unites him and his people in what may be a commonly experienced difficulty.

(e) Avery big problem for some pastors is the negative attitude and bad behaviour of their own children. This can sometimes weaken the pastor's influence, or even prevent him from working effectively. People are very ready to use the bad conduct of family members as a 'spear' to attack the pastor, or as a 'club' to destroy the value of any advice he may give. Where his happens both pastor and people need to acknowledge the problem and honestly try to understand and improve the situation.

We may conclude this chapter by studying the words with which Father Adrian Hastings summed up the chief task of the Church in relation to marriage and family life:

'Marriages can be shipwrecked upon the hard rocks of character, selfishness, the facts of human sin, of bad circumstances: political, economic, and accidental. In a situation of very rapid social change, of the breakdown of traditional ways of behaviour, of a world in which there are many nominal Christians and the Church's means of influencing them is limited, it is important not to set impossible goals for ourselves.

What *is* possible – and important – is to make sure that:

(a) the Church gives a true witness about marriage through her own teaching and the example of her committed members;

(b) the laws of the Church do not stop people from becoming part of the family of the Church;

(c) the Church does what it can to influence the laws and standards of society to support strong marriage and family life.'

STUDY SUGGESTIONS

WORD STUDY

1. What is meant by:
   (a) the 'cultural' aspects of marriage?
   (b) marriage as an 'order of creation'?

REVIEW OF CONTENT

2. Why is marriage so important in every society?
3. What are the chief differences between 'Church' marriage on the one hand, and 'customary' or 'civil' marriage on the other?
4. The report *Christian Marriage in Africa* listed three factors which form the essence or foundation of a valid marriage. What are these factors?
5. Which four 'social' factors are causing marriage problems in many countries?
6. In this chapter we discussed five chief ways in which a pastor can

help people with problems in their marriage and family life. What are these five ways, and which do you think is the most important?

BIBLE STUDY

7. The teaching about marriage in Matt. 19.3–9 differs from the teaching in Mark 10.2–12 in one very important way.
   (a) What is that important difference?
   (b) Why did the two evangelists give different teaching?
8. What teaching do we find in Prov. 18.22 and 19.14 about the choice of a wife?
9. In Gen. 2.18, the woman is described as a 'helper fit for the man'. What do you think this means?
10. Prov. 31.10–31 lists some of the characteristics or marks of a good wife. What are these characteristics, and which do you think are the most important? Which, if any, do you think are *not* important? What other characteristics, if any, do you think should have been included?
11. The Scriptures teach that marriage is generally God's plan for his people. However, it is clear that marriage is not God's plan for *every* person. Read Mark 1.29–31; 1 Cor. 7.1–9; 1 Cor. 9.1–18. What do we learn from these passages about the marital status of the following people?
   (a) Simon Peter (Cephas) (b) the Lord's brothers (c) Paul
   (d) Barnabas (e) the other apostles
12. Explain what you think each of the following passages means for husbands and wives today:
   (a) 1 Cor. 7.1,2 (b) 1 Cor. 7.3–5
   What difficulty, if any, do you see in applying either of these passages to people's lives today?
13. In 1 Cor. 7.32–35 Paul refers to a problem which married people face in their service for Jesus Christ.
   (a) What is this problem?
   (b) In what way, if any, does Paul's teaching in this passage conflict with the teaching of Gen. 2.24?

APPLICATION, OPINION, AND RESEARCH

14. In what chief ways are the features of traditional marriage in Papua New Guinea as described on pp. 174–177 (a) similar to, and (b) different from, features of traditional marriage in your own society?
15. Some people condemn the system of bride-price, saying it is a sort of purchase, so that it leads to the idea that a woman is a 'thing' to be bought and sold, rather than a person whom God loves and

values. (See pp. 176, 177). What is your opinion? Give examples to support your answer?

16. According to the report *Christian Marriage in Africa* one cause of marriage breakdown is lack of adequate pastoral care. Do you think this is true in your area? If so, how do you think the situation could be improved? What are the other chief causes of marriage breakdown in your area?

17. What is the attitude of your Church to customary or civil marriage? In what ways can customary or civil marriages become 'Christian' marriages?

18. In some countries premarital counselling is regarded as a 'Western importation', and therefore unsuitable for the local situation. What is your opinion?

19. How would you reply to a pastor who said, 'I cannot help people with their marriage problems because I have got problems in my own marriage'?

20. What are the legal requirements concerning marriage in your country? That is:
    (a) Who can legally conduct weddings or marriage ceremonies?
    (b) What sorts of marriage are legally valid?
    (c) At what age can people be married?
    (d) What is the law regarding divorce and remarriage?
    If there is no law laid down on any of these subjects, what are the accepted ideas and customs?

10
Sickness and Healing

Many things happen in people's lives which make it difficult to achieve the purpose of the Church's ministry: that all people should be set free from anything which prevents them from knowing God, and should come to a life of mature fellowship with each other in union with Christ. Faults and weaknesses in the ministry of the Church may prevent people from truly understanding and experiencing this abundant life. Personal problems and temptations may turn them away from God's plan for their lives.

For many people, *sickness* is one such problem. Sickness comes to most people in every culture at some stage in their lives. It is one of the big tests that people face. For all Christians, sickness comes as a challenge to faith and service. For pastoral workers, especially, it is also an opportunity to help people experience the power of the gospel in their lives.

THE IDEA OF 'HEALTH'

We can only understand sickness properly when we compare it to 'health'. 'Sickness' is really a negative idea, while 'health' is a positive one. However, in some countries, where nearly everyone is poor and suffering, people do not think much about the meaning of 'health' as such. In other situations, where people are more fortunate, they take their health for granted until they are confronted with sickness or suffering of some sort.

A group of college students in South-East Asia were asked the following questions:

(a) What does 'health' mean to you?

(b) How would you try to translate this word or idea into your own language?

These are some of their answers:

(a) For most of the students, 'health' meant being physically well and strong; being *not* sick; being free from disease and germs; being clean; having good sanitation. These ideas, they said, had developed mainly since Western-type schools and hospitals had been set up in the area. In the local schools, most of the teaching about health dealt only with medical matters such as hygiene, infectious diseases, and injuries. It did not cover the wider and deeper meaning in the *total* idea of health. These limited ideas were contrasted with traditional ideas about health as relating to a wider area of people's lives.

(b) In some local languages there was no word which could adequately describe the full meaning of health. However, some of the many different words that were used included ideas which went deeper than merely being free from physical disease, injury, or pain. In one language being 'healthy' meant being 'normal' in every way. In another language it meant being free from disorder or chaos. In a third example the word for health meant being in a good relationship with other people and with the spiritual powers of the tribe or clan.

The English word 'health' comes from the same basic root as the word 'whole', and the two are closely connected in meaning. To be 'whole' means to be completely 'sound' or in good condition, to be free from any defect or disease, to be well in body and 'sane' or normal in mind. Thus 'health' means soundness or wholeness of body, in which the various organs all function well; together with moral, emotional, and mental wholeness; and also spiritual well-being, welfare, and salvation. (The word 'Holy' is also from the same root, and means being spiritually whole.)

Example 35: This understanding of health and sickness is well illustrated by the case of Philip, a young African pastor who had a bitter quarrel with his bishop. Later he went overseas for further study, and while he was away, he heard that the bishop had become seriously ill and had died. This caused Philip deep disturbance, and disrupted his theological studies. Although he was an able student, he found himself unable to work, or even to talk with his fellow students. Eventually he was admitted to a mental hospital for a long period, and then flown back to Africa. Many months passed before he fully regained his health and was able to resume his studies. Because he had refused to be reconciled with the bishop, Philip felt guilty, and as though in some way he was responsible for the bishop's death.

So we see that 'health' relates to the whole personality and whatever affects people's well-being, and that 'sickness' is not limited to physical injury or illness, but includes emotional and social factors as well. Physical sickness is one way in which a person's total well-being or wholeness is disturbed, but it is only one way. A person may be healthy in body, and at the same time unhealthy in mind and spirit, and in relationships with other people. So a true 'healing ministry' will aim to bring wholeness to *every* aspect of a person's life and personality.

THE ROLE OF THE CHURCH

Healing the sick was an important part of Jesus's ministry (Matt. 4.23). This healing was part of the good news of the Kingdom of God. It was a sign of the coming of the promised Messiah, one of the blessings the Messiah would bring to all people (Luke 7.21, 22; Isa. 35.5, 6; Isa.

61.1–4; Luke 4.18, 19). Healing people was one of the ways by which Jesus showed that He was the promised Messiah, and that He was concerned for all aspects of people's lives.

So the Church has always seen the defeat of suffering and sickness as one way of proclaiming the good news of the Kingdom, while healing has been an important part of its work. By providing medical care, the Church can bring the love of Jesus Christ into people's lives, and open the way for them to hear and understand the meaning of the gospel in their own situation. Here are two examples:

Example 36: When the Church first came to the island of New Britain in New Guinea, the people believed that the only cure for many sorts of sickness was through sorcery and magic. When this failed there was nothing else they could do. When the missionaries set up dispensaries and hospitals the people were shy at first, but before long one of the missionaries was able to report that 'the people's confidence in our medicines is taking the place of belief in charms and witchcraft'. And a local Church leader commented: 'This work has opened the way into the hearts of the people as nothing else can do. It is remarkable how barriers are broken down, and to see the confidence people have in the medical workers.' This had a deep effect in many people's lives, and the same thing has happened in many other areas.

Example 37: In another place where the Church was giving medical care, some people accused the Christians of using it as a sort of 'bait' with which to win converts. But the Church leaders regarded healing work as an essential part of the good news 'in action'. They said, 'It is part of the duty of the Church, in showing the meaning of Christianity, not to neglect the service of a Christlike compassion. When the Church takes no part in this effort, the world says: "the Church talks at men's souls and lets their bodies rot away." When this happens, one of the Christlike marks of Christianity is gone. There must be the verbal explanation of the gospel, and also a practical exhibition of it in the form of loving care . . . as long as the Church exists and human need remains.'

Not all Christians, however, are agreed about responsibility for medical care. Some see caring for the sick as a basic part of the witness and ministry of the Church. Some see it as an 'extra' work which the Church should do only where there is no other organization, public or private, to take the responsibility. Others think that the Church should not involve itself in organized medical care at all.

The sort of care mentioned in the two examples above, is, of course, not the only way in which the Church can offer help to people who are sick in one way or another. Many Christians think of 'ministry to the sick' as being of three chief kinds: (1) practical, (2) pastoral, and (3) charismatic. They define these three as follows:

201

1. *Practical or medical care* is the expert help provided by trained doctors and nurses who work in an organized way to restore health to people who are sick in body or mind. This work includes preventing disease and injury, and providing conditions in which people can live healthy lives. Many individual Christians and Churches undertake this work, but so do many more people and organizations who are not Christian at all.

2. *Pastoral care of the sick* is an important part of the work of every pastor, whether or not his Church as a whole is actively involved in medical care and healing. A pastor is expected to visit those who are ill, whether at home or in hospital, to pray with and for them, and in some Churches administer the sacraments to them. Sometimes he must help to exorcise and free people from 'demonic' powers that bind them. Sometimes he must help a person to prepare for death, or to endure a life of continuous suffering. Often he must comfort and strengthen their families as well. This sort of work is usually regarded as a 'spiritual' ministry which a pastor undertakes alongside those who are providing medical care for people's bodies. In this way the pastor participates in the work of making people whole. Like the doctors and nurses he needs some training for it, but it is a work which every pastor expects to undertake.

3. *Charismatic or 'faith' healing* reflects the healing ministry of Jesus Himself. With the development of modern medicine, however, scientific discoveries about the way people's bodies function have led to the idea that 'healing', as distinct from pastoral care, is either (a) the job of the medical experts alone, or (b) a 'gift' bestowed by God on a very few extraordinary people only. Some Churches actively discourage their members from seeking this sort of healing – perhaps because it is too easy for impostors ('false Christs', Mark 13.22) to exploit the sufferings of the faithful. And it has not, in the past, been customary to commission ministers, as Jesus did his disciples, to 'heal the sick, raise the dead, cleanse lepers and cast out devils' (see Matt. 10.8 and Jas. 5.13, 14).

But more recently these ideas have been changing. In very many of the Independent Churches of Africa and elsewhere, for example, healing is regarded as an essential part of everyday ministry. As the Nigerian theologian, Dr Nathaniel I. Ndiokwere, points out in his study of prophecy in the African Independent Churches: 'faith-healing has been the centre of the activities of most of the new movements . . . the numerous miracles of Jesus, the healing activities and exorcisms reported in the new Testament, have influenced and encouraged the faith-healing mission in the Independent Churches. . . . Often it may not be necessary for the new "man of God" in Africa to be aware of the specific complaints of suffering individuals – the patients are healed by the power of the Spirit and by faith.' In the West, also, special services in Church for healing with prayer and laying on of hands are becoming a regular feature.

We must recognize that each of these three sorts of healing or ministry to the sick is valid. Some people mistakenly see them as incompatible with each other, and think that if we seek medical attention this rules out the need for 'faith', or that if we seek healing through prayer then we should not also go to the doctor because that would be to lack trust in God's power to help us.

The essential fact is that ultimately *all* healing comes from God, but He is not restricted to any one method. God may work through 'natural' means, i.e. the process of 'nature' by which all living organisms (including our human bodies) heal and repair themselves, and the skill and compassion of doctors and nurses who use the properties of plants, minerals, etc. to provide medicines and medical services to help on that process. Or He may work through 'supernatural' means such as prayer and the exercise of faith. God uses *all* means to bring 'wholeness' to people's lives, but the means themselves do not bring healing: it is God who heals through them. And the pastor who clearly understands this fundamental truth will contribute all the more effectively to the process of restoring people to health, by recognizing and encouraging the use of 'all means' for God's healing power to become real in people's lives.

In this chapter, however, we are concerned chiefly with situations where pastors and medical experts have an equally important but separate contribution to make, as they co-operate in this work. As we have seen, a pastor first needs to understand people's attitudes to sickness and health.

ATTITUDES TO SICKNESS

How people think of sickness depends on their 'world-view', that is, the way they think about themselves, the world around them, and the things that happen; and this world-view in turn depends on their cultural and religious background. A person's beliefs will strongly influence his thinking about the causes and the cure of sickness. Imagine two people who are suffering from the same disease. One perhaps believes that all sickness is caused by angry spiritual powers, so he will seek to be cured by propitiating those spirits. His attitude is quite different from that of his friend who understands that he has been infected by the germs of a particular disease, and knows that a specific drug will help him to get well.

The following examples from two areas in Papua New Guinea illustrate two such different ways of thinking.

'All healing comes from God . . . God uses *all* means to bring about wholeness in people's lives' (p. 203).

In Pittsburgh, USA, Kathryn Kuhler, a well-known faith-healer, brings hope to a large audience of believers. In Ghana many of the people who queue for treatment by the 'witch-doctor' are Christians who also attend the government health clinic. By what 'means' have you yourself experienced healing?

Example 38: happened in the early 1970s in a village in the Sepik region. A woman there called Monda became sick. Her skin was cold and clammy, her head and whole body ached. She was not vomiting, but did not want to eat. She lay on her bed very quiet. Kauyu, her husband, was much concerned, and called for Wilaki, the medicine-man. Feeling Monda's cold skin, Wilaki decided that ancestral spirits had affected her, and said that her sickness was the result of her bad behaviour. Kauyu's mother, who had died some years earlier, was tired of hearing Monda insult Kauyu and tell lies about him to the neighbours. The mother's spirit was angry with Monda because she was bad-tempered and lazy too, often hitting her children and failing to have food ready for Kauyu when he came home hungry from work. Wilaki told Monda that if she wanted to be well again she must try to change her ways. Then, placing his mouth over Monda's back and shoulders, he pulled out seven pieces of wood. He said that angry ancestors had shot these into Monda, and Kauyu's mother and others had taken part of Monda's spirit away from her. That was why her skin was so cold.

When Kauyu heard Wilaki's diagnosis he set about making his wife well again. He persuaded Monda to confess her wrong-doing, and earnestly prayed to God to send away his wife's sin, her sickness, and also the bad spirits. He blew softly on the painful parts of Monda's body, saying, 'Mother, go out of her!' Next day Kauyu picked some leaves and grasses from the garden where Monda had first felt sick. He tied them into a bundle and called to his mother and other spirits, 'Put back my wife's spirit so she will be well.' Then he went back along the track to the village, stopping every few yards and placing an upturned leaf with the stem pointing homewards, so that Monda's spirit could follow. Again, when he got home, he called on the ancestors to leave Monda alone.

Next morning Monda was well again, and a week later Kauyu came to a nearby mission to tell of his wife's sickness and ask for more teaching about the meaning of prayer. Kauyu prays often, both privately and at Church services in his village, and he often passes on to others what he has heard and experienced of God. He told the missionary that he had paid the medicine man Wilaki 50 cents, and that Monda is now behaving much better, as she is afraid of the ancestors. Monda does not claim to be a Christian, but Kauyu does, and he continues to attend services regularly.

Example 39: concerns the Elema people of the Gulf District where the Church has been working for over 25 years. The following description of their beliefs and attitudes is offered by the people themselves, who explain the ideas behind their actual practices. Some observations of missionaries and Church leaders who have lived and worked among them are also included.

The Elema people make a clear distinction between minor ailments or injuries, and the serious sicknesses that threaten a person's life. Minor ailments, they say, are common to all human beings, and are caused by coughs, colds, infections, muscular injuries, etc. Serious illnesses, however, have a different cause, and where any sickness gives anxiety for the sufferer's life, then a much deeper cause must be looked for.

Minor ailments are treated by simple remedies, usually involving the use of local plants which are either boiled, and the liquid then used to bathe the parts of the body afflicted, or burnt, and the scent is inhaled.

In serious sicknesses investigations are made into the cause of the sickness. The important question asked is *why* is this person sick? Not *how* did it happen, but what has the person done to offend someone? The cause is sought by asking *who* rather than *what* is the cause? Traditionally, people believe that all serious sickness arises from some agent who is manipulating spiritual or magical power.

Therefore, to effect a cure, some form of counter-magic or sorcery must be used against the harmful magic. A person able to perform 'white' magic is paid to counteract the 'black' magic which has harmed the sufferer.

Thus the Elema believe that whereas minor ailments affect only a person's body, serious sickness involves not only the life-spirit of the person concerned, but other spiritual 'beings' related to that person. Serious sickness means that spiritual forces and magical powers are at work which can either control and harm a person, or release him or her from the sickness. Someone somewhere is using the spiritual power for evil purposes, so that more than just a physical interpretation of the causes and cure of sickness must be found.

To sum up, we see that in any individual situation there are many different causes to which sickness may be attributed, and that these causes may relate to the beliefs and attitudes of the sick person, and those of the people concerned with his welfare. Thus there may be:

(a) physical causes, e.g. specific disease, infection, injury;

(b) natural causes, such as old age;

(c) emotional causes, such as worry, stress, fear, guilt, etc.;

(d) cultural causes, like the breaking of some traditional custom or taboo;

(e) moral causes, such as wrong-doing or breaking the law;

(f) 'spiritual' causes resulting from the use of magic and other spiritual powers.

Any one of these factors may be the basic cause, and the physical sickness caused by e.g. emotional or spiritual factors is no less 'real' than sickness which has an obvious physical cause. Sometimes sickness can only be explained by a combination of such factors. But whatever the cause, any serious sickness affects the *whole* person, body, mind, and spirit; and it can affect the person mentally, emotionally, and spiritually. Some people use the word 'psychosomatic' to describe this close relationship between the mind (the *psyche*) and the body (*soma*), which occurs when some mental disturbance causes physical illness, or some adverse physical condition upsets the balance of a person's mind. In such cases both body and mind must be adequately treated if a person is to be effectively cured.

SICKNESS AND SIN

Many people believe there is a close connection between sickness and wrong-doing. They think that sickness is sent by God as a punishment for sin.

Example 40: Late one afternoon, a boat carrying a very sick 18-year-old girl arrived at a Christian village on an island group in the Pacific region. The girl, Myra, was taken to the medical aid centre, where the nurse diagnosed her sickness as a very severe attack of cerebral malaria. The nurse, who came from a neighbouring island, also said that the girl had not received proper treatment before coming to the centre, and this was why she was so sick. The girl was delirious, and crying out with pain, and the medical staff decided she must be taken to the nearest hospital, a boat journey of several hours away. Surprisingly, the local boat-owners seemed unwilling to go, and said they should wait till next morning. The girl, however, became worse, and the nurse again requested the boat-owners to take her to hospital. Again the boat-owners refused, showing very little concern, and at last one of them explained: 'It's no use taking her to hospital. She will die anyway because she broke God's law by committing adultery with her uncle. That is why she is sick, and she is being punished for it.' In spite of the nurse's care, Myra did indeed die before any boat was ready to leave, and her death was clearly both expected and accepted by the local people. They saw her sickness and death as a direct punishment for breaking the Christian law and the clan law, both of which forbid adultery.

In the Bible, too, we find many passages where sickness and such other 'afflictions' as death, suffering, and accident are shown to be the result of some sort of wrong-doing. That is, these afflictions are seen as being caused by 'moral' failure, i.e. sin. Bible writers generally imply that the three chief causes of people's problems and suffering are:

1. The sufferer's own personal sins (Deut. 28.15–18; Jer. 31.30; Ezek. 18.1–4);

2, The sins of the sufferer's parents (Exod. 34.7; Num. 14.18; Jer. 31.29; Ezek. 18.2);

3. The sin of Adam, in whom all mankind have fallen and all are guilty before God. (This is implied in Rom. 5.12–21, and see also Gen. 3.17–19; Rom. 8.20–23; 1 Cor. 15.21, 22; Eph. 2.3.)

In the Old Testament, especially, the leaders and teachers of the people emphasized personal wrong-doing and the sins of the parents as the causes of sickness and other troubles, and most people at that time believed that these were the chief cause of the problems in their lives. For example, when Job was experiencing great pain and hardship, his friend Eliphaz, in trying to comfort him, asked: 'Who that was innocent ever perished? Those who plough iniquity and sow trouble, reap the same' (Job. 4.7–9). Eventually Eliphaz traced Job's afflictions to the sin of cruelty to widows and the fatherless (see also Job 8.20; 11.6; 22.5–10).

In the time of Jesus, the disciples asked the same sort of question about the man born blind: 'Who sinned, this man or his parents, that he was born blind?' (John 9.1, 2). Most people then regarded sickness as a punishment and a sign of God's anger.

But some Bible writers saw other causes also: e.g. the activity of Satan (Job 2.1–7), and of evil spirits (Mark 9.17, 25). The Interpreter's Bible Dictionary gives a good summary of biblical teaching on the subject: 'The Bible does not encourage a purely naturalistic [i.e. physical] theory of the causes of sickness [e.g. old age, lack of hygiene, inadequate medical care, etc.]. Other causes must be recognized, including the forces of evil, wrong-doing, and the power of the supernatural world.'

We may ask whether Jesus himself shared these ideas about sickness and disease. Some Christians would say that Jesus did accept them, because He fully shared in the life and thinking of His people. Others disagree, and some Bible passages seem to show that Jesus did not always accept the commonly held ideas of His time. According to John 9.3, He did not agree that the man's blindness was caused either by his personal sins or the sins of his parents. Jesus was more concerned with the love and power of God as shown in the man's healing, and made it clear that this was more important than searching for the causes of the affliction (see John 1.14 and 5.19, 20).

People then regarded sickness and disease as a *theological* problem. They asked '*Why* did God let this happen? *Who* caused the person to get sick?' But Jesus asked a different sort of question: '*How can this person be helped?*' Jesus gave His followers a living challenge and opportunity to help someone in need, rather than a theoretical problem to argue about.

Many people in the Church today still face the same problem. Sometimes there is a clear connection between sickness and wrong-doing. In other cases, even where there is no obvious physical cause, sickness cannot be traced to any moral or even psychological cause either, and the reason for it remains a mystery. But the attitude of Jesus is a continuing challenge for all Christians, and especially for pastoral workers. We have mentioned (pp. 105 and 202) that many people have found healing through the 'confession' and testimony encouraged by revival movements such as that in East Africa, and by similar Independent Church movements elsewhere. In very many cases the question 'why' people suffer cannot be answered; but the important question is 'what can be done to help them?' Often the exact cause of sickness is impossible to discover, but caring love and practical concern will always help to relieve people's suffering.

THE PASTOR'S CONCERN

UNDERSTANDING THE BACKGROUND

To help people effectively in times of sickness and suffering, therefore, a pastor needs to *know*:

1. The cultural ideas or 'world-view' of the person or people concerned;

2. The Church's ideas about sickness, and how these agree with or differ from the cultural ideas;

3. The role of medical workers in the area. A pastor should never oppose the work of doctors and other medical workers unless there are very strong reasons for doing so. He needs to understand, as far as he can, the nature of the person's sickness and the medical treatment being given. Where possible he should co-operate in this treatment and support the medical workers with prayer.

4. The social and economic situation of the sick person's family and other dependants, who may need practical help in carrying on their daily routine. Within the extended family system, especially, problems and questions may arise which affect the ideas and behaviour of the sick person's relatives. The pastor needs to be aware of this and try to help if he can.

UNDERSTANDING THE INDIVIDUAL

As we have seen, sickness affects different individuals in different ways. It not only affects the body, it also involves people's feelings and attitudes, and the way they behave to others. One writer distinguishes between a *disease* or injury as 'something which happens to a person's physical body'; and an *illness* as 'an experience involving the person's feelings and attitudes towards the disease and towards other people'.

Many doctors and medical workers show concern for the feelings associated with disease as well as the disease itself. But the chief concern of any medical worker is with physical suffering, and the need to restore health to the body. Where the Church is active in the work of healing, this must also be a concern of the pastor. But the pastoral worker will be chiefly concerned with the sufferer's feelings and attitudes, and the feelings and attitudes of those closely connected with him. *Both* aspects are important because right (or positive) attitudes can help a sick person to recover more quickly, and wrong (or negative) attitudes can make him worse.

Before you read further, write down what your own attitudes and feelings are when you yourself are sick. Then compare what you have written with the following summary description of the feelings most usually experienced as a result of falling sick.

(a) *Fear* of pain and suffering, especially when the cause and likely outcome of the sickness is not known. Many people, and especially those in a rural or village situation, are very much frightened by the idea of going to the unfamiliar surroundings of a hospital or medical centre, and fear they will never come home again. Friends who have themselves come through a period of sickness, and know the benefits of hospital treatment, can often give sick people courage to overcome such fears and feelings of hopelessness. Often a pastor will know which members of his congregation have had this experience, and can persuade them to visit and encourage a sick person in this way.

(b) *Anxiety* about the possible causes and results of sickness. People wonder how their family will cope without them. Who will look after the children? What will happen about unfinished work or studies? What about money? All these worries can affect not only the sick person but also their family and workmates, whose anxiety will in turn affect the sick person's state of mind. Here again the understanding and practical support of friends and neighbours can reduce a sick person's anxiety and give a peace of mind that will help them recover. And here again the pastor is in a good position to persuade people to help.

(c) *Isolation* from family and friends, especially when they must spend a long time in hospital. Loneliness is a big problem for the sick, and can cause them to try and avoid treatment, or act in ways which slow down the process of healing. Some quite healthy people have a morbid fear of sickness and sick people, and dislike visiting even their closest relatives in hospital. A pastor who persuades such people that visiting sick people is one way of responding to God's love (Matt. 25.34–46) is not only helping the sick, but can also help the healthy to have a more positive attitude towards sickness.

(d) *Uselessness:* Skilled people who normally lead a full and busy life can become very frustrated and depressed when prevented by sickness from following their usual activities. They feel useless and despairing because they are treated as incapable of working. Sometimes, of course, they really are too ill to do anything at all. But even chronic invalids can adapt to a less active life (see Example 43), and there are many ways a pastor can encourage even those in hospital to feel useful: e.g. by suggesting they write to cheer up someone else who is sick, or say special prayers for someone in trouble, or help raise Church funds by knitting, handicrafts, etc.

(e) *Anger:* Sick people often feel resentful towards those who are well, or angry with the doctor and other medical workers – or even with themselves, if they feel their illness was caused by their own wrong actions and attitudes.

(f) *Hopelessness:* When sickness is prolonged, people can lose hope and can hinder their own recovery by an attitude of defeatism. We have seen above some ways in which they can be helped to change such attitudes.

(g) *Escapism:* There is one other emotional factor in sickness which a pastor needs to recognize, and that is when people fall sick almost 'on purpose', as a way of avoiding responsibility or escaping from an unpleasant situation, or in order to attract attention or gain certain privileges. They themselves may not realize why they are sick, but in such cases it is quite possible for them to *want to remain sick* rather than get well. Perhaps this was one reason why Jesus, in his healing ministry, often began by asking: 'Do you want to be healed?' (John 5.2–6); or 'What do you want me to do for you?' (Mark 10.49–51). At first, the answers seem obvious. But Jesus was teaching people to face up to their sickness as well as offering to heal them. Besides wanting an end to their suffering, were they really ready to accept the new responsibilities that health might bring? In the same way a pastor can often support the doctors by encouraging sick people to *want* to get well, or on the other hand, to face up to the prospect of continued suffering. If a person's attitude to recovery is a negative one, even the best medical and hospital care may fail; and anxiety, fear, or frustration can hinder the healing process.

By taking whatever practical steps he can to encourage positive attitudes in the sick person, and where necessary in his family, the pastor can help to relieve the sick of those feelings which prevent recovery.

BEING ACCESSIBLE

Often the mere fact that a pastor, or a group of Church elders, or even just one fellow Christian, is *there* can bring a sense of help to someone in need. Through them, as representatives of the Church which is the total family of God, the healing powers of fellowship, faith, and prayer are made accessible. Newly appointed pastors sometimes wonder what to say at such times. They feel that 'words are cheap'. But love and concern are more important than words, and the presence of a sympathetic pastor can even help to *prevent* sickness from developing. If someone is seen to be upset, or anxious, or behaving in a strange way, an alert pastor may be able to bring help before the problem grows and real sickness takes hold.

USING THE SCRIPTURES

The words of the Bible can be a great source of help in times of sickness, provided they are used properly. Here are two examples of how the Bible can be used.

Example 41: Pastor Amos was asked to visit a very sick woman in hospital. He did not know her, and she did not belong to his Church. She was so ill that he was told that he should not even talk to her. However, she had asked to see a minister because she realized she was going to die. So Amos went to the ward where she was lying very sick. He took a small Bible from his pocket and held it up in front of her, to show the gold cross on the outside cover as a reminder of God's love. When she saw it she gave a weak smile and reached out and took the pastor's hand. He prayed very briefly for her, and remained sitting there for a few moments before he left.

Example 42: Pastor Jordan went to visit a man who was being treated at home after being badly injured in an accident. The man was still in a shocked condition, and was very weak and tired, so the pastor knew he should not talk to him much. The pastor asked him, 'Is there anything I can do for you, or would you like to say anything?' the man replied, 'Thank you, but not now. I feel very tired.' Pastor Jordan remained standing, holding the man's hand, and said quietly: 'Jesus said, "Come to me all whose work is hard, whose load is heavy, and I will give you relief. I will never leave you or forsake you"' (Matt. 11.28.) The man said in a weak voice, 'Thank you, thank you', and after a few more moments, the pastor left.

These examples show how the Bible can be used as a symbol of hope and divine strength, and also to comfort those who cannot read for themselves. People too ill to move or speak are often fully aware of what is happening around them, and even when people are deeply unconscious the words of Scripture can sometimes get through to them.

People who can read, of course, can be encouraged to read suitable passages of Scripture for themselves. Some Churches print leaflets with verses specially selected to help the sick or suffering. Pastors can select their own sets of verses to suit their particular pastoral situation (see p. 283).

PRAYER, SACRAMENTS (AND THE QUESTION OF FAITH-HEALING)

We have already studied some principles concerning the use of prayer in counselling, particularly in connection with the Scriptures (pp. 149 and 154). Some Churches prescribe special prayers and forms of service for use with the sick, e.g. the Order for the Visitation of the Sick in the Anglican Book of Common Prayer. But a spontaneous approach related directly to the particular situation is more appropriate today. In praying for the sick, the principles to follow are:

(a) *Thank God* for His presence and concern and understanding in every situation.

(b) *Affirm* that healing is part of the good news, and that God wills to see people made whole.

(c) *Affirm* that divine resources of healing are available to all who are ready to receive them.

(d) Honestly *recognize the true needs* and feelings of the sick and their families, without hiding their fears and anxieties or suggesting that all is well when the situation is serious.

(e) *Acknowledge and support the work of doctors*, nurses, and any others who share in the work of healing.

These are positive principles, which turn people's thoughts to the great possibilities of healing that God provides. Prayer can be offered in confidence that God's healing presence and power are available today as they have always been, whether we experience them directly through the prayer of faith, or through the human means of medical care and pastoral support, or through a combination of means.

HEALING AND 'FAITH'

However, this does not mean that physical healing will *always* be the outcome of prayer, or indeed of medical attention. There is a dangerous teaching which says: 'If you have faith, you will be healed, so if you are not healed, this shows that you must be lacking in faith.' This over-simplistic viewpoint can cause depression, a sense of failure, and despair, when people are not healed even though they do believe and have prayed themselves and others have prayed for them. In all prayer for healing, God's sovereign plan must be acknowledged. It seems that there are some sick or disabled people whom God does not choose to heal physically, and we cannot *demand* healing from God just because *we* say *we have faith* that He is able to heal. There is no general answer to the question of why some people are healed while others are not, and this will remain a mystery until we have a fuller understanding of God's purpose in our lives, and a more complete knowledge of the way our bodies and minds work.

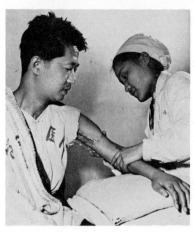

'In many cases the question *why* people suffer cannot be answered . . . the important question is what can be done to help them? . . . There are some people whom God does not choose to heal physically' (pp. 209 and 213).

The spastic girl receiving Communion at Lourdes came hoping for a cure – but continues to need her wheelchair. A Chinese workman lost hope when he lost his arm in a factory accident – but through the 'miraculous' skill of surgeons and patient care of physiotherapists he will soon use it again. What sort of counselling could help each of these people to achieve still greater wholeness?

We shall experience full and final release from sickness and suffering only when the Kingdom of God is fully revealed in the 'end of time' (Rev. 21.4). Until then we share in the pain and travail of the creation, and this includes the fact of disease and disability (Rom. 8.19–23). To expect or demand complete physical healing in this life is to confuse our present imperfect experience with the fuller blessings which will only be given when God's Kingdom is perfectly revealed.

Even so, people do sometimes come to see quite clearly why God has chosen to let them remain 'un-healed':

Example 43: Joeli, a house-builder, had been a faithful Church member and a leader in the congregation for many years. One day, as he was working on a roof, he slipped and fell, hurting his arms and back. After several weeks in hospital he was fit to come home, but was told he would never again be able to use his hands and arms properly. His days of working on buildings were over. He just sat on his verandah and watched other people working. What else could he do? Because of his interest in those around him and his concern to help them, many people came to visit Joeli as he sat there, seeking his advice about their problems. They found he had plenty of time to listen, and his wisdom and knowledge of life, and of God's grace, were really helpful to them. Joeli could no longer build houses, but he found that God had given him a new skill – the gift of wise counsel which enabled him to help people to know God better, sort out their problems, and rebuild their lives. And through using this gift he became a more mature and more *whole* person himself, even though he had not been healed in body.

Too often people think that 'healing' means physical healing only, and when this does not happen, their faith is shattered. They try to find reasons, such as their own lack of faith or failure to repent, to explain the 'failure' of their prayers. However, if we think of healing as 'wholeness' (see p. 200), we can see that it may sometimes be quite wrong to ask for and expect physical healing. Many sick people are more in need of *inner* healing as a means of returning to a right relationship with God or with others, rather than the overcoming of physical handicaps. What we can affirm is that God *is* present, and His healing power *is* available in every situation, but we cannot know in advance how this healing will be accomplished. It may be through the removal of physical sickness. It may be through the experience of inner healing of bad memories, unhappy relationships, or deep personal wounds, even while the physical sickness remains.

To try to avoid expecting or demanding physical healing to result from prayer, some people begin or end their petitions with the conditional phrase, 'If it be thy will', e.g. 'If it be thy will, O God, take away this person's sickness and restore them to strength.' Such a prayer acknowledges that our own wisdom is limited, and that God knows best what is good for us, but it can weaken our confidence that God is offering healing in every situation, though it may come in ways we do not expect. Perhaps a better way to pray is to affirm that God wills wholeness for everyone, and ask only that He will bring His healing power into the lives of those who are sick, so that they may be made whole in whatever way He sees as best for them.

At the same time we must be careful not to underestimate the importance and power of faith. In spite of all the problems and dangers involved, a strong faith in the love and power of God in Jesus Christ certainly can and does make a great difference in any situation where healing is needed.

WAYS OF PRAYING

So – is there a right way and a wrong way to pray for those who are sick? This is difficult to say, because each situation is unique, and the particular factors in each situation will determine what sort of prayer should be offered. However, it can be useful to study the sort of prayers which could be offered for the sick, and note carefully the points emphasized and the underlying principles on which the prayers are built. This is valuable because all prayer reflects people's beliefs and ideas about God, about human beings, and about the world we live in. The following examples of different prayers which could be offered in two different situations are given for purposes of evaluation.

Example 44: Pastor Lawrence received a message that Zakia, one of the Church leaders, had suffered a heart attack, and had been taken to hospital. The pastor hurried to the hospital but Zakia had been sedated and was sleeping. The doctor told the pastor that Zakia was seriously ill and must stay in hospital for several weeks; and even after that would have to rest for some time before starting work again. Zakia's wife Leah was at the hospital, and Pastor Lawrence asked how she was feeling and what she would do. Leah was very upset and anxious, and did not know how she would manage without her husband. Some of Zakia's friends, too, had come to find out how Zakia was, so the pastor drove them and Leah home to Zakia's house where the rest of the family were waiting. Pastor Lawrence went inside with the others, to offer prayers for them all in their time of sadness and difficulty.

Example of prayer (a): O Father, you are closer to us than we can understand. Help us to know that you are with us always, in joy and in pain, in sickness and in health. May your love be the rock on which we can stand when the way seems dark and the days ahead difficult. In this time of trouble, help us to find the strength that you alone can give us, so that we can continue to live our lives day by day. Help our dear Zakia in his sickness, and all his family. We commit him to you, and also those who are looking after him. In his pain give him the sense of your love and power which is at work for his healing. Through Jesus Christ our Lord.

Example of prayer (b): Help us, O God, not to be overcome by self-pity. Give us the courage to forget our own problems and suffering, and be moved by the greater need of those who are starving and dying in other parts of the world. Help Zakia's wife and family to remember that sufferings are sent to us to make us stronger in our Christian faith and character. If it is your will, restore your servant Zakia to peace and good health. Heal him, Lord, that he may continue to serve you and help others. Help us Father, to use this difficult time to think more clearly about your will for us. Bless all in this house. Through Jesus Christ our Lord.

Example 45: A young married teacher, Elias, had been sick for several weeks. At first the doctors could not discover the cause of his illness, so they sent him to hospital for a series of tests. The results showed that he had a cancer in his stomach, and would need several operations to remove it and stop it from spreading to other parts of his body. Elias was recently appointed as headmaster to a new school in a remote rural area, but had not been well enough to take up his new appointment. His wife Gwen was a regular member of the congregation, and their two children came to Sunday School. Elias himself did come to church, but only occasionally.

Pastor Jackson visited the family when Elias had just returned from hearing the result of the tests. The doctor had arranged for him to enter hospital in two days' time, and he and Gwen were both upset and worried about what might happen. They could not understand why this sickness had come to Elias. After talking with them, Pastor Jackson offered prayers for them and their family.

Example of prayer (c): O God, we praise you for the love of Jesus Christ which is for us all. We remember how Jesus faced hardship and pain, but did not complain or give up, knowing that all that happened was part of your will for Him. We think too of other people who have continued to believe in you in spite of many burdens and problems – blind people, deaf people, and sick people. Now we have this problem of our own to face, please help us to follow the example of those others who have experienced your strength in their lives, sometimes with great difficulty and trouble. We ask you to strengthen our faith and send your help and blessing on Elias as he goes into hospital, and to grant that he may eventually be restored to health. Through Jesus Christ our Lord.

Example of prayer (d): Lord God, we thank you that every part of our lives is known to you. You understand all our thoughts and feelings, and all our ways. So we realize that you know all about this problem facing Elias and his family. We pray that you will help Elias to face going into hospital with courage and hope, even though he has to accept some pain and his family may experience hardship. We pray you to help the doctors who will operate on Elias, and the nurses who will look after him. And especially, O Father, we pray that you will strengthen Elias and Gwen and their children to live through this time with cheerfulness, and accept whatever may happen as being in accordance with your will for their lives. In this time of trouble we thank you for all the good things you give us, and especially for your great love which never leaves us. For Jesus' sake. Amen.

THE SACRAMENTS

Where chronically ill or disabled people cannot attend services in church, pastors may need to arrange for them to receive the Lord's Supper at home or in hospital. Some hospitals provide facilities for regular Communion services for long-stay patients.

Sometimes, too, a very ill or dying person may express a strong desire for formal Confession and Absolution if they belong to a Church where this is practised, or for Holy Communion, and may be greatly comforted and strengthened as a result, physically as well as spiritually. It is wise for pastors to consult with the doctor or hospital authorities before arranging for this. If the pastor himself feels that a person is in need of these sacraments, he should be careful to make the suggestion tactfully and at an appropriate moment, so as not to frighten the person (or their family) into supposing their sickness is *more* serious than it really is. This is specially important where the pastor does not know the sick person very well. The doctor or nurse – (or a member of the family) – can often advise about timing, and where possible should naturally be consulted about the person's condition before administering Extreme Unction.

STUDY SUGGESTIONS

WORD STUDY

1. What is meant by a person's 'world-view'?
2. Which of the following words would you use to define 'health'?
   desire   wellbeing   happiness   security   peace   soundness   freedom   renewal   wholeness
3. List four words which mean the *opposite* of 'health'.

REVIEW OF CONTENT

4. Give two examples of each of the following:
   (a) a 'moral' cause of sickness;
   (b) a 'physical' cause of sickness.
5. What sort of sickness is sometimes described as 'psychosomatic'?
6. Describe three different 'positive' attitudes which can help people recover from sickness more quickly, and three 'negative' attitudes which are likely to hinder the process of healing.

BIBLE STUDY

7. Compare the teaching in John 5.14; John 9.3; and Luke 13.3. What connection, if any, did Jesus see between sickness and sin on the one hand, and repentance and healing on the other?

8. What was said to be the cause of sickness, as described in each of the following passages?
   (a) Deut. 28.58, 59   (b) Josh. 22.16–18   (c) 1 Sam. 1.1–7, 12–18   (d) 1 Sam. 16.14–23   (e) Jer. 31.29, 30
   (f) Mark 7.25–30   (g) Luke 8.27–33   (h) 1 Cor. 15.22, 45.

9. Read Luke chapters 4, 5, 6 and 7. From these chapters choose two examples of healing from the ministry of Jesus, and explain how these acts of healing can be interpreted as signs of the coming of the promised Messiah.

10. What do we learn from the following passages in Acts about the Church's responsibility for the ministry of healing?
    (a) 3.1–16   (b) 5.12–16   (c) 8.4–13   (d) 28.7–10.

APPLICATION, OPINION, AND RESEARCH

11. (a) What are the commonly-held ideas about 'health' in your cultural situation? Do people think and talk much about health? If so, in what ways?
    (b) If you live in a country where the establishment of medical services, either by the Church or by government, has changed people's basic ideas about health and sickness, briefly describe these changes.

12. To what extent, if at all, do you think that the Church as an organization should be involved in healing and medical work? Give your reasons.

13. Consider what you know of the work of doctors and other medical workers in your own locality, and the relationship of pastoral workers to them. Do you think there is enough co-operation between them? If not, in what practical ways could they work more closely together in the task of healing?

14. Some people say that praying for the sick is useless, either because they think that modern medicine has made prayer unnecessary, or because they believe that God's will for every person is already fixed, and prayer cannot change it. What is your own opinion of these two points of view?

15. Read again Example 38. Imagine that Kauyu has come to you as a pastor, for help, and you are visiting Monda at home in her sickness. Would you tell her to go to the medical doctor to be treated for fever, or let Kauyu call the medicine man? Or would you do both? What do you chiefly learn from this example about ministering to people who are sick?

16. Compare the Elema people's ideas about sickness (see Example 39) with the common belief of your own people. In what ways are they the same, and in what ways are they different?

17. (a) Which of the two prayers suggested in Example 44 do you think would have been most helpful for that situation? Give reasons for your choice.

    (b) Which of the principles listed on pp. 154 and 213 were followed in each of the two prayers suggested in Example 45?

    (c) What, if anything, do you find in the four prayers suggested in Examples 44 and 45 which might *not* have been helpful in the particular situation?

18. Write a short prayer for use in each of the following situations. For each prayer, say which of the principles listed on p. 213 you have followed.

    (a) A sick villager is afraid of going to hospital for an operation;

    (b) A sick man believes his sickness was caused by sorcery;

    (c) A woman has hurt both her legs in an accident, and is not expected to be able to walk again; she has to face a lifetime of pain and disablement.

19. For each of the three situations given in Question 18, choose a passage of Scripture from the lists on pp. 283f, which you might read to the sick person involved.

11

Death and Bereavement

Just as death is the one certainty which no one can deny or hope to escape, so the experience of loss and grief when somebody dies is common to all people, whatever their cultural background or social status. We can say that death is a *crisis*, not only for the person who dies, but also for the living who remain. As the anthropologist Raymond Firth has pointed out, though the outward object of any funeral is the dead person, in fact it benefits not the dead but the living.

So, too, the pastor's ministry in times of death and bereavement can be said to fall into two parts:

1. On the one hand there is the final phase of his ministry to the person who dies (for whom he may also have been caring during a period of sickness), that is, the arranging and conducting of the funeral ceremony (which also marks the beginning of his ministry to the living who are bereaved).

2. At the same time there is his *continuing* pastoral concern and care for the bereaved, perhaps over a long stretch of time.

In this chapter we shall look at these two aspects in the reverse order, chiefly discussing the care and counselling of the bereaved, with a final section about the purposes and conducting of funerals.

But before we go on to consider the experience of bereavement as one which causes many people to need counselling help, it will be useful to carry out the following study-exercise. If possible, get a friend or fellow-student to do the exercise at the same time, so that you can discuss each other's answers.

EXERCISE A

Part 1: Imagine that you are resting at home with your family. Suddenly a man runs to the house, shouting: 'In five minutes this house will be blown up, and everything in it will be destroyed. You have five minutes to leave, and you can take only *five* things with you!'

(a) Write down the five things you would choose to take, and say why you would choose those particular things.

(b) Repeat the exercise, but this time choose only *two* things to take with you. Again give your reasons for choosing those two – and for leaving three of your previous choices behind.

Now discuss your answers to this part of the exercise.

Part 2: Imagine that a close friend of yours, who has been sick for some time, comes to see you. He is very upset, and tells you that the doctor has just told him he has only six weeks to live, or even less. He asks you two questions:

    (a) What should he do?

    (b) What would you do if you were he?

As before, write down your answers, and then discuss them, if you can, with another person.

Part 3: Write down what you have learnt from Parts 1 and 2 of the exercise, about:

    (a) Your own sense of values – that is, the things you think are valuable and important;

    (b) Your attitude to the possibility of your own death.

Once again, if you can, discuss with a friend the answers you have given.

THE EXPERIENCE OF BEREAVEMENT

DEATH AS LOSS

The feelings of grief we experience when someone close to us dies are feelings which we experience, though less strongly perhaps, in other situations also. The word 'grief' itself comes from a Latin root meaning 'weighed down' or 'afflicted by heavy wrong'. So a person who 'grieves' is one who feels deep sorrow, distress, or misery.

These feelings of grief occur when we *lose* something or someone valuable to us; for example, if we lose our job, or our status and authority. We may grieve for the loss of friends or relatives who move away to another city, or for the loss of some treasured possession that is stolen from us or damaged beyond repair. Many different events produce a sense of loss, but the strongest feelings of grief are usually caused by the loss of a *person*, a close friend or relative, who dies.

PERSONAL BEREAVEMENT

The word we chiefly use for those who have suffered this sort of loss is 'bereaved', meaning deprived or robbed of something, being made destitute; and the sorrow that follows a death is often called 'bereavement'. (Note that the word 'grievance' has a different meaning from 'grief', and is normally used for some injustice or cause of complaint which makes people think they have been treated unfairly, and so feel pain or distress accompanied by anger or resentment.)

The following exercise may help to clarify this point still further.

EXERCISE B

Think carefully about each of the six events listed below, and for each event write down the answers to the following questions:

(a) What sorts of loss would you suffer in this situation?
(b) What would be your strongest feeling as a result of that loss?

Event 1: Your brother is killed in a car accident.

Event 2: You have completed a diploma course and will soon be leaving college. You realize you won't see many of your fellow students again.

Event 3: You are a parent, and have just said goodbye to your child who is going to study overseas for a few years.

Event 4: You have been dismissed from your job, where you have worked for many years.

Event 5: You have just broken your engagement with your girlfriend (or boyfriend).

Event 6: The doctor has just confirmed that you are very sick and must go into hospital for an operation.

The experience of grief as loss, and the need to care for people who have suffered bereavement, has been summed up by one writer as follows: 'Any experience which forces us to do without something or someone important to us can cause mourning. The grief we feel concerns our loss. It can happen as we face the loss of our own life, or suffer the death of a friend; with the loss of our health, a limb, our youth, our self-esteem. . . . Any of these things . . . which have become an integral part of our lives, and therefore a part of us, are involved in our identity. They help to make us what we are. To lose some or all of them is like losing something of ourselves. We feel depleted by the loss.'

GRIEF

As we have seen, people experience grief in many different situations. In this chapter we are chiefly concerned with grief experienced in the crisis of death and bereavement, when people are in particular need of pastoral care and counselling. The counsellor must understand the emotional needs of people facing death, and of people bereaved as a result of the death of someone they love. Both the dying person and those close to him or her face loss. The dying person faces the end of life, and the approach of death usually means the end of important relationships. The bereaved, and those expecting to be bereaved, face the loss of someone close and dear to them, and must adjust to the fact that their lives may be changed.

For the bereaved, grief is not merely a brief sensation which is quickly over. Usually it is a *process*, in which various emotional needs and responses are experienced over a period of time, perhaps a few weeks, but for most people many months or even years. Sometimes people become 'blocked' or trapped in one part of the process. The death of a marriage-partner may involve years of 'working through' the different stages of the process, before the widow or widower can make an adequate adjustment to their new situation.

COMMUNAL BEREAVEMENT

We should note that grief and bereavement can be a communal as well as an individual experience. Every culture recognizes the role of the community in times of bereavement. Although death chiefly affects the immediate family, many others share in the experience. This is especially so in extended family or clan systems. Then the whole family or clan mourns, and those most deeply affected receive comfort and help through the community which shares and participates in their grief. And when a national or community leader dies, the people as a whole go through the same stages of the grief process as individuals do. 'Idealization' of such leaders or famous personalities may be expressed by a whole community or by a group of admirers or fans, and a person's greatness will be loudly proclaimed but little or nothing said of their faults and weaknesses. (Or occasionally the opposite may occur, especially in the case of political leaders – e.g. Stalin and Mao Tse Tung – if their policies are discredited after their death.)

STAGES IN THE GRIEF PROCESS

Each person experiences grief in their own way, and there is no set pattern which everyone will go through. But three main stages in the process of grief have been noted by social and pastoral workers, and these stages will help us to understand what bereaved people usually experience. These stages are:

1. To start with, immediately following the death, a stage of *shock*;

2. A period of *disorganization*, in which normal living patterns are upset. For example, when the father or mother of a family dies, the bereaved members are often too confused and upset to carry on the daily routine, and the whole life of the household becomes disorganized;

3. A period of *reorganization*, during which the bereaved gradually return to a normal pattern of living.

SHOCK

The state of shock is a physical as well as an emotional condition, in which people experience a feeling of weakness, emptiness, and sometimes even collapse. If death is sudden and unexpected, then the shock may be severe, even for those not immediately connected with the person who has died. People will then feel 'stunned' by the fact of death, and may react in surprising ways. Some will weep uncontrollably, wail, shout, hit the wall, slash trees. Some refuse to believe that the death has happened; others lose the capacity to feel anything, or become confused about what has occurred; or they just sit in silence as if trying to sort out their thoughts. Feelings will be withheld or expressed, depending on each person's personality and the suddenness of the death. Pastors need to remember that people in a state of shock are often not able (or not fully able) to control their own actions and reactions.

If the death has been expected and awaited, however, shock may not be severe. In some situations death may even be welcomed by both the dying person and the bereaved, so that few if any of the feelings suggested above will be experienced.

DISORGANIZATION

The disorganization stage begins after the actual shock has passed. During this stage various aspects of people's lives may be affected, and a number of different emotions be felt.

(a) *Physical health* may suffer. Bereaved people often find it difficult to concentrate, or to sit still, or to sleep. They continue to feel weak, as in the period of shock. They may be full of aches and pains, have little or no appetite for food and no energy for work, and feel sick at the thought of meeting with other people.

(b) *Feelings and emotions* continue to be affected. As we shall see when we consider mourning customs, ways of expressing sorrow vary in different cultural situations. In some areas the bereaved are expected to express their feelings freely in crying and wailing. In Papua New Guinea one young man, attending the funeral of his uncle whom death had released from a painful illness, was literally forced to cry by his relatives, even though he himself felt happy because his dear uncle was no longer suffering. In that area anyone failing to weep was thought to lack love towards the dead person. In some other cultures, however, the open expression of grief may not be considered 'manly', so men are expected to keep their feelings under control, and leave the weeping to women.

(c) *Depression and loneliness* are very commonly felt in bereavement, and may be acute in the dead person's close relatives. 'There's nothing left for me now', they say. Or 'God doesn't care', or 'Why should it happen to me?' or even 'No one else was ever so lonely as I am!' Many of the Bible writers describe this feeling of being 'isolated' both from other people and from God. (See Pss 42 and 43: 'My soul is cast down and disquieted within me', and 'Oh God, why hast thou cast me off?'; and also Ps. 10.1: 'Why dost thou stand afar off, O Lord?') Jesus himself felt isolated and forsaken (Mark 15.34), and though the reason for these feelings was different from the depression felt in bereavement, the feelings expressed are similar.

(d) *Feelings of guilt and remorse* are common at this stage. People feel they could somehow have prevented the death by giving more care and attention, or that they neglected or behaved badly towards the person who has died. They may even feel directly responsible for the person's death, even though they had nothing to do with it and have no reason to feel guilty. Often they have a deep sense of remorse or regret for something they have said or not said to the dead person, and now feel it is 'too late'.

These feelings of guilt usually reflect the ideas and standards of the group or society to which the person belongs. If people have neglected to act in certain accepted ways, they they feel ashamed of having failed to fulfil what they think is expected of them. Christians who feel they have fallen short of Christian standards (and who has not?) often feel the need for confession and forgiveness in times of bereavement. Sometimes the feelings of guilt are so strong as to be 'neurotic' – that is, they either have no basis in fact, or they are out of all proportion to the bereaved person's actual involvement with the person who has died (see Example 35, p. 200).

(e) *Resentment and anger* are natural reactions when people are deprived of something valuable or important to them. When the 'loss' is through death this resentment may be directed towards any nurses or doctors who may have been caring for the deceased, or against members of the family or other people involved, or against the pastor (perhaps for failing to persuade God to spare the person who has died!), or even against God Himself.

A further problem may arise in cultural situations where there is a tradition of 'pay back' or vendetta. In such situations anger may be expressed in terms of 'an eye for an eye and a tooth for a tooth' (see Exod. 21.23–35; Matt. 5.38). Where members of another family or tribal group are involved, the cause of death will be investigated, and there can be no end to mourning until some form of vengeance is taken or compensation received from those held to be responsible. Such a system may lead to continued reprisals, and can poison relationships between clans and families over many years or even lifetimes.

(f) *Exaggerated fear or respect for the dead* is quite common. In areas where people believe that the spirits of the departed remain with or near the living there is often great fear of the dead, and special care is taken to show respect for the spirits so that they will do no harm. Rather similar to this is the 'idealization', or even 'idolization', of the dead, especially when one partner to a marriage dies, or one of a pair of friends who were greatly dependent on each other. Then the past relationship is treated as having been perfect in every way, all past differences and faults are forgotten, and the dead person becomes the central object in the life and thoughts of the bereaved. This attitude can prolong the period of disorganization, and prevent the bereaved from returning to normal relationships with others.

(g) *Anxiety* about the practical problems resulting from someone's death is a natural and common reaction. Who will do the work of the farm now? Who will earn the money to pay the rent and buy food and clothing? Who will do the cooking and look after the children? What decisions have to·be made about the future?

Because of this feeling of uncertainty and anxiety, people often try to make quick decisions while they are still in a state of disorganization and unable to judge the situation clearly. A pastor can help them to calm down and take things easily until they are able to take a more balanced view.

REORGANIZATION

The period of reorganization begins gradually, as the bereaved start to take up normal activities again. The dead person is still remembered, but the bereaved have accepted their loss and can now resume their own lives again.

They do not, however, return to life exactly as if nothing had happened. We sometimes say that bereaved people are 'themselves again', or that they have 'got over' the death and are now 'back to normal'. But this is rarely so. Bereavement is a deeply traumatic experience, and people become more mature in their lives – or less so – according to how they respond to it. Some people actually refuse to enter life again and remain, as it were, shut in with the dead. They continue to live in the past, and cut themselves off from present reality. Some even refuse ever to accept that the person they loved has really died and that their relationship has really ended. They then live in a sort of make-believe or fantasy world, behaving as if the dead person was still alive. When this happens, true reorganization may be delayed, or may never really take place.

In some cultures there are social customs which can hasten reorganization by helping to relieve the bereaved of their loneliness, and their fears and uncertainty about the future. In some island groups in the Pacific, and in some parts of Africa, the brother of a man who dies is expected to marry the widow as a matter of course, or at least to take her into his household. Some of the traditional customs, too, which involve offerings, including food and drink, to the spirits of the dead, can actually help the bereaved to accept the fact of physical death. Like the Christian custom of placing flowers on the grave or making a memorial gift to charity, these ways of regularly *remembering* the dead often enable people to reach the stage of reorganization more quickly.

UNDERSTANDING THE BACKGROUND

When people come face to face with death, perhaps more than at any other time, they stand in special need of pastoral care. More even than in times of sickness they need the help and support of an *understanding* and caring 'shepherd', and the reassurance that God is with them in their desolation. In 2 Cor. 1.3–7 St Paul emphasized the great importance of this ministry of comfort: 'the God and Father of our Lord Jesus Christ . . . comforts us in all our affliction, so that we may be able to comfort those who are in any affliction, with the comfort with which we ourselves are comforted by God. For as we share abundantly in Christ's sufferings, so through Christ we share abundantly in comfort too. If we are afflicted, it is for your comfort and salvation; and if we are comforted, it is for your comfort.'

Although the emotional reactions to bereavement through death, and the stages in the grief process which we have discussed, are common to all peoples, a pastor needs to *understand the particular background* to each situation if he is to help and counsel the bereaved effectively. Just as in helping the sick, there are certain things he needs to *know*. These are of four main sorts:

1. *The mourning (and funeral) customs* of the people concerned. (In most areas he should also be familiar with the local facilities for burial, cremation, or other funerary arrangements.)

2. *The ideas and beliefs about death and the afterlife* held by the person who has died and by the bereaved family. These may or may not be those generally held in the area. In most areas accepted mourning customs reflect the generally-held ideas about death, but where social customs are changing there may be a conflict between the two which the pastor will need to recognize.

3. *The teaching of the Church about death and the afterlife*, and about mourning and funerals, and especially how this teaching agrees with or differs from the ideas and beliefs of the bereaved and of people in the area generally.

4. The pastor also needs to know something of *the social and economic situation of the bereaved*, who may need practical help in making arrangements for the funeral, as well as long-term support through the various stages of the grief process and the reorganization of their daily lives.

Much of this knowledge the pastor will gain in the course of his everyday ministry, from observing and listening to the people he

'Some traditional customs can help the bereaved to face the fact of physical death' (p. 227).

The Hindu custom of making offerings to the spirits, like the Christian custom of placing flowers on the family grave, can help the young man in Sri Lanka and the father and child in Sweden to reach the stage of reorganization more quickly. What are the chief differences in the ideas about death on which these two customs are based?

meets. But some details he may have to learn in the immediate situation, for example, as may happen in a town or city, when he is asked to conduct a funeral or give counsel for a family he knows only slightly or perhaps not at all.

Often formal mourning has already begun by the time the pastor is called to the bereaved, so it will be helpful to look at some examples of typical mourning customs in different parts of the world, before we go on to discuss in more detail the ideas and beliefs about death and the afterlife on which such customs are based.

MOURNING CUSTOMS

Every culture has its own particular mourning customs, or formal ways of expressing people's emotional reactions to death. These customs, as we have said, reflect the generally held ideas about life and death, and in mixed societies they may also differ according to people's religious affiliation. What is accepted in one area and by one group may be regarded as improper in another. Ways of mourning also change over time, following changes in people's ideas and social behaviour. The following are some examples of such customs, and show some of the similarities and differences between them.

Example 46: In the Gulf region of Papua New Guinea the time of mourning, and especially of burial, is a very solemn and holy time, similar to the Holy Day of God. No work is done, and there is no singing, talking, or noise. The whole community mourns quietly together. In the New Hebrides, too, mourning is a time for quietness and silence, with no talking or singing, and everyone mourns for the grieving family. But here the mourning period lasts for at least a week, during which no work will be done. Everyone remains in their houses, and immediate family members may stay indoors even longer than the prescribed week. Some of the Eskimo peoples in Northern Canada keep very quiet and do no work for several days after a death. And they refrain from using any sharp or pointed tools such as knives, axes, or needles, for fear of injuring the ghost of the dead person, which is thought to remain near the body and to be likely to harm any mourner who strikes or angers it.

Example 47: We can compare these examples with customs in one area of the Philippines, where the close family members stay awake for three days and nights, keeping watch around the dead body. During this time there is much crying, and also much talking, especially by people outside the family who come to visit the bereaved and pay their respects to the dead. But this often becomes an opportunity for more noisy activities such as table games and gambling, and conversing with new friends. Similarly the 'wakes' or vigils beside a corpse, which are still the custom among rural people in some Western countries, have sometimes been accompanied by music and revelry, as relatives and friends gather together to honour the dead by attending the funeral.

OTHER CUSTOMS

In many countries mourning is marked by some outward sign, such as the wearing of special clothes, especially by widows. In the New Hebrides men grow beards, family members refrain from washing for a certain period, and the women put wet ash on their foreheads. In most countries of the West it was until recently customary for both men and women to wear black clothes, and many men still wear a black tie, hat-band, or arm-band at a funeral. The custom is now dying out except for very formal occasions, though among poorer people of the eastern Mediterranean countries a widow, unless she remarries, will probably wear black for the rest of her life.

In some Aboriginal tribes in Australia, and also among some North American Indians, the bereaved change their names, either for a fixed period of mourning or permanently, so that the ghost of the dead person will not recognize and trouble them. For the same reason many American Indian peoples traditionally refrained from mentioning the names of the dead for fear the ghosts would come at the call, and this taboo is still a part of present-day mourning customs. It has even been the custom in some areas for close relatives to express their grief by self-mutilation, such as lopping off part of a finger, or an ear-lobe.

IDEAS ABOUT DEATH

Obviously people's ideas about death vary according to their cultural background and religious beliefs.

Many people today, especially in the developed countries of both East and West, believe that 'death is the end'. They think that when a person dies their life is totally extinguished, like the light of a candle when it is blown out. Those who call themselves scientific humanists, for example, and many Marxists, do not believe in any sort of afterlife at all. They do look forward to a perfect society where all men will live in peace and plenty. But they expect human beings to achieve this 'heaven' for themselves, in this world, by political or technological means – provided of course that warring nations do not destroy themselves and the world itself in the meantime.

People who follow the great Eastern religions, Hindus and Buddhists, for example, believe in the doctrines of *samsara* and *karma* – a long process of recurring deaths and rebirths. Each soul or being, they say, goes through many quite separate lives or states of existence depending on the good or evil they have done, before finally attaining to *moksha* or *nirvana*, the state of supreme bliss and freedom from change.

Both Jews and Muslims, like Christians, believe in a day of judgement and an afterlife in which God will 'reward the obedient and punish transgressors'. Jews also believe in the coming of a Messiah and the resurrection of the dead, but not until some time in the future.

At present, however, many people, especially in the West, seem unwilling to accept the idea of death, and tend to treat any direct reference to dying and death as taboo. Instead, when a person dies, they say he has 'passed on', or 'departed', or is 'resting in peace'. Even among Christians, phrases like 'fallen asleep' or 'gone to be with the Lord' are used to express the fact of death (see 1 Thess. 4.13).

SOME TRADITIONAL IDEAS

Nearly all the peoples who follow 'traditional' religions believe that the spirits or ghosts of the dead live on, either in 'heaven', or close to their former homes, or in a special 'land of the departed' which different peoples associate with different locations. Some believe it to be below the earth, or on special mountains, or beyond the sea or a great river.

Unlike Westerners, most of these peoples regard death in a very realistic and factual way. Children as well as adults are in constant contact with death and accept it as a part of living. The death of older people, especially, is accepted as a perfectly normal occurrence: 'he had reached the end of his road', or 'it was her turn to die', they say.

The death of younger people, however, is regarded very differently, and is usually believed to be caused by some sort of sorcery, either by another person, or directly by the spirits. This is because they also believe that the spirits of those that have died have power over the living, either to protect, or to harm anyone who disturbs their resting place or angers them by breaking some tribal law or custom. Often there is extreme fear of special sorts of death, e.g. by witchcraft, or the death of particular people such as sorcerers or warriors. When a young person dies, therefore, the death is carefully investigated to find out who was responsible, and if evidence of some bad action is found, then this must be 'paid back' or avenged. The following example from Southern Africa shows how many bereaved families feel and behave in areas where belief in the power of spirits is strong. (It also shows how Christians are often unable to offer any real comfort, or to convince others of the power of Christ over all creation.)

Example 48: As we visit a house where one of the family has died, even in their first shock and sorrow the relatives soon begin to ask questions which will determine what they will do next: 'What is the reason for the death of our loved one? Who is responsible? An enemy? Or the ancestors? Why did it happen?'

As these thoughts take shape, some will call in a diviner to find the evil cause, some will meditate on the question themselves, but fear and suspicion creep into all hearts. No one accepts death as a natural event until a person reaches the normal age limit. Everything that happens to a person before that time is believed to be caused by either good or evil supernatural powers, At this time of crisis the family believe that the utmost caution is needed to prevent further evil from coming. As peace and balance are lost, the evil power may strike again. To protect against this, every word and move must be watched.

In some situations the faith of any Christian friends and neighbours present ought to prove its healing power, and calm these fears. The Christians show compassion, sitting silently or discussing the events in a low voice. They offer all kinds of neighbourly help, and in general show a marvellous solidarity. But others do the same, either because it is customary or from fear that to hold back might cause suspicion, or out of love or friendship. No one speaks openly of their fears, but the general sense of helplessness and apathy is expressed in such phrases as 'God must still be there'. When Christians continue to express the traditional outlook in similar terms: 'It must be God's will', they have no real comfort to give the mourners. They rarely take their Bibles with them to a house of mourning, and even those who do intend to testify to Christ's power to comfort and heal, often fail to do so.

Clearly, then, the subject of death raises many questions for Christians: questions regarding traditional beliefs about the spirits of the departed, about the relationship between the living and the dead, and about the meaning of the gospel hope of eternal life. The pastor who seeks to help people at this time needs to study these questions, and clarify his own ideas, if he is to offer guidance about the truths of the Christian gospel which may help people to resolve their fears and confusion. This task is perhaps especially important in countries where the coming of modern education, and the change from rural to city life, have been undermining the whole system of traditional beliefs and practices relating to death and the afterlife, but do not offer any single undisputed system of beliefs in its place.

FROM TRADITIONAL BELIEF TO CHRISTIAN HOPE

Where Christians are really strong in their faith, however, they *can* overcome the fear of spirit powers, even in areas where the Church is in a minority. The following examples show how Christians have interpreted the gospel as bringing victory over the forces of death and evil, and how traditional religion can sometimes provide a foundation on to which gospel truths can be built.

Example 49: In the late 1960s a Christian graveyard cult developed among the Enga people in the Highlands of Papua New Guinea. Unlike the many 'cargo' cults which have developed in the islands of Melanesia, it offered its members no expectations of material wealth, like the 'cargoes' brought by traders and missionaries, to come to them from across the sea. This cult remained, as it began, within the Church; yet it raised many questions for Christians. Here is a description of its activities:

'Dawn is breaking on Sunday morning. The Christians have washed ceremoniously and put on their best clothes. Now they form into a long line and walk silently and reverently along the path to the village to the well-kept cemetery. There, they sit in rows while the pastor leads in singing a traditional chant with Christian words:

> We live in darkness,
> Yes we sat there,
> We were spoiled there,
> Lord Jesus, you shine like the sun in heaven,
> Come – come, and redeem us.

Then they pray, thanking God for sending Jesus, who has released them from the power of darkness and evil spirits. The cult leader then tells of his latest vision, in which Christ revealed that, from now on, cult members should wash their hands before eating, and after going to the toilet. Next, the leader reads Matthew 10, emphasizing that Jesus, who was sent by God, in turn commissioned men to go out and do God's work, and especially to: "heal the sick, cleanse the lepers, raise the dead, cast out devils; freely you have received, freely give." It is our task, the leader says, to go into the world to do the work of Christ. Christ has delivered us, we must go out to cleanse and deliver others.

'Then the leader asks: "Who has been delivered by Christ?" The congregation reply: "We all have." Again he asks: "Are you willing to go out in His name?" And they reply: "Yes, we are!"

'The leader continues to question the people: "In the past when strangers came, did you welcome them hospitably?" "No!" "What will you do now?" "We will take them into our homes and look after them. Even the Europeans may live freely among us."

'The preacher then works through the Bible passage in detail, ending with yet another question: "Have we all received Christ?" "No, many have cast Him out."

'"Have all the people received our teaching?" "No, many are rejecting it."

'Finally the worshippers sing another chant. Prayers are offered, and they say the benediction. Some worshippers then wander back to the village, others sit talking of the things God is doing among them.'

This cult began when a local school-teacher and leader in the Baptist church, named Pyanjuwa, received a series of visions. Christ, he said, appeared in bright clothing and told him to clear away the undergrowth and plant a lawn in the old graveyard near the church, and hold dawn services there twice a week.

These services became very popular, and people came from other Churches in the neighbourhood.

The cult received a strong impetus when a pastor's handbook was published in the local language, containing a newly translated Scripture reading (1 Thess. 4.13–18) in the section on Christian burial. Pyanjuwa specially emphasized vv. 16 and 17: 'For the Lord Himself shall descend from heaven with a shout . . . and the dead in Christ shall rise first. Then we who are alive and remain shall be caught up together with them in the clouds.' To the Enga people this was a thrilling confirmation of what they had always believed about the essential unity of the dead and the living. In the traditional religion of the area, ancestor spirits were believed to live around the houses and gardens, joining in feasts, and regulating much of the villagers' social lives. The living and the dead would be finally united in the spirit world. Graveyards for many miles around were cleaned up and shrubs planted, and it seemed likely that the movement would spread.

Many pastors saw this cult as an opportunity for renewal in the Churches, but others condemned its emphasis on beliefs from the old religion. The Church District Executive agreed that to ban the cult would send it underground, but decided not to encourage it either until there had been time to observe its results.

The practice of holding regular services in graveyards has developed elsewhere too.

Example 50: On Easter Sunday at Msealama in South Africa the Christians meet at the Church, but instead of going inside they walk in silent procession to the graveyard, led by the pastor. There, as the sun rises, a short service is held, with hymns, prayers, Gospel reading, and sermon, as the people sit among the graves. The Pastor recalls the first Easter, linking it with their own lives, the rising sun, and the dead below – proclaiming Christ's victory over all. The people truly feel one brotherhood, united in joy and hope with their Christian ancestors. After the final prayer and hymn of adoration, they all shake hands and greet each other in the Name of Christ, in love and reconciliation where before there was suspicion and fear. Then they place flowers on the graves before going home.

This sort of service has become customary in many places, and means much to many Christians. But some other Christians have doubts about what really takes place at such services. They ask such questions as: 'Don't you see that the people are actually worshipping their ancestors? Why do they put cups on the graves? Why do they prefer the graveyard instead of the church nearby? Why do they flock together in such large numbers, while at regular services which should proclaim Christ's victory every Sunday, the church is often empty?'

We too may ask questions about these new sorts of service: Is this a valid way of expressing the gospel? Or is it dangerous? Is it bringing a new type of paganism into the Church? These questions have been troubling Christian leaders for many years. Many have concluded that Christian beliefs and ancestral rites are wholly opposed to each other, and most of the Churches have given a strong 'no' to any suggestion that prayers for ancestors should be incorporated in the Church ritual. Some Church leaders have refused even to discuss the matter.

But this has not solved the problem. The traditional beliefs and rituals have not ceased, and even where they have 'gone underground', they still appear in ceremonies connected with funerals. Sometimes they are performed in secret apart from the Christian services, or they may be disguised, and given a Christian flavour, or joined with elements of Christian worship.

The overall result is *confusion*, as the old beliefs and the new either exist side by side or are mixed together. This is a pressing problem for many young Christians, and especially for Christian pastors, who have a strong love for their newly independent countries, and may feel that some return to the traditions of the past is actually a part of their national duty. As one Church worker in Africa has written: 'Today, many African Christians are experiencing a sort of "schizophrenia", in which conflicting ideas and actions exist side by side. As different needs arise in their lives they derive comfort from more than one source. Believers may enjoy the Easter service, but in times of distress they will ask a diviner to pray for them to the ancestors over whom Christ's resurrection power has been proclaimed. Thus the uniqueness of Christ's victory is at stake. Christianity becomes something to be put on at certain times and in particular circumstances, but has nothing to do with other areas of life.' However, a student in Kenya noted that for some Christians the opposite is true: 'They do often accept traditional customs, but when faced with death which they know they cannot avert, their Christian faith is their ultimate refuge.'

Example 51: comes from a Roman Catholic missionary in Melanesia: 'Sometimes people come to the parish priest asking him to pray and say Mass because their pigs are dying, their children are sick, or the harvest is failing. But often this is the second step. They have already killed a chicken or pig in the cemetery. Now they want to try the Christian way in case the traditional way does not work. In European thinking these two things do not go together. In the thinking of the people they fit quite well. What can we do if people use both ways of praying?'

As Louis Luzbetak describes it, this 'double standard' found in some new (and also in some not so new) Christian communities is a result of what he calls 'uneven culture change'. In many countries there are individuals who attend Church services and religious instruction very faithfully, but who also consult diviners, offer sacrifices to ancestors or major gods, and attend seances in order to communicate with the dead. While professing the Christian doctrine of heaven and hell they still somehow feel that the departed souls of their relatives have joined their pre-Christian ancestors and live with them in the ancestral burial place.

Pastors therefore need to analyse the traditional beliefs of their people and the mourning and funeral practices based upon them, rather than giving an authoritarian 'no'. They need to ask such questions as: What ethical and religious truth, if any, do these beliefs and practices embody? What was and is their psychological and social value to the community? What should be the pastor's approach to these beliefs and practices, and how far must they be rejected as contradicting the truths of the gospel?

These are questions which pastors need to ask in the so-called 'secular', 'materialist', and 'rationalist' cultures of the West, as well as in areas to which Christianity has come only recently. As the sociologist Peter L. Berger has pointed out, what a true 'rationalist' would call 'superstition' is still very strong in Europe and America. In a fairly recent study of American students, only 48% admitted to a belief in the God worshipped by Christians and Jews alike, but 80% expressed a 'need for religious faith'. In an opinion poll in West Germany, 68% said they believed in God, but 86% admitted to praying; and according to studies made in England, nearly 50% of those questioned had consulted a fortune teller, more than 15% believed in ghosts, and 6% claimed to have seen one! Indeed, in some places where Christianity is fairly new, it is the new Christians who most strongly reject the old ideas.

Example 52: The sound of crying came from the house of Nikodemo, a well-known Sudanese Christian. 'Oh, O-o-oh! Rebekah has died! Oh my dear wife Rebekah! Oh my mother, my mother! Oh dear, oh dear, O-o-oh!' The neighbours ran to find out what had happened, and quickly carried the news to Christian friends. Everyone felt very shocked, because everyone loved Rebekah – a good wife, a wonderful mother, and her faith was strong. But in spite of their sorrow the Christians began to praise God, because He had taken Rebekah to be with Him in heaven. 'Death is not the end of all things,' they said. 'We mustn't be too sad. We are sure she is with the Lord now.' So they sang as they carried her body to the graveyard, remembering that though Rebekah's body would be buried, her spirit was alive in Jesus. But when they returned to the house the traditional mourners arrived: 'Ai-ee!' they wailed. 'What shall we do? Rebekah is dead. Who has bewitched her? It must have been a jealous enemy! We must avenge her. Ai-ee!' The women mourners rolled on the ground, and the men threw dust on their heads, dancing and beating the drums. Rebekah's children had been comforted by the Christian's singing, but now they began to cry again, and Nikodemo felt his heart would burst. But then he took courage and stood up. 'My friends,' he said, 'it is good you have come, but I don't want you to mourn like this. We have a new way of life in this home, and Rebekah now has a new life in the family of Christ, in the home He has prepared for her in heaven. So we are not crying loudly like people who have no hope. I don't mean that the old ways are all bad, but for us Christ has made everything new.'

Clearly, the subject is a very complex one, and the conclusions we reach may vary from one situation to another. But the problems involved are so important for pastoral care that every pastor needs some understanding of how they affect the people he serves, and what his own ideas and attitudes should be in each situation.

VALUES AND DEFICIENCIES IN
TRADITIONAL BELIEFS

The following are some of the ways in which the social and religious *values* in traditional beliefs can be compared to those we find in the Christian understanding of death:

(a) Traditional beliefs in the ability of ancestors and spirits of the departed to influence daily life answer the deep human need for a living contact with the unseen world. They reflect man's awareness that he is not the master of life, but depends on a higher power than himself, a watchful and protective power which demands his respect, obedience, and worship. The South African 'poet of protest', Dennis Brutus, may have been thinking of political power rather than divine power when he wrote:

Not in my hands
Is the clay of my life.

But these words express very clearly what many people believe.

This approach to life, with the idea of a close relationship between the living and the dead, is very different from much Western thinking, in which man is regarded as self-reliant, self-sufficient, and free from the influence of any spiritual or supernatural power.

(b) Traditional beliefs answer some of man's uncertainties, and seem to justify his compelling natural instinct to survive. Death is not seen as the end to life, but simply as a transition to another sort of living.

(c) Traditional beliefs ensure that the ties which bind a clan or tribal community together are preserved, even when people die and leave this present life. The tribe thus becomes an unending fellowship, bound together by the continual inter-action of the living and the departed, and by their common respect for tribal traditions.

(d) Belief in the power of departed ancestors and other spirits to punish the living for breaking the tribal law and custom helps to preserve moral values. It also provides a supernatural foundation and framework for the group's ethical system, and thus a religious basis for ethical training.

(e) Belief that departed ancestors can act as intermediaries reflects the idea that man needs always to approach the Supreme God in a spirit of reverence and fear.

(f) These traditional beliefs preserve a 'world view' which treats both this present life and the spirit world seriously. In some ways such beliefs provide a starting point for the revelation of God in the Christian gospel.

Does all this mean that these traditional beliefs can be so adapted and interpreted that they actually *become* the gospel for those who hold them? These beliefs certainly keep religious and spiritual attitudes strong. But do they provide fully true answers to people's questions about life and death?

In contrast to these positive values, pastors will recognize certain *deficiencies and dangers* which are common to many of the traditional beliefs about death and the after-life. For example:

(a) Where belief in ancestor spirits is strong and actively practised, there is a danger that people will start to think of these spirits as if they were gods. From regarding the spirits as 'intermediaries' between God and man, people come to see them as holding the authority and power which really belong to God alone. And soon they begin to think that God Himself is far removed from their daily lives, and very different from the description we find in the Bible, where He is shown to be not only all-powerful, but ever-present and working, loving and sustaining His people in every situation.

(b) Very deep respect for ancestors can sometimes lead people to worship them in place of God. Many people insist that they give respect rather than worship to the ancestors and departed spirits. But there is always a danger that respect will merge into dependence, and worship will be given to God's creatures, rather than to the Creator Himself. Man must love God above all else, and no spirits can become a substitute for Him.

(c) Although departed spirits are believed to have magical powers, they are still regarded as having the same human characteristics as when they were living on earth. They have no more than human wisdom and sinful human reactions to offer. So how can they provide the answers 'from outside ourselves' which we all seek? Only God Himself can provide the true wisdom to answer human need.

(d) The spirits are believed to protect the traditions and values of the group, and to punish any neglect of customary rites and laws unless they are propitiated by sacrifices and other rituals. But there seems to be no suggestion that God Himself offers forgiveness to those who have rebelled and offended against His laws, if only they will repent of their sin and return to Him in love and humility. Ritual accuracy is what the spirits call for, rather than true repentance.

(e) Although some people feel respect and gratitude towards the spirits, many others fear them, and are chiefly concerned to escape their unpleasant and threatening influence. There seems to be little real desire for close communion with the departed, nor any idea of the loving relationship which God offers.

(f) Most people seem to approach departed spirits in the hope of gaining material benefits and security. This reflects the universal human need for survival, that is, to maintain physical life in this world (Greek: *bios*). But it has little to do with the higher sort of life which God offers through the gospel, that is, eternal life and communion with Him in Christ (Greek: *zoe*).

(g) Belief in ancestral spirits may be strong, and the supposed powers of the spirits very great. But the influence of these spirits is nevertheless limited to the people who belong to the particular group concerned. The benefits of these beliefs are not open to 'outsiders'. They stand in direct contrast to the good news of the gospel which offers to *all* people the hope of belonging to the one world-wide fellowship of God's family.

FROM DEATH INTO LIFE: THE GOSPEL TEACHING

As we have seen, a pastor must be able to offer systematic teaching of the gospel message if he is to minister effectively to the bereaved. The following summary of the gospel truths which chiefly need emphasis in this situation may be used as a basis for further discussion and study.

GOD THE CREATOR

The God shown in the Scriptures is the one great living God who is Creator and sustainer of the whole physical universe, including our planet Earth, and of all things in it: the world of nature, the world of human beings, and the world of spiritual beings also. No part of Creation is outside His constant concern, and all life comes from Him. Many people recognize Him as Creator, but not all take Him seriously. Some think of Him rather as an absent land-owner, who long ago set the world going and then left it to run according to certain laws, with man in charge to manage it on His behalf (Gen. 1.27, 28; 2.15). But

God is not absent or ineffective, and He has not transferred His powers to any other beings. As Creator, He rules and is present in all the events of life.

SIN AND DEATH

According to the Scriptures, death was not God's original intention for man. Death came into the world because man disobeyed God's command (Gen. 2.16, 17; 3.6). 'Death spread to all men because all men sinned' (Rom. 5.12), and with death came suffering and fear. Only when we recognize the seriousness of our sin and rebellion against God can we fully understand the seriousness of death. And only when we recognize God as Creator do we understand that when we rebel against Him we are guilty of idolatry. This happens whenever people give to some part of God's creation (e.g. heavenly bodies, spiritual forces, physical objects, or man himself) the respect and fear and obedience that are due to God alone. Then we 'exchange the truth about God for a lie and serve the creature rather than the creator' (see Rom. 1.25). Only God Himself can save us from the consequences of our rebellion, that is, from the power of death. And He does this through Jesus Christ. By His own death and resurrection Jesus has overcome the power of sin, and He offers victory over death to all who will receive new life through Him (1 Cor. 15.55–58). Jesus holds the keys of death and of the place of the dead (Rev. 1.18). Without Christ, death is final, but through Him death is conquered and the power of departed spirits is controlled. This means that those who know and accept the power of Jesus in their lives have no need to fear the presence of the dead or the power of departed spirits.

JESUS: 'LORD OF ALL'

By His resurrection Jesus shows Himself to be 'Lord both of the dead and of the living' (Rom. 14.9). By His descent into Hades, the place of departed spirits, and by His ascension to the Father, He shows Himself to be victor over all powers, all angels, all spirits, and all natural and supernatural forces (1 Pet. 3.18, 19 and see Eph. 4.8–10). He is 'pre-eminent' and supreme over all things (see Col. 1.15–18). He has broken the influence of all evil spirits (see Col. 2.15: 'disarm the principalities and powers', RSV; 'strip the spiritual rulers and author-ities of their power', TEV). When we accept that all these spiritual forces are under Christ's control they have no power to harm us. Nor do we need to seek help from any spirit in order to approach God, because direct access to the Father's grace is given us through Jesus Christ (Eph. 2.18). We need not pray to any spiritual beings, nor seek to please or placate them by special offerings, rituals, or taboos.

JESUS: 'MEDIATOR', 'GREAT HIGH PRIEST'

In some African tribes the people were not allowed to approach the chief except through a headman. This applied to everyone except the chief's son, who could go direct to his father. Under the gospel there is no need for any such 'headman' to act as intermediary between man and God. The New Testament contains many descriptions of Jesus as a 'forerunner' who goes first to prepare the way for others to follow. This idea of Jesus as one who opens the way into a new life (see below) is strengthened by the further descriptions of Him as 'a merciful and faithful high priest' (Heb. 2.14–18; 4.14–16), the 'mediator between God and men' (1 Tim. 2.5), who is 'able for all time to save those who draw near to God through him, since he always lives to make intercession for them' (Heb. 7.25). By His sacrifice, Jesus becomes the new and living way to the Father. Having Himself lived a fully human life He perfectly understands us. He is able to bring God's mercy and help to all needy people, and also to bring their needs and requests to God. He is always available as our high priest and mediator, so other mediators or spirit helpers are unnecessary.

JESUS: 'PIONEER', 'LEADER', 'FORERUNNER', 'FIRSTBORN'

The Greek word *archegos*, which is used to describe Jesus, is translated as 'pioneer' in Hebrews 2.10 and 12.2, and as 'one who leads' in Acts 3.15 (TEV). As William Barclay explains: 'It describes someone who originates and initiates something. . . . The *archegos* is the first to do something or discover something . . . the person who blazes the trail for others to follow.' Jesus Himself told His disciples: 'Where I am going . . . you shall follow afterwards. . . . I go to prepare a place for you . . . that where I am you may be also' (John 13.36; 14.2, 3). And Paul in his letters emphasized the closeness of the link between Jesus and those who are His followers. Jesus is not only the pioneer who is above all others and first in all things. He is so closely linked to man that we can think of Him as 'the firstborn among many brethren' (Rom. 8.29); 'the beginning, the firstborn from the dead', that is, the eldest brother in God's family, who becomes the beginning of the new creation (see Col. 1.15–18): 'the first fruits of those who have fallen asleep . . . in whom all shall be made alive' (1 Cor. 15.20–23).

We notice that all these descriptions show Jesus as one who is *first*, with the whole of Creation, all powers and spirits, and all who accept Him as Lord, following after. He is also *before* all others in time. So every Christian becomes joined to One who is before and superior to any tribal or national ancestors. Those who are 'in Christ' share in a history which goes back beyond any tribal memories, beyond even the creation of man. They are members of their own earthly family and tribe or nation, but they also become members of a larger family of whom Christ is the firstborn, the pioneer.

And not only is Jesus *first*, he is also *last*: 'I am the Alpha and the Omega' (i.e. the first and last letters of the Greek alphabet) '. . . who is and who was and who is to come', 'the beginning and the end' (Rev. 1.8; 21.6). He dominates the past, the present, and the future.

JESUS: THE 'SECOND ADAM'

St Paul, in his letters to the Romans and the Corinthians, explained more fully this idea of Jesus as pioneer and 'author of life' (Acts 3.15, RSV), and also 'the same yesterday and today and for ever' (Heb. 13.8). Paul showed how the reconciliation of sinful man with God, by Jesus as representative of all mankind, on the cross, is to be understood in the context of world history: 'At the right time . . . while we were yet sinners . . . we were reconciled to God by the death of His son. . . . As sin came into the world through one man and death through sin. . . . So by one man's obedience many will be made righteous. . . . So that grace might reign through righteousness to eternal life' (see Rom. 5).

The first Adam belongs to the 'old order', representing the sinful human race whose rebellion against God brought death and sin into the world. Jesus, by His act of justification, has founded the 'new order' which is open to all mankind under God's grace. 'The first Adam . . . came from the earth: the second Adam came from heaven' (1 Cor. 15.45, TEV), and 'as in Adam all die, so in Christ shall all be made alive' (1 Cor. 15.22).

So we see that Christ as the second Adam may be called the one great ancestor, the 'chief ancestor' who is before and above all other ancestors. This order or line is based on grace, not on natural birth. As men and women become joined to Him they become members of His 'new creation' (2 Cor. 5.17), the new family of God which is the Church. This new community over-rides all cultural, racial, tribal, and national boundaries, and membership of it is open to all who respond to Christ, its chief and head. As in tribal societies where the riches of the chief are owned and shared by all, so in the Church the riches of Christ's salvation are owned and shared by all who follow Him. And as Christ stands solid with them, so He enables them to stand solid with each other, bound together in a common commitment to Him who is their common ancestor and their hope for the future. This does not mean that under Him the human ties of traditional societies and nations are destroyed; on the contrary, they are fulfilled and trans-formed.

THE GOSPEL AND THE ANCESTORS

To sum up, what do these facts of the gospel which we have been discussing mean as far as belief in the power of ancestor spirits is concerned?

1. Christians no longer need to fear or propitiate ancestor spirits. Christ is supreme over all spiritual powers; He is the source of all genuine spiritual help.

2. Those who have died in Christ, together with the living, belong to one family under Christ their head. Those who have died in Christ are seen as mothers and fathers in the faith; and are to be honoured, respected, and greeted in fellowship, especially at such times as Easter and in the Holy Communion. They are part of the 'communion of saints', in which the living and the dead are united as they look towards the second coming of Christ. The living and the dead 'saints' in Christ share a relationship not only of common blood ties, but of the Holy Spirit.

3. We may ask: What then is the relationship between Christians and their ancestors who did not know Christ? This is not an easy question to answer, but we find some references in the New Testament to those who have died without knowledge of the gospel. They are not shut out from the wide scope of Christ's salvation. He is Lord of the spiritual realm (see 1 Pet. 3.18–22). These verses have been interpreted by some Christians to suggest that in some way the gospel has been made known to those who lived before Christ, and who have passed to the spirit world. They too have been given the opportunity to accept or reject the gospel. Romans 2.6–26 shows that the standard by which God judges is related to the knowledge of the light which has been received. God judges in mercy those who have tried to live according to the light they have received. All who die, with or without knowledge of God's salvation, will come to His judgement (2 Cor. 5.10; 1 Pet. 4.5, 6). And the Scriptures affirm the general principle that 'the Judge of all the world shall do right' (Gen. 18.25).

It is quite clear, then, that for Christians Jesus Christ is the only Saviour, and the fulness of God's salvation is to be found only in Him. But human wisdom is limited, and the full details of how God's purpose and plan for His creation will be fulfilled are beyond our understanding. It is difficult to say more in a brief way without interpreting the Bible text in ways to suit our own wishes and inclinations.

Pastors need to proclaim these facts of the gospel in their regular teaching and preaching, and not only when counselling the bereaved or in funeral and memorial addresses. Unless people have some basis of Christian truth on which to build, effective pastoral counselling on matters relating to death and to the relationship between the living and the dead is difficult to give.

In very many areas today, people who claim to be 'in Christ' nevertheless continue to regulate their lives in ways which show that they still believe in the power of spirits of the dead, or the stars, or other spiritual forces, to influence events on earth (see p. 237 above). The Scriptures teach that this is wrong, and therefore should not be part of a Christian's daily practice (see Col. 2.8–23). However, we cannot deny that certain people do seem to be gifted with a spiritual sensitivity that most of us do not have. Nor can we deny that God may choose to reveal Himself and His purposes to particular individuals in ways we do not understand. But it does mean that the Pastor's own attitude to those who claim to be spirit mediums, or to receive visions and other mystical experiences, should be an open yet cautious one.

THE CHRISTIAN ATTITUDE TO MEDIUMS

Many people claim to be able to contact ancestors and other spirits. In the West, there are 'spiritualist' groups who meet regularly with such mediums in the hope of receiving messages from departed relatives and friends. In countries where continuing contact with the dead is an integral part of traditional religion, mediums may hold a respected and powerful position in society. Many of them support their claims by strange behaviour, and utterances which suggest that they are speaking under the control of a spiritual power.

However, pastors should not simply accept these claims to contact and spiritual knowledge without careful evaluation. They may be true or they may be false. Some of those who claim to be mediums are really seeking to gain power over others, or they simply want to make money. On the other hand, a pastor should not reject such claims merely because he cannot understand them. Some people do have abilities which others do not share, and always the question should be asked: 'Are these claims true?'

Even more important, the pastor needs to ask: 'In what name and by what power does the medium exercise these abilities? Do the messages and revelations come from God, or from Satan?'

The New Testament teaches that the spiritual forces could be demons, not departed spirits. Satan is a master of disguise, even appearing sometimes as an angel of light (2 Cor. 11.12–15). So the pastor needs to 'test the spirits' to see whether or not 'they are of God' (1 Cor. 12.2, 3; 1 John 4.1–3). New Testament writers warned the early Christians against being deceived by spirits posing as good, when they are in fact harmful (1 Tim. 4.1; 2 Cor. 11.3, 4, 14, 15; Rev. 12.9). So the pastor must ask: 'Is the revelation received through this medium in harmony with the revelation of God given in Jesus Christ? Does it contradict or support the plain teaching of Scripture? Does it call for the offering of a sacrifice or worship to spiritual beings rather than Christ Himself? Does it encourage trust in Christ, or the use of other powers through ritual and magic?

THE ROLE OF THE PASTOR

Earlier in this chapter we referred to the role of the pastor in times of death and bereavement by quoting Paul's words to the Christians at Corinth: 'To comfort those who are in any affliction with the comfort with which we ourselves are comforted by God' – the God 'who raises the dead' (2 Cor. 1.4, 9). Of course the various attitudes and methods of counselling discussed in previous chapters are to be considered and applied at this time, as the pastor thinks best. But pastors may also find that some of the words in 2 Corinthians 1 give special clues to the ways in which a pastor should go about his ministry in a bereavement situation. Besides the knowledge and *understanding* which we have already discussed in detail, the pastor's ministry to the bereaved will include a *sensitive, sympathetic and sharing presence* (2 Cor. 1.7), *prayer* (2 Cor. 1.11), use of the *Scriptures* (2 Cor. 1.20), and sometimes *practical support* of one sort or another (2 Cor. 12.14–18).

A SENSITIVE PRESENCE

This is especially important while people are going through the shock stage, and on into the disorganization stage. In many areas Church members expect their pastor to visit them immediately when a death occurs, and perhaps even to remain with them for a whole day or night. Sometimes even 'nominal' Christians, who are not regular church-goers, will expect this, and feel that it is a very important part of a pastor's ministry. They may not want to *say* much to the pastor in this early stage. If he understands and accepts their feelings and emotional expressions, this will be more helpful to them than any direct preaching. Some pastors do tend to 'preach' at this time, rather than encourage the bereaved themselves to talk, regarding it as an opportunity to remind people of the gospel. This may have some value, but only if the pastor knows the people well enough to understand what they need to be told, and if they do not think of him as a stranger coming in from outside the situation. In any case it is usually more helpful at a later stage.

As always in counselling, careful *listening* is important. By being ready to listen, a pastor can encourage people to express their deepest feelings. This will help to relieve their tension and shock, as well as enabling him to respond to their real needs rather than merely following his own ideas about them.

The pastor who is willing to learn, not only what ideas and beliefs people hold, but what those beliefs mean to them in their daily lives, will be able to express the gospel message of hope in ways that will really give them comfort and strength. Even when people's beliefs conflict with Christian teaching, the understanding pastor will acknowledge the importance of those beliefs to the people who hold them. This does not mean that he agrees with such beliefs; he will probably go on to show that they are inadequate when compared with the truth of the gospel. But if he simply rejects such beliefs and refuses even to discuss them, he may lose the opportunity for a continuing dialogue which could comfort the bereaved and also help the Christian community as a whole to gain a better understanding of their faith in Christ.

In this way the pastor stands for a time 'alongside' those who grieve. He is 'there', so that family members can talk over their feelings, ideas, and problems with him. In such a ministry the pastor must be prepared to encourage sharing and discussion, rather than silencing people, if they wish to talk about what has happened.

The value of this sort of 'supporting' ministry will depend very much on the pastor's own feelings and ideas about death and dying. If he feels uncomfortable, or afraid of discussing the subject of death, this may mean that he has not yet tried to think through the possibility of his own death. He may not have felt the power of the gospel releasing him from his own fears, and may himself feel insecure when the matter is brought out in open sharing of thoughts, and discussion, especially with people whom he does not know well. Some pastors, when this happens, do all the talking themselves, and so fail to help the bereaved to express their own deep feelings and possible emotional and spiritual problems. As we have said, people can derive comfort from the mere fact that the pastor is *there*, and it is certainly better to say too little than too much.

Example 53: Pastor Simon was told that Sara, the young daughter of a woman in his congregation, had died after some weeks of sickness. He had not known Sara was ill, nor that she had recently expressed a desire to be confirmed. He went at once to visit the family, and found the house full of relatives – about fifty people – whom he did not know at all. At first Simon felt nervous. How should he counsel them? How long should he stay? He sat down near the mother, and asked one or two questions about the girl, speaking quietly with her and her husband. Then he kept silent for a time. Finally he spoke out briefly to the whole room, about death and its meaning for Christians. Later he took the funeral, and always afterwards on Sundays the mother came to him after the Service and said quietly, 'Praise the Lord!' – and he knew that she was comforted in her loss.

Often other commitments make it impossible for a pastor to stay with grieving people for very long, but if he can, he should continue to visit them from time to time. For the first few weeks after a death, friends and relatives are usually very ready to visit and comfort the bereaved. But often it is later, when the first shock and numbness begins to wear off, and people enter on the stages of disorganization and then adjustment to life again, that they suffer from times of depression, and chiefly need the support and help of a caring pastor.

Sometimes, too, a pastor can help people even if he is not able to visit them in person. A letter can be a good means of expressing care and understanding, and assuring people of your prayers for them. Some pastors have developed a very effective ministry of letter-writing, particularly to the bereaved, though of course this should not be used merely as a short cut to save the time and trouble of visiting.

A pastor may also find ways to help the bereaved indirectly, by tactfully suggesting to neighbours or other Church members that they should visit and help them, or, as the bereaved begin to adjust to life again, invite them out for a meal or other social occasion. This sort of 'help' can work effectively in both directions: one of the best ways of helping the bereaved can sometimes be to encourage them to help and comfort others who have suffered a similar loss, or affliction of some kind.

USING PRAYER AND THE SCRIPTURES

PRAYING WITH AND FOR THE BEREAVED

Many of the points discussed in earlier chapters about prayer generally, and for the sick in particular, apply equally to the ministry of prayer with and for the bereaved. But one or two additional points should perhaps be remembered.

In the period of shock immediately following a death, some people are so upset that they feel unable to pray at all – but this of course does not prevent the visiting pastor from praying silently for them himself. With others, prayer is the first thing that is expected of him. If the pastor knows the bereaved family well, he will probably want to visit them regularly for a time, and pray with them in person. Perhaps he may have to help them to pray for themselves. Others may only need to be assured that they are remembered in the pastor's own prayers and perhaps those of their fellow Church-members. For others again the pastor may pray effectively himself, even though he cannot let them know it.

'When people come face to face with death they stand in special need of pastoral care and reassurance . . . in the period of shock some are so upset they feel unable to pray at all' (pp. 228 and 248).

What sort of 'reassurance' could a pastor give to this young Brazilian woman whose husband and children were drowned and her home destroyed by disastrous floods? What sort of prayers could he use?

Example 54: On Christmas day Bertie, the student son of an Indian engineer who had taken a post in England, woke up feeling very ill. Next day he saw the doctor, who diagnosed leukaemia and sent him straight to hospital. On New Year's Day he died. Pastor Stephen, who knew the family well, had visited Bertie regularly, and he reached the hospital that day just in time to meet the bereaved parents coming away from the ward. He embraced them in their grief, and spoke with them for a time about Bertie, and about the difficulty of understanding why God should let him die so young. At this stage the pastor didn't try to answer this question: 'Why?' But he gently reminded the parents that it was only Bertie's body they had just left in the ward – not a person any longer. Bertie himself was alive. The father's first reaction was that he must give up his job and go back to India as England would now have such unhappy memories for the whole family. But the pastor suggested he should not decide too quickly: surely they wouldn't want to forget Bertie, but to remember all the happiness they had enjoyed together. Then they prayed, thanking God for Bertie's life, and later, when Pastor Stephen took the funeral, it was not a miserable occasion but one of assurance and joy. Many of Bertie's student friends were there, and told the family how popular Bertie had been at college and how he had helped new students from other countries to feel at home. His life had been short, but a full and useful one, and his parents felt they now knew their son better than ever before.

USING THE SCRIPTURES

As in times of sickness, the pastor needs to know how to use the Scriptures to bring comfort and hope, both in counselling bereaved individuals and families, and in the course of sermons and addresses at funerals. He must of course be careful to select passages which are suitable for the particular situation. We have already discussed many of the passages which underline the truths of the gospel about death and eternal life (see pp. 241–243), and others are included in the general list on pp. 283f. In addition to those, the following are some of the most important passages for use at this time:

1 Thessalonians 4.13–18: Some Christians have taken verse 13 in this passage to mean that Christians ought not to grieve at all when someone dies, and that to express grief shows a lack of faith. But a truer interpretation of the verse is that it is natural to grieve, but people should not lose heart and behave 'as others do who have no hope' that 'through Jesus, God will bring with him those who have fallen asleep'.

In some situations, as we have seen, it is customary to 'grieve' openly (and even to hire paid mourners to weep and wail, though this is often for purposes of show or to drive evil spirits away, rather than as a genuine expression of feeling). Jesus Himself expressed grief when He saw Mary of Bethany and others weeping because of the death of His close friend Lazarus (*John 11.28–36*). Pastors should not attempt to prevent people from expressing their natural feelings. Sometimes the effect of hearing a Scripture reading will be to *release* people's tears, rather than drying them, and this can often bring more true comfort than encouraging them to 'bottle up' their grief.

Matthew 5.4: Some Christians find this a surprising verse, because it suggests that those who mourn are in fact 'blessed' by God. William Barclay points out that the Greek word *penthein*, here translated 'mourn', is 'one of the strongest words in the Greek language.' It means 'mourning for the dead. A sorrow which is piercing and intense . . . visible sorrow which can be seen in a man's tears . . . a sorrow which will be shown because a man cannot help doing so.' How then is it possible for those who mourn in this way to be 'blessed'? The 'blessing' they receive is the gift of comfort from God Himself. There are many passages in the New Testament which help people to understand and experience this blessing for themselves.

In *John 11.21–26* and *12.24–26*, for example, Jesus was Himself comforting and consoling Mary and Martha and His disciples with the clear promise that death is *not* the inescapable 'end', though we all feel it to be so when we lose a close relative or friend. In *John 14.1–3*, as we have seen, Jesus was encouraging and strengthening His disciples with the promise that after His death and theirs they would be together with Him.

In *Romans 8.38, 39*, Paul repeated the promise that nothing can separate us from God's love and care, and in *Romans 14.8, 9*, that both the living and the dead belong to Christ, so that in Him they are not separated from each other.

When an older person has died, *Revelation 14.13* may help the bereaved to feel comforted for the sake of the dead person now at peace. When a child or young person has died through accident or illness, the sense of desolation and 'waste' which families so often feel may be overcome by the suggestion in *Revelation 7.15–17* that early death has perhaps spared them from some greater suffering.

The 'blessing' which comforts Christians, even while they grieve, is the 'living hope' which is perhaps best described in *1 Peter 3.7*.

PRACTICAL SUPPORT FOR THE BEREAVED

In some circumstances the pastor may have to give practical support to the bereaved, or arrange for others to do so.

One pastor, who was called in when a man working far from home was killed in an accident, had to order the coffin and arrange for the body to be transported back to the man's family, because there was no one else with the authority to do so. This sort of help may be needed especially in cases of sudden death, when relatives are too shocked and distressed to act for themselves. Another example occurred in an island community when sixteen men were drowned in a cyclone, and the villagers were too upset to organize themselves properly. The pastor from a neighbouring island commandeered boats and brought all the people back to his own island, where they were fed and looked after until they could return to their own place.

When a pastor is called in immediately after a death, he should try to make sure that the bereaved know what has to be done, and are able to cope with the situation or have friends or relatives to help them. If not, he may tactfully offer such help as he can, or arrange for neighbours or fellow Church-members to do so. This is especially important if there are money problems or legal difficulties to be solved.

In some congregations the members themselves organize 'neighbourhood' groups, who help and support one another in times of difficulty. Such groups can be especially helpful in 'sharing' the affliction of bereavement during the stages of disorganization and reorganization. Usually it is best for such groups to be run by the members themselves, rather than by the pastor. But often it is up to the pastor to encourage their formation, and perhaps to arrange for some money to be regularly set aside from Church funds for the purpose of helping people who are in temporary financial difficulty as a result of bereavement (see 2 Cor. 8).

ARRANGING AND CONDUCTING FUNERALS

The purpose of a funeral is not merely to dispose of the dead body. It also provides accepted forms of marking the formal end of a human life and of demonstrating the sympathy and solidarity, not only of the bereaved family, but of the community as a whole.

Like other mourning customs, funeral practices vary from place to place, but they fulfil a number of common needs in all cultures, and show many similar features in widely separated parts of the world. We therefore start by looking at some of the common features which characterize funeral customs generally, before going on to discuss Christian funerals in particular. Then we shall note some of the questions which pastors need to consider when planning and conducting funerals and funeral services, whether in church, in a 'funeral parlour' or other public place, or in the home of the bereaved.

GENERAL PURPOSES AND FEATURES OF FUNERALS

1. The basic purpose of any funeral is the disposing of the dead body in such a way as not to endanger the health of the community. For Christians this has usually been by burial, but in some circumstances cremation (that is, burning) or entombment are more practical.

2. Funeral rites and ceremonies are basically religious. They reflect the generally-held beliefs about life and death, and about man's relationship with God and the world of spirits. Even in some of the countries where the cultural background is mainly secular and humanist, funeral rites tend to be basically religious in origin.

3. In many areas they have a double purpose: to mark and facilitate the passing of the dead person from this life to the after life, and also to protect the living from any evil influence which the dead person or other spirits might exert at the time or in the future.

4. As we have already said, a funeral is often a communal as well as a family affair, and provides an occasion for regulating and maintaining economic as well as social relationships within and between families and the community as a whole. The feasts provided for mourners and other participants serve partly as marks of respect for the dead, and partly as a sign that the family is carrying out the responsibility expected of it by society. (Quite often those who have been estranged or cast off by their families as wrong-doers are given expensive funerals, as if to compensate for years of ill-will and perhaps to avert the vengeance of the spirit of the deceased.) Sometimes, too, the feasts which form part of the ceremonies in many areas may start as an occasion for demonstrating grief, but if they last for several days, may simply become an occasion for the family to show off its status and wealth.

5. Funeral ceremonies often include some sort of procession, from the home of the deceased to the church or temple where the funeral service is held, or to the graveside. The idea behind this custom is usually that it enables relatives and friends to accompany the dead on their last journey. When a well known person dies there may be a public procession, which anyone wishing to pay respect to the dead may join or watch.

6. Funerals sometimes provide an opportunity for friends and relatives to view the body, as a way of saying goodbye. Again, when a national leader dies, a public 'lying in state' may precede the funeral, so that anyone who wishes may view the body or the coffin. (A secondary purpose of this custom is to give proof that the deceased really has died. This can be important for the heirs, who may inherit property or succeed to a title or office of some kind.)

7. Funerals can indirectly provide a reason for bringing an incurably sick person 'home' to die, or for bringing home the body of someone who has died elsewhere. In some parts of the world this is very important. Many people are afraid of dying in a strange place, or among strangers. And many believe that unless the dead are buried according to custom in the family or tribal graveyard, their spirits will be unable to rest and will return to trouble the living. Many Christians,

253

too, find it easier to bear their bereavement if those who have died afar are brought to a final resting place close to their homes. A striking example of this was reported in many newspapers when the inhabitants of an island group in the Pacific would not allow their island home to be taken from them for development by an international mining company. The company offered to pay them very large sums of money and move them all to new homes on another island, but the islanders refused to go and leave their ancestral burial places untended, or to live where they would themselves have to be buried apart from their ancestors.

CHRISTIAN FUNERALS

In addition to the purposes and features common to all funerals, Christian funerals proclaim (or should proclaim) the distinctive Christian beliefs about death and life after death. They remind people of the good news of the gospel for both the living and the dead. At this time of crisis in their lives, many Christians feel that their faith is shaken. But in fact they do not always find the comfort they seek in the funeral service, because they do not fully understand its purpose and meaning.

These difficulties arise especially in countries where Christians are few and the traditional ideas and customs of others are strong. As a writer from Africa has noted with concern, mourning customs and funeral rites can become 'the broad highway on which a new form of paganism can force its way into many congregations'.

At this time Christian and traditional ideas are mixed together, so that for many people the Easter message of the victory of God in Christ over the powers of evil, sin, and death is accepted as a form of head-knowledge, but fails to become a meaningful force in their lives. The writer likens this situation to the first Easter morning, when: 'some early witnesses tried to report what they had seen, but were not understood until the risen Christ, by His presence, confirmed their report among the disciples. Much of Church life in Africa today is like that of the disciples behind the closed doors.' People have *heard* the facts of the gospel, but have not fully experienced them.

These problems are increased when, as sometimes happens, traditional customs which actually conflict with Christian teaching are included in the ceremony, such as killing an animal, preserving bones, or decorating the grave with traditional symbols to ensure the protection of departed spirits rather than their enmity.

THE PRACTICAL ARRANGEMENTS

In developed countries the detailed arrangements for the burial or cremation are usually made by the Undertakers (or 'funeral directors' as they prefer to be called) in accordance with rules laid down by the government health authorities. In most other areas, too, these functions will be carried out by specially designated groups among the people themselves. So the pastor's job will be chiefly concerned with the religious ceremony.

Just as mourning and funeral customs differ from one area to another, so too, different Churches have somewhat different ways of conducting funerals and funeral services. Most Churches have a set form of funeral service, and the pastor has only to adapt points of detail to each situation. But some Churches provide general guidelines only, so that ministers may themselves have to work out a form of service suited to the occasion.

Even funerals which follow the form of service set by the Church, however, do not always bring the meaning of the gospel clearly before the people. The very fact of having a set liturgy may mean that the pastor is tempted to use it without giving much thought to its real purpose and meaning.

The actual manner of conducting the ceremony is important also. If the minister performs the rite in a casual way; if he fails to prepare and present a sermon or address which the people will really understand; if he chooses unfamiliar hymns, then the funeral will not serve its proper purpose, the dead will not be honoured, nor the bereaved comforted. And what is worse, the Christian hope of eternal life through Jesus Christ will not be proclaimed.

A pastor should therefore carefully evaluate any order of service for funerals set by his Church (and indeed any other form of service which refers to the relationship between the living and the dead). Does the service clearly present the certainty and hope of the gospel in ways that are relevant and applicable to the cultural situation, and in words which the people of the area will understand? Or is it merely a translation of a Western form of service, with no reference to the questions which perplex the people to whom the pastor is ministering? This is quite literally a 'matter of life and death', and the pastor needs to make sure that any funeral service he conducts really does fulfil the purpose for which it is intended.

STUDY SUGGESTIONS

WORD STUDY

1. (a) What is the exact meaning of the word 'bereaved'?
   (b) What word is used to translate this idea into your own language or another language you know?

(c) Give two other words in your own language which can also be used to mean 'bereaved'.

2. 'The "idealization" or "idolization" of the dead' (p. 226). Which three of the following words have the same meaning as 'to idealize', and which three have the same meaning as 'to idolize'?
worship   admonish   admire   deify   honour   disembody
esteem   hallow

3. What is the difference between 'grieving' and 'grievance', as described in this chapter?

4. Explain the meaning of each of the following terms, as it is applied to Jesus:
(a) forerunner   (b) firstborn   (c) high priest   (d) the 'second Adam'

REVIEW OF CONTENT

5. 'Grief is the feeling we experience as a result of loss.' Give two examples from everyday life to illustrate this statement.

6. (a) What are the three main stages in the grief process?
   (b) Explain briefly what most people feel, and how they are likely to behave, at each of these stages.

7. (a) What are the four chief areas of *knowledge* a pastor needs to study before he can counsel the bereaved effectively?
   (b) What sorts of *customs* does he need to study in order to arrange and conduct funerals effectively?

8. How would you describe a 'sensitive presence'?

9. Give *three* examples of practical support which a pastor can give the bereaved.

BIBLE STUDY

10. Some people think of Jesus as one who was removed from the problems and sorrows and disappointments of life. In what ways do the following passages show that this idea is false?
(a) Mark 14.32–37   (b) Mark 14.60–65   (c) Luke 4.1–4
(d) Luke 22.63–65   (e) John 19.28–30.

11. Select *one* of the following passages, and explain how it could be used in ministering to grieving people:
Psalm 23   John 11.32–36   Romans 8.35–39

12. What was the 'loss' which caused the grief described in each of the following passages?
(a) Matthew 26.69–75   (b) Mark 5.35–40   (c) John 11.32–36
(d) Acts 20.16,17, 25–37.

13. Read the following passages in the order given. What ideas about death and life after death do you find in (a) the group of Old

Testament passages and (b) the group of New Testament passages? What are the chief differences between the New Testament ideas and the Old Testament ideas?

OT: Ecclesiastes 9.4–6, 9.10   Psalm 88.10–12   Isaiah 14.4–21 (esp. 9–11)

NT: 1 Peter 1.3, 4   1 Corinthians 15.51–57   2 Timothy 1.10b

14. Select *two* of the following passages and explain in your own words how each of them helps you to understand the Christian idea of death.

    1 Corinthians 15.12–20   1 Corinthians 15.21–23   1 Corinthians 15.35–50.

15. Read again 2 Corinthians 1.3–7.
    (a) What does this passage teach us about the source and nature of true comfort?
    (b) List some of the ways in which the bereaved can experience the comfort described in this passage.

APPLICATION, OPINION, AND RESEARCH

16. (a) If a Christian graveyard cult like that described in Example 49 arose among members of your own congregation, what do you think should be done about it? Give reasons for your answer.
    (b) Compare the Easter service described in Example 50 with the Easter services in your own Church. What is your opinion of each? Which do you think best helps people to understand and respond to the message of Easter?

17. Describe the traditional mourning and funeral customs of your country. Which of them, if any, do you think Christians ought *not* to follow? Give your reasons. If you are the only Christian in your home, how should you respond to the traditional mourning when someone dies?

18. (a) Is it 'wrong' to wail when someone dies?
    (b) In her will the Queen of the Netherlands stipulated that everyone should wear *white*, for joy, at her funeral, not black for grief. For what reasons should people be joyful at the death of a Christian?

19. What are the ideas and attitudes of your own people about death? Is the subject regarded as 'taboo' – or is death freely talked about?

20. What, if any, is the official teaching of your own Church about:
    (a) The role of ancestral spirits and belief in the power of the spirits of the departed for good or evil?
    (b) Dependence on fortune tellers, astrologers, and other forms of divination to regulate daily life?

    If such teaching is given, to what extent is it effective? Do you agree with it? If there is no such teaching, do you think there

257

should be? What do you yourself truly believe on these two questions?

21. How would you answer someone who said: 'In some Churches Christians are taught to invoke the prayers of the Virgin Mary and other saints, as well as praying directly to God Himself. I can see no difference between this teaching and the custom of petitioning the ancestral spirits to carry our prayers to God.'?

22. In a discussion about the purpose of a Christian funeral, a group of ministerial students made the following suggestions.

The purpose of a Christian funeral is:

(a) To offer comfort to those who have died and commend them to the care of God.

(b) To benefit the living, not the dead: to proclaim the hope of the resurrection, which is good news for the living, not the dead.

(c) To proclaim that death is not the end, life goes on.

(d) To remind people that their present life is leading to a definite conclusion, and they need to look carefully at their lives, as a preparation for their own death.

(e) To proclaim that God's love and power is stronger than death, and that all the powers of death have been overcome.

(f) To provide comfort for those who mourn.

(g) To give thanks for the life of the dead person.

(h) To declare the seriousness of life and the reality of judgement before God, and call people to repentance and faith.

Which of these suggestions do you agree with, and which, if any, do you disagree with? Give your reasons in each case. Do you think those students omitted any important point?

23. Some ministers and pastors will only conduct funerals for those whom they know to be practising Christians. They refuse to conduct a Christian funeral or burial service for non-Christians or non-Church members. What is your opinion about this? Give your reasons.

24. 'Much of Church life in Africa is more like that of the disciples behind the closed doors. Christians have heard the facts of the gospel, but have not experienced them in their own lives' (p. 254). Is this true of people in your own Church? If so what do you think are the reasons? How might the situation be changed?

12

Right and Wrong: Adapting to Change

In chapters 9, 10, and 11 we have discussed ways of counselling people who need pastoral help in overcoming problems which arise in three particular sorts of situation: in their marriage and family relationships, in times of sickness, and in times of death and bereavement.

In chapter 3 we noted very briefly another sort of situation in which people often have problems to face, and may therefore be in special need of pastoral care. That is, when they experience *change* from one place or one way of living to another, and are confronted by unfamiliar surroundings, strange people, new ideas and beliefs, perhaps even a language they do not understand. In this present chapter we look more closely at some of the ways in which such changing circumstances can affect people's lives, and at the role of the pastor in helping them to 'hold to their faith' and 'do what is right' (see 2 Cor. 13.5–7).

CHANGE AS LOSS

When people are separated from their usual surroundings, and from the ideas and traditions to which they are accustomed, they become upset. They are afraid, and cannot feel 'at home' in the new situation; they lose their sense of security and well-being. This often happens when people move from a village to a big town or city, and vice-versa. They find it difficult to adjust to new ways of thinking and living. Their need for security is no longer fulfilled; they are uncertain what new role or roles will be expected of them, and even their self-image may become blurred if their new neighbours or workmates treat them in ways they do not expect.

A striking example of such problems was described by Jacob Loewen, when he was working in South America among the Chulupi Indians of Paraguay, who had experienced drastic changes in their patterns of living.

Example 55: The Chulupi had formerly been hunting and gathering nomads. Now they had changed to a settled village life near to the European settlements where they found employment. Besides work, these settlements offered new ways of living and thinking. The problems of liquor, prostitution, and other aspects of a semi-urban way of living gradually brought changes to the Chulupi's traditional patterns of life, and they became more and more dependent on and subservient to their European employers. They had exchanged their nomadic freedom with its problems of poverty, hardship, and drought, for a more settled life and regular work, but this did not bring them the freedom they were seeking. Instead it brought them a feeling of being slaves and prisoners. Their slavery to poverty and hardship had been exchanged for a new slavery to their European bosses, and this created a deep discontent among them.

Jacob Loewen asked the Chulupi: 'What is the most important desire that you carry in your innermost hearts?' One of them answered with great feeling: 'One wants to become a human being.' Several others said the same thing: 'Yes, one wants to become a human being,', and as Loewen listened, group after group made similar confessions. It was clear that something very important was threatening the status and security of the Chulupi people.

The problem was that the Chulupi's self-image was being attacked and threatened. They had the feeling of being 'lost'. They had lost their former security and identity, and had become 'nothing people', who did not really belong in the new situation. They had lost their role as independent people, and had accepted the role of underpaid workers. They felt they were being treated as things, rather than as human beings able to control their own lives. This was a crisis situation for them. They felt like second class citizens, and they wanted to regain a secure self-image as first class citizens. How could they achieve this? Was a new self-image possible? These were the sort of questions they were really asking.

Changes in cultural traditions and social patterns always produce changes in roles, and this is why any rapid changes in our way of life create problems and tensions for our sense of selfhood and our self-image. Jacob Loewen researched many situations similar to that of the Chulupi, and found similar problems in many different parts of the world.

The problem of changing role or self-image is not limited to any one group of people. It is found in many different countries, and affects both groups and individuals.

Both educated and uneducated people are affected wherever rapid changes are taking place. Students often find that education leads to disillusionment with the traditional world-view and the ideas of right and wrong they inherited. As more and more of their 'home town' or 'village' faith and moral standards are challenged by new ideas, they experience feelings of uncertainty, insecurity, and even rebellion. This is often felt most powerfully by educated people from areas where traditional religion was strong, and the result is a feeling of loss or 'lostness'. Such people experience major personal crises, as many of their traditional beliefs wither and die as a result of new scientific learning. When these people are cut loose from tradition, they do not always become free. Instead, they experience what Loewen has called a 'lostness in human values, a sense of lack of belonging, a lack of direction in behaviour'. Many such 'lost' people have been produced by detribalization and urbanization in Africa, Asia, and Latin America – like the Chulupi they are seeking how to become 'first class citizens'.

One writer has compared this sense of loss or 'lostness' which is experienced as a result of any big change in people's lives, with the experience of bereavement through death and the ways in which such bereavement can affect them. He has also pointed out that just as the feeling of bereavement can turn to one of assurance and joy when we recognize it as part of God's plan for our lives, so too the feeling of loss resulting from change can be seen as an opportunity to find and follow new directions to which God is pointing us.

In order to help people see and recognize change in this way, the pastoral counsellor needs to recognize that there are different sorts of change, and to understand the difference between *social* change and *individual* change. By 'social' change we mean change and development in the *general* cultural and economic conditions experienced by society as a whole, from which no one can wholly escape. By 'individual' change we mean the *particular* changes which occur in the individual lives of each separate person or family.

SOCIAL CHANGE

In the early 1970s the East Asia Christian Conference organized a Workshop on training people for ministries to crucial areas of social, political, and industrial life in Asia. One of the speakers recalled that Pope John XXIII had pointed to three major 'signs of the times' (see Matt. 16.2–4), in which we may discern God's action leading man towards the fulfilment of His designs. These signs, resulting from the great changes that have taken place in modern times in science and technology, and also in man's understanding of his own history and behaviour, are:

1. *The demand for socialization:* Working people all over the world are no longer content to be treated as mere instruments of production. Like the Chulupi, they want a say in the decisions that affect their work and their lives, a share in the profits of their labour, and access to the power that will give them a stake in the political life of their nation.

2. *The demand for sexual equality:* Women in many countries are no longer content to be treated as inferior to men. They want an equal opportunity to participate in all aspects of life, a share in decision-making, and an active role in society.

3. *The demand for de-colonization:* Nations which formerly were, or still are, colonies are no longer content to endure any vestiges of political or economic dependency or inferiority. They want a

genuinely equal status with the older nations, and a full say in the running of world affairs.

In addition to these three, we might add a fourth sign:

4. *The demand for freedom of expression* in speech and action within the law. Racial, religious, political, and other minorities in many countries are no longer content to suffer discrimination and oppression. They want equality of opportunity to participate in whatever aspects of life they may wish, and freedom to express their views and beliefs and follow their particular ways of life without harassment or hindrance, so long as they keep within the law of the land.

Obviously, these trends, and the technological and political and cultural changes which gave rise to them, will show themselves in different ways in different countries and cultures. But in very many parts of the world today their influence takes one or other of the following forms:

Urbanization and development are weakening traditional social and kinship structures, as people leave their village homes to find work among strangers in towns and cities.

Extension of school and university education is tending to weaken or even destroy the authority of parents and relatives, and to undermine the traditional respect for age and experience. 'Knowledge' is coming to be regarded as more important than 'wisdom'.

The spread of Western and other cultural influences based on different social and marriage customs is upsetting traditional customs in Third World countries especially. This makes people unsure of themselves in their social and working relationships with other people, and confused about the meaning of marriage. The resulting problems are specially difficult to overcome in areas where some of the people have been more strongly affected than others by these influences.

Christian teaching has brought different standards of right and wrong to be observed in many aspects of life and in personal relationships generally, as well as different ideas about the purpose of marriage, and about the proper status of women both within the family and in the community.

At the same time, *the spread of materialist ideas* has led to a weakening of Christian attitudes to life in general and marriage in particular, especially among younger educated people in the West. In many countries money has become the standard by which every activity is measured. And in many of the new nations marriage and divorce are now regarded as wholly secular matters, which must be legally ratified by government officials, but which have nothing to do with religion.

The worldwide economic recession of recent years has reduced the demand for goods and services in many countries, halting the speed of development and causing widespread unemployment. People's hopes of attaining a higher standard of living through hard work and education can no longer be fulfilled.

The introduction of electronic techniques, in the developed nations especially, is another factor reducing the number of jobs in offices and industry, and even highly skilled people are having to face redundancy or 'go back to school' for re-training.

Totalitarian governments and the idea of the one-party state, instead of giving power to the people or to wise and benevolent statesmen, have created new élites whose power is based on brutal and oppressive police methods, and who demand unquestioning loyalty to the dictates of the state. In many countries the poor have no hope of ever improving their living standards, and those who disagree with government policies live in constant fear of arrest and imprisonment, or even death. This in turn has resulted in:

The increasing use of terrorism and violence by national and political minorities to achieve what they see as their legitimate aims.

Here are some actual examples of the problems these changes can cause:

Example 56: Margaret was the daughter of a Church Elder in East Africa who was also a prominent businessman and politician, and who prided himself on being 'modern' in his views. He rejected any idea of asking a bride-price for his daughters, but they insisted that he should not cheapen them in this way. So he agreed, but asked a very small sum only. Margaret looked forward to a happy marriage, but soon found that her husband was drinking heavily. He often beat her, and refused to let her meet any of his friends or their wives. Because he had paid so little bride-price he considered her to be of no value as a person, and treated her as if she were his servant. Margaret took her problem to the pastor, who encouraged her to persevere with the marriage, and tried to reason with her husband. But things got no better, and finally Margaret left her husband and obtained a divorce. Her sister had no prospect of marriage at all, although she had several children, not all by the same man.

Example 57: Elemu was brought up in a country where everyone believed it was better to allow people who are old, and no longer able to work, to die when they become ill, rather than trying to prolong their lives and make them well again. When he went to study in Europe, he had to work at night to supplement his scholarship money, and the only job he could get was as porter in a hospital. At first he found it almost impossible to understand that, in this very different culture, to allow people to die when they could be saved was considered as wrong as murder, and that many beds in the hospital were occupied by very old people who would remain there all their lives. Elemu was so upset to think that this meant some younger people might have to be refused treatment, that he nearly gave in his notice. It was only after he had discussed the matter with the college chaplain, who explained the Christian teaching about the value of *all* life as being God's gift to man, that he decided to continue in the job. Even then he was not altogether convinced, but was anxious to continue earning in order to keep on with his studies.

Example 58: Patricia lived in a West African country where it had long been customary for women to engage in trade. She had done well in school, and was now keen to work as a teacher in a Church college. To help her prepare for this she wanted to study Education at university. However, her father, an elderly shop-keeper, put great pressure on her to train in commerce and secretarial skills instead. As Patricia had been brought up to believe that a daughter should obey her father in all things, she did as he asked. But she began to feel very frustrated, and still believed that God was calling her to teach. Knowing her father's mind, she felt she could not consult him about this, so she went to the local pastor. The pastor recognized that there was not only a generation gap and sex difference between the girl and her father, but also a big educational gap. The father had his daughter's respect until he pretended to be an expert in matters he knew nothing of, and tried to influence her on the basis of parental authority alone. The pastor lent Patricia a book about the changing relationships between parents and children in the modern world, and showed her that it was right for her to respect her father in matters about which he was wise, but to make her own decisions in matters of which he was ignorant. At the same time he encouraged her to try to explain to her father all her reasons for wanting to teach.

Example 59: Carlos was a middle-aged railway mechanic working in the repair shop. Now the system was to be electrified, and the Railways Board offered free training to all existing staff who would be servicing the new type engines; in future such training would only be open to apprentices. Carlos thought he knew all there was to know about locomotives, and refused to opt for the special re-training scheme. As a result he lost his job and his right to a company pension. After 18 months he is still unemployed. He spends one evening a week helping at the Church youth club, but has little else to do and has become very disgruntled.

In spite of problems like these, however, we should not be tempted to assume, as the Church has sometimes done, that change is necessarily a bad thing in itself. To be alive at all, means that people have to change and grow. St Paul told the Romans that 'in everything God works for good with those who love him, who are called according to his purpose' (Rom. 8.28). The tension and conflict we experience in life can help to prepare us for the 'good' which God holds in store for us.

But any big changes in people's cultural, and economic background mean that they themselves have to change some of their ideas and ways of behaving, and this process of adjustment can be very painful, or at least, uncomfortable. The pastor himself is likely to experience this, and the experience should help him to show people how to adapt to new ways without losing hold of their faith, and how to interpret the basic Christian principles of right and wrong in terms of their new situation.

INDIVIDUAL CHANGE

In some ways, and for some people, the sort of 'general' changes we have been discussing are easier to adapt to than the particular changes of circumstances which affect their individual lives. For one thing, in situations of general change people are not alone. *All* the workers in an industry are affected when new techniques are introduced, or when jobs are hard to find in times of high unemployment. *All* parents find it difficult to bridge the generation gap when their children break away from traditional patterns. *All* young couples face uncertainty about the 'rights and wrongs' of personal relationships when the long-accepted marriage customs and moral standards of their country have broken down.

When individual people have to face big or unexpected changes in their way of life, however, they are usually without the support of anyone else to share the experience. As we have seen, changes of this sort nearly always mean *loss* of one sort or another. The sense of loneliness which follows change – for example through divorce or separation from a marriage partner – may not be so severe as that resulting from bereavement through death. But it does make it more difficult to adapt to the new situation.

Of course, not all change involves only loss. Often there is gain as well. For example, there is greater freedom for a young person who leaves home to take a job somewhere else. There is greater responsibility and 'job-satisfaction' for someone who is promoted at work to be in charge of others. There is greater security and a higher standard of living for someone whose financial position changes for the better. There is greater fulfilment for an artist whose work is appreciated for the first time after a long period of adverse criticism. Even separation can bring relief from conflict and tension (see Example 30).

But nearly all such changes involve some change of role, and as we saw in chapter 4 (p. 58), this can be upsetting. For example, when we start a new job we accept a subordinate role under the direction of a boss. As we gain experience we may become foreman, or even the boss, ourselves, and this means a new role and changing relationships with our workmates. As we move into different situations we have to adapt our behaviour according to whether we see our role as that of an equal, a servant, an employer, or whatever it may be.

Similarly, such changes may lead to changes in our self-image. These, even more than changes of role, may upset and unsettle us, especially when the change is one that we feel reduces our importance, or our usefulness to others.

Here are some examples:

Example 60: Joan, aged 38, had been a buyer for women's fashions in a large chainstore, travelling about and earning a good salary, with her own apartment and prospects of becoming head buyer before long. She left her job to marry Robert, an accountant. At first she was very happy, furnishing their new home where Robert also had his office, and entertaining her husband's clients. But soon she became bored, and found it very frustrating to be tied down to domestic affairs, with no real responsibilty or independence. In her working life it had been 'right' for her to give orders and make decisions, and she found it difficult to refrain from telling Robert how she thought he should run his business. She became very bossy and interfering, and when he reproached her for this she became moody and subject to fits of crying. Robert was very worried, and suggested she should see a doctor, but Joan flatly refused. In the end Robert consulted their pastor, and found that he too had noticed how discontented Joan had become. The pastor saw that Joan's chief trouble was her failure to adapt to her new situation and her new role as a married woman, so he suggested that she might go back to some part-time work. At first Robert was unwilling even to consider this. Eventually, however, he recognized the truth of the matter, and himself encouraged Joan to take a part-time job with an ex-client of his who was starting a dress-shop in the neighbourhood.

Example 61: Edmund had formerly been a leader in the congregation he belonged to, but had handed over his duties to someone else when he was promoted at work to a post which gave him little spare time. Now he was due for retirement, and his wife mentioned to the pastor that Edmund was worried about this, thinking of himself as finished and useless. His time would be empty, with nothing good to occupy his mind; and he could see little purpose left in his life now that his working days would be over. So the pastor called to see Edmund, and suggested that he could once again work for the Church, as he would have plenty of time free to do so. The congregation wanted to start a neighbourhood group for helping the elderly, and Edmund would be the ideal person to run it. In this way he was enabled to find continuing satisfaction and feel useful to others, and this helped to prevent a possible crisis developing in his life.

As these examples show, further change to a new and active role can often help people to overcome their sense of loss, and so regain a positive self-image.

'NO ONE CAN SERVE TWO MASTERS'

There are other situations, besides those resulting from change, in which people may need counselling help because they find it difficult to know what is 'right' and what is 'wrong', or cannot see what God is calling them to do. We are often faced with choices in our lives when two or more courses of action that are open to us seem equally good or equally bad. We have to choose between 'conflicting goods', or conflicting loyalties; or we have to try and decide which is the lesser of two evils.

Jesus said that no one can serve two masters (Matt. 6.24), meaning that if we are to serve God faithfully we must turn away from the people – and the habits and actions and attitudes – which separate us from Him. Sometimes it is easy for us, and for the pastor, to see which is the 'right' thing to do. Sometimes the problem is not so easy. Here are some examples:

Example 62: Don and Maria had struggled hard to make a good home for their children. They were both working, and their two elder sons would soon be taking the school certificate exam. Suddenly Don's employers decided to shut down part of the factory where he worked. Most of the employees in Don's section would be made redundant, but he and two others were offered the choice between promotion if they were willing to move to a new factory in a town many miles away, or accepting subordinate jobs at much reduced wages in another department if they wished to stay on where they were. If Don took promotion either he would be separated from the family just when the boys most needed a father's help, or they would all have to move, upsetting the boys' education, and Maria might not find a job in the new town. If he took the subordinate job the family's standard of living would be much reduced, and they might have to give up many things they had worked so hard to obtain.

Example 63: Elsie and her twin sister Jane had left school and just started training, when their father was killed in a motor accident and their mother so badly injured that she would need care for the rest of her life. Elsie was at a Church college preparing for work among refugees, and Jane, who was a talented pianist, at a college of music. The problem was: should one or other of the two girls give up the career she had planned, in order to look after their mother, and if so, which one should do so? Where did God's call lie in the situation?

Example 64: Nathan, was a government employee working in the Ministry of Trade, and had lately been made an assistant in charge of issuing import licences. Here he was immediately faced with the problem of corruption. Very many of the firms applying for a licence offered some sort of bribe, hoping to get speedier service or an extra quota. Though this was a wide-spread custom, the government was trying to stamp it out, and anyway Nathan knew it to be wrong, and unfair on the smaller firms who could not afford to keep on bribing officials. So he steadfastly refused to accept offers of either money or goods – even though one company actually delivered a parcel of toys for his children to his home! Gradually Nathan ceased to receive such offers, but he saw from the files that some firms were still getting preferential treatment, and guessed that applicants were now bribing his senior colleague instead. Nathan was in a dilemma. What was the right thing to do? Should he tell the head of the department? Or speak to his colleague himself? Or simply say nothing? To whom did he chiefly owe loyalty?

Example 65: A rather similar conflict of loyalties was experienced by two government officers in an island group in the Pacific: Lopeti and Smithson were friends who had gone through university together and now held good positions in the public service. They had also been to the same Church school, and the Christian faith and Church activities were important in their lives. They were now closely involved in preparing for the fourth general election of a new central government to take place since their country gained its independence. They remembered with pride and joy those first wonderful weeks and months 15 years ago in a newly independent country. Since then the government had introduced new programmes of economic and industrial development, and the future looked full of promise. But Lopeti and Smithson were becoming aware of the growing temptation to take 'short cuts' in achieving the desired goals. Some government officials (who were their friends) were very ready to accept 'rewards' in return for supporting certain programmes or favouring a particular group. The central government itself was putting pressure on people to 'obey the government line', or 'put the nation or party first', whatever the issues involved and regardless of whether an action or policy seemed morally right or wrong. Decisions were being made and policies evaluated according to whether or not they favoured the government position. If they did, then they were 'OK' even if other groups were harmed, and larger questions of right and wrong were being forgotten. Some political leaders who strongly opposed the government were threatened with arrest. Lopeti and Smithson began to ask themselves: was it really legitimate for the government – or any political party – to demand a blind obedience if this meant rejecting Christian teaching about the rights of others? Could they themselves, as Christians, accept this demand and still remain committed to God's service as the first priority in their lives? As they discussed all this together they realized that the situation was different now, not only from colonial days when the people had no say in their country's affairs, but also from the inspiring times immediately after independence when hopes of freedom and justice were so high. Now they were free to make their own decisions, but were faced with a clash between selfish interests and a wider concern for the rights and freedom and well-being of *all* people in the country.

'Not all change involves loss' (p. 265).

Women in Khartoum protest against Soviet interference in African affairs. What have these women *gained* from the great social changes that have taken place in their country?

'Sometimes it is easy to see what is the "right" thing to do; sometimes it is not so easy' (p. 267).

An elector casts his vote for the parliamentary candidate of his choice. How far do the 'choices' made by the Sudanese to protest, and by the British elector to support a particular political party, depend on their ideas about 'right' and 'wrong'?

269

THE ROLE OF THE PASTOR

When people seek counselling help because they are facing the sort of dilemma we have been describing, they often come expecting that the pastor's approach will be an authoritative one. They hope that he will give them a direct *answer*, and tell them exactly what they should do to solve their problem. And indeed the choice sometimes seems so clear-cut that the pastor is tempted to do just that, even when the client really needs to be helped to reach his or her own solution. But to give a 'snap answer' may not be the best way, and may even lead to worse problems, unless the client is someone the pastor knows very well indeed, and the pastor is already familiar with the whole background of the problem.

In all cases, just as in times of sickness and times of bereavement, it is essential for the pastor to follow the pattern we have suggested in earlier chapters; that is, he should:

1. Make sure that he fully *understands* the general background, the immediate situation that gives rise to the problem, and the particular person or people concerned (see pp. 119–123).

2. Make himself *available* as a caring, sensitive, and supportive *presence* to whom those concerned feel ready to turn as the situation develops (see pp. 95–101).

3. Make appropriate use of prayer and the Scriptures (see pp. 146–154).

4. Make sure that those in need receive any practical support which he or other members of the congregation can offer (see pp. 154–157). In many of the dilemmas people face they can be helped if someone who has been through the same experience will discuss things with them, or perhaps speak for them to the authorities. This may be the pastor himself, but often a fellow Church-member with special knowledge, authority, or skill can be more useful.

METHODS TO USE

As always in counselling, the pastor will have to decide what method best suits the particular situation (see chapter 7).

For people whose problems result from the sort of major cultural and economic changes described on pp. 261–263, however, the *identification* method is specially useful, though it may be necessary to combine it with another method as well. Nearly everyone finds that adapting to new ideas and new ways of living becomes very much easier once they realize that the problem is not theirs alone, and that hundreds if not thousands of other people have the same difficulties to face.

In many situations the best method will be *non-directive*, that is, the counsellor's chief task will be to *listen* while people talk over and analyse the rights and wrongs of their situation and the possible alternative courses of action open to them. He may make observations as they go along, and suggest points of view they may have forgotten. But he should always remember that the problem is *theirs*, and *they* are the ones who will have to live with the consequences of the choice or decision they make. If people are to grow in maturity they may need guidance, but they also need to be allowed to make the choice or decision for *themselves*, and gradually adapt *themselves* to their changing circumstances.

If, however, the situation is such that the pastor feels he is required to give people clear guidance or direction in reaching a decision, he should also make sure that they themselves know and fully understand the following aspects of the situation:

(a) the *background* causes of their problem or their need;

(b) the *reason or reasons* why the pastor suggests that a certain course of action would be 'right' and another 'wrong'; and

(c) the likely *consequences* of whatever action they may decide to take.

Finally, whatever method you use, always remember the presence of God the Holy Spirit in the situation. So long as people honestly try to do what they believe is 'right', God can redeem what may afterwards seem to be a 'wrong' or mistaken decision. This does not mean God will correct all our mistakes. It means what Paul meant by saying 'in everything God works for good' – perhaps remembering when the 'problem' of his imprisonment 'really served to advance the gospel' (Phil. 1.12).

STUDY SUGGESTIONS

WORD STUDY

1. A teacher of Ethics said: 'Accepted patterns of correct behaviour are different in different cultures, but certain actions are considered right, and others wrong, wherever we are.' Give examples to show the difference in meaning between the words 'correct' and 'right' as used in that statement.

REVIEW OF CONTENT

2. What are the chief differences between the *general* changes that we can regard as 'signs of the times', and the *particular* changes that affect the lives of individual people?

3. Which counselling method is specially useful in helping people to adapt to major cultural or economic change?

4. What are the three aspects of any situation calling for adaptation to change, which both counsellor and client should understand before any choice of action is decided upon?

BIBLE STUDY

5. Read Mark 3.31–35. Do you think Jesus meant that if we have to choose between undertaking a job for the Church or looking after our family, we must necessarily put the Church first? If not, what did He mean? (Notice that neither Mark, Matthew, nor Luke tell us what Jesus actually *did* after He had spoken those words.)

6. 'People hope that the pastor will tell them exactly what they should do' (p. 270). What connection, if any, do you see between that statement and St Paul's words to the Corinthians: 'God . . . has made us . . . to be ministers of a new covenant, not in a written code but in the Spirit; for the written code kills, but the Spirit gives life '(2 Cor. 3.6)?

APPLICATION, OPINION, AND RESEARCH

7. (a) What are the chief *cultural* changes that have occurred in your country in the past 50 years, and what are the chief *economic* changes that have occurred in the same period?

   (b) In what chief ways have these changes affected people's lives? In what ways, if any, have they affected your own life?

8. Read again Examples 62, 63, and 64. If you were counselling (1) Don, (2) Elsie, (3) Nathan,

   (a) What method or methods of counselling would you use in each case?

   (b) What passages of Scripture, if any, would you use in counselling each person?

   (c) What advice, if any, would you give to each person?

9. One person who read Example 65 remarked: 'But when the Pharisees asked Jesus if they should obey the government and pay taxes to Caesar, He told them to "Render to Caesar the things that are Caesar's." Doesn't this mean that if I work for the government then I must always obey the government?' What do you think about this matter?

10. Some people say that when we are faced with difficult decisions caused by changing situations, we should always follow the advice of Walt Disney's 'Jiminy Cricket', and 'let our conscience be our guide'. Do you think that this is a satisfactory answer? If not, why not?

Epilogue:
Evaluating our Ministry of
Pastoral Care

UNDERSTANDING OUR MINISTRY

Before we conclude this study by looking at some of the ways in which a pastor can evaluate the effectiveness of his ministry, readers may find it useful to repeat parts of the exercise undertaken at the start. This should help you: (a) to sum up what you have learned as a result of your study, (b) to formulate clearly in your own mind some of the ideas about the purpose and practice of pastoral care and counselling that have been discussed, and (c) perhaps to see in what directions some of your earlier ideas and opinions have changed and developed, and what new understanding of the subject you may have achieved.

As before, *write down* your own answers to all the questions, and note the important parts of any discussion of them you have had with other people. When you have completed the exercise (but not before), take out your earlier answers and notes, and compare them with the new ones. If it is also possible for you to discuss your conclusions with the same people with whom you discussed the earlier exercise, so much the better.

CONCLUDING EXERCISE

1. *Your own experience in the life of the Church:*
   (a) Are you a full member of the local Church? How regularly do you attend services? Are you involved in any special activity in the congregation?
   (b) What are the *good* points in your local Church which you find helpful in your own life?
   (c) What are any *weak* points in your local Church which you would like to see improved?

2. *A pastor's work in the Church:*
Which of the following statements do you agree with, and which do you disagree with? Think out your reasons in each case, and discuss your answers with at least one other person, comparing your ideas with theirs.
   (a) A pastor is chiefly responsible for the spiritual life of the Church; he should not have to worry about such worldly matters as money and property.

(b) Every pastor needs a good theological training if his work is to be effective.

(c) There is no difference between a specially ordained or appointed pastor and any other Church member; each has their own gift to use.

(d) Everyone is equal in the Church, and a pastor should not expect any special privileges.

(e) We should think of the pastor as 'overall director' of the congregation.

(f) Most pastors are lazy, and care more for getting their money than caring for people.

(g) Most pastors are not paid enough for the work they have to do.

3. *Lay people in the Church:*
As with Question 2, say whether you agree or disagree with the following statements, giving your reasons, and then discuss and compare your answers with a friend.

(a) Pastors should allow lay people a greater share in the work of the Church. Most pastors want to keep the leadership role and its power all for themselves.

(b) Most lay people are too lazy to do anything for the Church. They let the pastor do it all.

(c) Lay people should support the work of the pastor in three chief ways: by (i) praying for him, (ii) giving money, (iii) attending services regularly.

(d) Few well-educated people would choose to do the work of a pastor nowadays. Ordinary lay members can do better work for the Church than pastors can, because they can really understand what is going on in the world.

4. *Judging the work of pastors:*
Based on your own experience and other people's opinions, make two lists, one containing the good points and the other the bad points, commonly found in the work of pastors. (Do not name any pastors, simply record your views.) Discuss the lists with another person from your own congregation, and if possible with someone from a different area.

5. *Your own feelings:*
Write down your own feelings about yourself as a pastor or would-be pastor – your hopes and fears, doubts and problems. Then discuss what you have written with two other people.

6. *Sum up your own thinking:*
Try to clarify your own ideas about the aim or purpose of the Church. What is the Church really trying to do? How does its work relate to

God's plan in the world today? (In completing this question you may find it helpful to try and define each of the following subjects: the main work of a pastor; the main work of lay people; the main task of the Church in the world as a whole; the main task of your own Church in the local situation; your own feelings about the work of a pastor as you complete this course of study.)

EVALUATING OUR MINISTRY

Paul told Timothy 'Train yourself in godliness . . . Practise these duties, devote yourself to them, so that all may see your progress . . . take heed to yourself' (1 Tim. 4.7, 15, 16).

In most sorts of work a person's 'progress' is judged by others. His employers or superiors may commend or rebuke him, and if they think he has done well, promote him or increase his wages. A farmer can measure his success by the quantity and quality of the harvest he reaps, a businessman by the profit he makes. But it is not always so easy for a pastor to be sure that his ministry is effective, and that he is both shepherding his congregation in the way God intends, and providing them with the leadership and care which they themselves feel they need.

In Churches where ministers are appointed 'from above', and a pastor is ultimately responsible to a higher authority (for example where the overall structure is episcopal, presbyterian, etc.), that authority will no doubt make some evaluation of his work, especially when any new appointments are to be made. And similarly, where the structure is 'congregational', and appointment is 'from below', the congregation themselves will evaluate the work of their pastor.

But neither of these sorts of evaluation can do away with the need for pastors to stand back from time to time and 'take heed' to their own performance and progress; that is, both their personal growth in 'godliness' and their development in the exercise of their 'duties'. Some pastors prefer to carry out this sort of evaluation by themselves. A pastor who is working closely as a team with lay leaders in the congregation may want to involve those leaders in the process of evaluating their joint efforts, and perhaps in evaluating his personal effectiveness too.

Some pastors make a practice of regular 'self-examination', not only with regard to their personal life, but also their work. Some do this very often, others perhaps only at intervals of several months, or once a year.

EVALUATING TEAM WORK

When pastor and people come to evaluate *together* the effectiveness of the congregation's and the pastor's ministry as a whole, it can be useful to start by discussing one or two general background questions which are confronting Christians today in many areas of the world. As an example of how this can be done we look at one such question, or rather a double question, which was asked and answered by various groups in the Pacific region: (1) What sort of ministry is needed today, so that the people of God in a particular situation can communicate the meaning of the gospel to people in words and actions? (2) What sort of pastors do we need to care for people and counsel them in the problems and crises of their lives?

1. Answers given to the first part of the question by Christians in island groups of Melanesia and Polynesia fell into three main groups:

(a) *A combined ministry:* today's ministry must include both ordained and lay members of the fellowship. Ordained or appointed leaders are important, but they must give emphasis to sharing the work with others.

(b) *A ministry that fits the situation:* both pastors and people need much more education and training if they are to understand the many changes that are taking place, and apply the meaning of the gospel in the light of these changes.

(c) *A balanced ministry:* the coming of change does not mean throwing away all the past ways of working. Pastors and people must look carefully at what they are doing and how they are doing it, to see what that is good can be kept, what needs to be changed, and what needs to be scrapped.

How far, we can then ask, does the pastoral ministry as now carried out meet these requirements?

2. Concerning the second part of the question, first of all we summarize 'answers' given by groups in the United Church in Papua New Guinea and the Solomon Islands, in the following further set of questions, which could well be used as a basis for evaluating team-work.

WHAT SORT OF PASTORS?

(a) Are our pastors getting, or have they got, sufficient education and training to understand and help people with their problems?

(b) Are the pastors willing to share their responsibilities as leaders and work as a team with lay people; are lay people in the congregations willing to share in the work of leadership; and are they being trained to carry out such work effectively?

(c) Are the pastors and lay leaders true Christians of sound faith and good character, and do they give a good example of mature Christianity in their lives?

(d) Do they have a real concern and show respect for people of all ages and all groups, and are they willing to come 'down' to the level of the ordinary people? Or do they regard themselves as 'superior' to those whom they are called to serve?

(e) Do they really communicate with people, not just by learning and using the local or common language, but by taking the trouble to understand their real problems and needs, and by making sure that people fully understand the teaching they give?

(f) Are they active in the life of the community as a whole, as well as within the Church?

(g) Are they giving a good lead in the services, meetings, and general organization of the Church?

(h) Are they willing to share their knowledge with the people, and are they using their knowledge to train others to be good Christians in their daily lives?

(i) Are they able and willing to look after the financial and business affairs of the Church carefully and honestly, and to represent the Church effectively in its dealings with the government?

Once again, pastors and lay leaders can evaluate their own work, and each other's, by asking themselves how far they can truthfully answer 'Yes' to all these questions.

Secondly, we suggest that the pastor and his helpers might find it useful to do the following group exercise based on the 'Johari Window' (see pp. 61–65).

GROUP EXERCISE

This exercise is chiefly useful for small groups of four to six people who are working together as a team or preparing to work in that way, e.g. in a joint ministry of pastoral care or counselling. It will only be effective among people who know each other well and who have a good relationship of sharing and open-ness between them. All must be willing and able to 'speak the truth in love' to each other, to accept each other's criticism, and to grow from the insights gained from others in the group. (see Eph. 4.15).

Each person starts with 2 sheets of paper, Sheet A (for understanding onself) and Sheet B (for understanding others). See diagrams.

Step 1: On Sheet A, each member of the group fills in on the left-hand side what they think are their assets (good strong points), and the liabilities (bad weak points) in their own lives. These are written on the left-hand side under 'self'. At this stage *nothing* should be written on the right-hand side under 'others'. After completing the 'self' assets

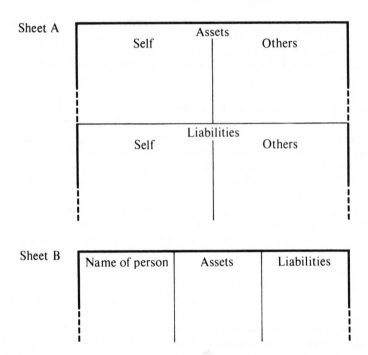

Sheet A

Assets	
Self	Others

Liabilities	
Self	Others

Sheet B

Name of person	Assets	Liabilities

and liabilities, each person keeps their own Sheet A. It is *not* shown to anyone else in the group.

Step 2: Each member of the group now completes Sheet B by listing in the left-hand column the names of all the others in the group. Then against each of these 'other' names, each person writes down two major assets (in the middle column) and two major liabilities (in the right-hand column) which they see in the life or character of the person named.

Step 3: After each member has completed Sheet B, all these B sheets are given to the leader of the group (who need not be the pastor), who then reads out the various names, with the assets and the liabilities they have been given. (An alternative way of carrying out this step is for the B sheets to be passed around the group, so that each can see for themselves what others have written about them.)

Step 4: As each name is read out or the sheets are passed around, each person copies onto their own A Sheet what the others in the group have seen in their lives. These assets and liabilities as judged by the others are written down on the right-hand side of the sheet, under 'others'.

Step 5: After all the information on the B Sheets has been read out or

278

passed around and copied onto Sheet A by each member, all the group members discuss together the information they have received about themselves, i.e. their assets and liabilities as others see them. They can then compare this with their own evaluation of their lives. Each should share their feelings about their own evaluation and the evaluation made by others.

Step 6: The exercise should end with prayers together, each person seeking God's help in becoming stronger in their 'assets' and more aware of their 'liabilities', and seeking to encourage each other in ways of serving and helping those in need, and supporting each other in their growth in Christ and their service for Him.

Where any team continues to work together over an extended period, it can be useful to repeat this exercise, perhaps at intervals of a year, as a way of measuring how far the team is becoming more effective in its ministry as a result of experience and practice, or whether any members are slipping into bad habits, perhaps without realizing it.

EVALUATING INDIVIDUAL MINISTRY

To help Methodist pastors and leaders to understand their work better, John Wesley set out the *'Twelve rules of a helper'*. He did not mean these 'rules' to be treated as strict laws to be obeyed without thought, but rather to serve as guidelines and suggestions. 'The work of a Christian minister', he wrote, 'is to watch over souls as he must give an account to God for his work, to feed and guide the flock. How shall he be fully qualified for this great work?'

It was in order to answer this question that Wesley produced his twelve rules. Because these rules touch on many important aspects of ministry, pastors today may find them equally useful as a sort of yardstick by which to examine and measure their own achievement.

The rules are:

1. Be always at work. Never be idle or lazy. Do not waste your time on things which are not important.

2. Be careful in your speech. Watch your words at all times, remembering that often your words show your character.

3. Do not speak too much with women, especially with young women. [This rule shows the sort of relationship that was accepted between men and women in Wesley's time. It was not thought proper for a man to speak to a woman or girl in private. This same idea is still held in many parts of the world today, and the rule remains valid everywhere as emphasizing that pastors should always be careful in their relationship with the opposite sex, and not do or say anything

which could cause problems or cast doubts on a pastor's integrity and moral life.]

4. Do not think about getting married without prayer to God, or without talking about this with your brothers in Christ.

5. Do not speak evil things about any other person. If you want to say some hard things to a person, then wait until you come to that person, and speak to him, and not to everyone else.

6. Tell people what you think is wrong in their lives, but do this in love. Speak the truth plainly . . . do not keep the thing in your mind, or it will become like a sore, and will spoil your life.

7. Do not expect others to wait on you and serve you. You are not to think that you are free from all work. Your task is to be the servant of all.

8. Do not believe evil things about any other person, unless there is truth in that thing. If you hear bad things about another, do not think they are true unless you can prove it. Always try to think the best about others.

9. Do not be ashamed of anything you do or say. The only thing you must be ashamed of is wrongdoing. Do not be ashamed of doing lowly jobs like chopping wood, drawing water, cleaning shoes, or any other job you are asked to do.

10. Always be on time for your work. Do not come late to meetings. If you say you will meet at a certain time then keep to that time. Keep yourself as a good example to your people.

11. Your main work is to save the souls of men. You are to give yourself to this work. In doing this you must go to all people to help them. Do not just go to the people you like – go to all, even those you do not like, and those who may not want to see you. Go to all who need you, especially those who need you most.

12. Act wisely as a servant of Christ. Be in fellowship and peace with your fellow workers in the Church. Obey the desires of Synod [the governing body of the Church]. Be prepared to work in the place where you are appointed. Always remember that your main task is to save as many souls as you can, to bring sinners to repentance, and to build them up in holiness, so that they can truly see and know the Lord.

We can use Wesley's rules for evaluating our own ministry by asking ourselves: 'How far have I or have I not followed each of these rules in the period under examination?' Some pastors find it helpful to keep a record of how they have answered each time, and then note their progress over a period of some months or years.

Others, however, may feel that this sort of evaluation could lead them to worry more about their own performance in the work than about the work itself. As with all such evaluations, we should remember that these rules are meant to challenge and inspire to greater effectiveness, and not to discourage.

Of course, using Wesley's rules is only one method of evaluation. If you do not find them helpful, then draw up other questions which may be more applicable to your situation. But whatever method you follow, beware of the temptation to *avoid* the more difficult questions. Growth in ministry will only come as you are prepared to evaluate the situation as it really is. Any such evaluation could usefully be followed up by reading again, either individually or with a group of lay leaders, the whole of Paul's Letters to Timothy, because they deal so clearly with many important aspects of the pastoral ministry.

A PERSONAL NOTE

There will be very few pastors who find that they can truthfully answer all these questions and arrive at an 'honours' or 'high distinction' mark. You will probably feel that you have found both strong and weak points in your ministry. There are two chief temptations to avoid. One is to imagine that your ministry is without fault, and become 'puffed up with conceit' (as Paul warned Timothy). The other is to become so discouraged by your failures that you want to give up altogether. Both of these conclusions are wrong, and can only be met by recognizing that effective ministry will always depend on the forgiving and strengthening love of God. A 'good minister of Jesus Christ' is not necessarily one who never experiences or feels failure, but rather the one who is honest in his dependence on God's grace, and who sincerely tries to be effective in the many different tasks he performs. So long as you truly have this desire, then you can continue to approach your pastoral task with confidence.

'For to this end we toil and strive, because we have our hope set on the living God, who is the Saviour of all men, especially of those who believe' (1 Tim. 4.10).

Suggested Scripture Passages for Use in Counselling

The passages suggested below have been grouped roughly according to different sorts of need or problem. Many of them will be suitable in more than one sort of situation, and pastors need to select very carefully those most appropriate to the particular problem or problems each client is facing. In any case the list should be treated only as a starting point for building up a list of your own.

Guilt, Remorse, Failure

A sense of guilt, need for forgiveness, and the assurance of God's love.

Psalm 103, 1–5; Heb. 4.14–16; 1 John 1.8–10.

Remorse; desire to atone following discovery of guilt and/or punishment for wrong action.

Acts 2.36–38; Luke 19.1–10.

Sense of inferiority and failure; oversensitivity to opinion of others, especially in position of leadership and other responsibility.

Josh. 1.1–9; Isa. 40.27–31; Matt. 10.29–31; Rom. 7.15–25a; 2 Cor. 12.9, 10; Eph. 2.4–5; Phil. 4.13.

Anxiety, Worry, Depression

Anxiety and worry about problems and troubles; fear that God does not care; hopelessness; lack of meaning in life; need for comfort and encouragement.

Matt. 11.28; Luke 12.28–32; John 10.10; Rom. 8.35–39; 2 Cor. 4.16–18; Phil. 4.6, 7; 1. Pet. 5–7.

Fear of Political Oppression and Persecution

Worry about obeying the laws of the country; conflict between Church teaching and state requirements.

Luke 20.19–26; 1 Pet. 2.13–17.

Fear of ridicule and contempt for being a Christian.

Rom. 1.16; Matt. 10.32, 33.

Fear of actual persecution and even death for one's faith.

Rom. 8.14–18 & 35–37; Matt. 10.28.

Fear of Evil

Fear of evil generally and need for strength to stand against it.

Ps. 91; Eph. 6.10–20; Phil. 4.13; Heb. 2.14, 15; 13.5b, 6.

Fear of evil spirits.

Mark 1.21–27 & 32–34; Gal. 4.3–9.

Wrong Attitudes

Desire for revenge; hatred; jealousy; anger against others.

Matt. 5.21–24; 5.38–48; Rom. 12.14–21; 1 John 4.7–12.

Sense of superiority; pride, arrogance, and boastfulness.

Rom. 12.3; 14.10–12; 1 Pet. 5.5.

Anger against God for apparently not answering prayer, or for permitting trouble.

Luke 11.1–13; Rom. 8.28; 11.33–36; James 5.

A materialist outlook, i.e. greed for money, possessions, or status; meanness; self-centredness.

Matt. 6.19–21; Mark 10.21; 1 Tim. 6.9, 10.

Laziness; carelessness over work.

Eph. 6.5–8.

Temptation

Need for strength to meet strong temptation of any kind.

1 Cor. 10.13; Heb. 2.17, 18; James 1.12.

Temptation to 'follow the crowd' and submit to influence of others.

Prov. 29.25; Rom. 12.1, 2.

Temptation to lose faith and follow false teaching.

1 John 4.1–6; Gal. 3.1, 2; Eph. 4.11–15; Jude 17–21.

Family Problems

Parents and children.

Mark 10.13–16; Luke 18.20; John 19.25–27; Eph. 6.2–4; Col. 3.20, 21; 1 Tim. 5.3–8, 14, 16.

Avoiding family conflict; inter-personal relationships generally.

1 Cor. 13; Gal. 5.13–15; Phil. 2.1–5; Col. 3.12–15; 1 Tim. 5.1–8; Titus 2.1–6; 3.1, 2, 9; James 1.19; 2.1–5; 3.13–18; 1 John 3.11–18.

Marriage

The meaning of marriage as part of God's plan.

Gen. 2.18–25; Mark 10.4–9; John 4.13–18; 1 Cor. 13; Eph. 5.21–23; Col. 3.18, 19; 1 Thess. 4.4–8; Titus 2.3–6; Heb. 13.4.

Problems in the sexual relationship inside marriage.

1 Cor. 6.15–20; 7.3–6; Eph. 5. 1, 21–23; Col. 3.12–14.

Sexual relationships outside marriage.

1 Cor. 6.12–20; Eph. 5.3.

Adultery.

Exod. 20.14; Mark 7.21, 22; Luke 18.18–20; John 8.3–11.

'Mixed' marriages.

1 Cor. 7.14–16; 7.39; 2 Cor. 6.14; 6.19, 20.

Conflict of all kinds between marriage partners.

1 Cor. 13.4–7; Eph. 4.31, 32; 1 Tim. 3.2, 12; 5.9–14; Titus 1.5, 6.

Divorce, and the question of remarriage.

Matt. 19.3–9; Mark 10.2–12; 1 Cor. 7.10–16.

Suffering, Pain and Sickness

In time of actual suffering or sickness.	Ps. 139.7–12; Matt. 11.28–30; Rom. 8.35–39; Col. 1.24.
Fear of going to hospital, an operation, etc.	Josh. 1.9; Ps. 23; Rom. 8. 31–39; Phil. 4.13.
Suffering as sent by God.	Job 7.7–10; John 9.1–3; 2 Cor. 12.7–10; Rom. 5.3–5.
Call to prayer for the sick.	Jas. 5.13–16.

Death and Bereavement

Fear of death and dying.	Ps. 23; Isa. 43.1–3a; John 11.25; Rom. 8.35–39; Phil. 1.19–23.
Bereavement; sorrow over the death of a relative or friend.	Phil. 4.6, 7; 1 Thess. 4.13–18; Rev. 21.1–4; Rev. 22.1–5.

Index of
Case Studies and Examples

Chapter 11
Death and Bereavement

Chapter 12
Right and Wrong: Adapting to Change

Key to Study Suggestions

Chapter 1

1 *Pastor*: See p. 3, lines 4–22; p. 9, section headed 'The work of the Shepherd'; and p. 21, lines 3–25.
Incarnation: See p. 11, last 12 lines; and p. 13, lines 1–22.
Pattern: see p. 11, paras 3 and 4; and p. 17, lines 4–14.

2 (a) Favour, benefit, right, advantage.
(b) Duties, obligation, concern, tasks.

3 Perhaps: Caring, sympathizing, sharing, mixing, loving. (See p. 13, lines 1–22.)

4 See p. 14, last line; and p. 15, lines 1–4.

5 See p. 9, numbered paras 1–6 and last para.

6 See p. 10, paras 2, 4, 5 and 6.

7 See p. 13, lines 6–10; and p. 15, numbered para. 8.

8 See p. 15, numbered para. 8, lines 2–6

10 (a) He grew up physically and mentally like any human child, joined in social events like weddings, attended the Synagogue, experienced fatigue and sorrow.
(b) He interpreted the Scriptures in new ways, possessed special insights and special gifts of healing, performed miracles – and He was without sin.

11 (a) Crowds – concern and compassion.
(b) 'Good' religious people – love, but also candid criticism.
(c) Soldiers – acceptance and respect.
(d) Those who would follow Him – encouragement, but also sternness.
(e) Poor and 'ordinary' people – understanding and sympathy.
(f) People of other nations – acceptance of *all* human beings, not only His own people the Jews.

12 Active concern, gentle persuasion (rather than stern power), humble selflessness.

Chapter 2

1 (a) See p. 21, lines 3–27; p. 24, last line; and p. 25, lines 1, 2.
(b) See p. 20, last 4 lines; and p. 21, line 1.
(c) See p. 22 (whole page).   (d) See p. 23, 4th para.
(e) See p. 22, lines 28–32.   (f) See p. 21, last para.

2 (a) See p. 21, lines 13, 14.   (b) See p. 21, lines 21, 22.
(c) See p. 21, line 18.   (d) See p. 21, line 26.

3 (a) See p. 22, paras 1 and 2.   (b) See p. 22, lines 24–33.

4 See p. 23, para. 2.

5 (a) See p. 23, lines 15, 14 from foot.
(b) See p. 23, last para.; and p. 24, paras 1 and 2.

6 (a) See p. 24, 4th para.   (b) See p. 24, last para.

7 (a) See pp. 28, 29, pattern 1; and p. 30, pattern 4.
  (b) See p. 29, pattern 2.   (c) See pp. 29, 30, patterns 3 and 4.

9 See p. 26, 4th para.

12 (a) See p. 26, paras (a)–(d); and p. 27, first para. (e).
   (b) See p. 27, paras (a)–(d) and second para. (e).

Chapter 3

1 See pp. 34, 35, para. (b); pp. 40, 41, para (g); and p. 41, 2nd and 3rd complete paras.

2 See p. 41 last 2 paras; and p. 42, 1st 3 paras.

3 See p. 37, para (d), Example 1, and last 2 lines; and p. 38 lines 1–15.

4 See pp. 47, 48, section headed 'Defence mechanisms'.

5 See p. 34, paras (a) and (b); and p. 35, paras (c) and (d).

6 (a) See pp. 35–38, sections (a)–(e).
  (b) See p. 38, section (e), 1st 2 paras.

7 See p. 44 last para.; and p. 45, lines 1–4.

8 See p. 47, section headed 'Defence mechanisms', 1st para.

9 (a) See pp. 35, 36, Truth (a).   (b) See p. 36, Truth (b).
  (c) See pp. 36, 37, Truth (c).   (d) See p. 38, Truth (e).

11 (a) See p. 50.

12 Based on pp. 47, 48.

13 See p. 51, paras 2 and 3.

Chapter 4

1 Place, position, relationship.

2 *Ambivalent*: See p. 67, para. (b); and following para.
  Unique: See p. 56, 3rd complete para.; and p. 69, last para.

3 (a) and (b) See pp. 55, 56, section headed 'Selfhood and self-image'; and p. 58, sub-section headed 'Group identity and self-image'.

4 (a) A very small hidden area and a correspondingly large public area (see Fig. 3 on p. 62).
  (b) A very small blind area and a correspondingly large public area (i.e. the *opposite* of Fig. 4 on p. 64).

5 (a) See p. 66, para. numbered 3 and 2 following paras.

6 (a) See p. 68, para. (d) and 2 following paras.
  (b) See p. 66, para. 3; and pp. 67, 68, para (c).
  (c) See p. 67, para. (b) and following para.

7 (a) Faith, and faithfulness before God.
  (b) Humility.   (c) The Holy Spirit is available to *all* people.
  (d) It is God's grace and forgiveness which saves us, not our own keeping of the law.

10 See p. 69, last para. but one.

Chapter 5

1 See pp. 77, 78, paras (a)–(d) and 2 following paras.

2 Friendship, sharing, discussion, trust, partnership.

3 (a) See p. 85, para. (b) and Examples 6 and 7.
  (b) See pp. 85, 86, para.(c) and Examples 8 and 9.
  (c) See pp. 86, 87, para. (d) and Example 10.

4 See p. 78, para. 2.

5 See p. 76, 3 paras following the Examples; p. 85, para. (a); and p. 87, para. (e).

6 See pp. 82, 83, numbered paras 1–7.

8 (i); (a) Moses counselled the people: (b) Clarifying, supportive, educative, crisis, confronting.
  (ii) (a) Jethro counselled Moses: (b) Clarifying, confronting.
  (iii) (a) The Judges counselled the people: (b) Clarifying, supportive, educative.

9 See p. 87, para. (e) and Example 11: The paralytic needed clarifying counselling as well as confronting, and both he and the rich man needed spiritual counselling.

10 (a) (i) Jesus counsels the disciples: (ii) *Nouthesia.*
   (b)(i) Jesus counsels the Pharisees: (ii) *Nouthesia*; (i) He also counsels the woman: (ii) *Paraklesei* and *Nouthesia.*
   (c)(i) Paul counsels the Galatians: (ii) *Nouthesia.*
   (d)(i) Paul counsels the Galatians: (ii) *Nouthesia.*

11 Having a sure faith in God. Putting one's trust in Christ rather than in oneself or in other people. Working with Christ to understand God's will for us and to do it. Relying on God's wisdom, not human wisdom, and trusting in God's Spirit to give one strength.

12 The Holy Spirit gives truth, dwells with and in people, teaches God's will, reminds us of God, bears witness to Christ.

14 Based on pp. 80–84, section headed 'Traditional or "cultural" counselling'.

Chapter 6

1 (a) See p. 97, paras 3 and 4; and p. 98, para. 1.
  (b) See p. 107, last para.; Example 16; and p. 108, 1st para. following Example 16.
  (c) See pp. 99–101, section headed 'Hope and Expectation'.
  (d) See p. 105, last 3 lines; and p. 107, paras 1 and 2.

2 (a) and (b) See pp. 110–112; and also p. 67, para. (b) and following para.

3 See p. 95, line 4 to end; p. 96; and p. 97, lines 1–5, section headed 'Positive Attitudes' and sub-section headed 'Respect'.

4 See p. 94, last para. but one.

5 See p. 104, paras (a)–(d).

6 See p. 104, last 2 paras; and p. 105, lines 1-3

7 See pp. 110, 111. subsection headed 'The client'.

8 See p. 111, last para.; Examples 17 and 18; and p. 112, para. following Example 18.

9 (a) To comfort the bereaved with gospel hope.
  (b) To avoid temptation, and help people to recognize their sin.
  (c) To correct and rebuke sinners.

10 Jesus *answered*, He did not turn the question back to the questioner. But the questioner did not follow Jesus's counsel.

11 1.21–28: (a) Jesus cured a man by ordering an unclean spirit to depart; people were amazed, and His fame spread. (b) He showed authority.
1.29–31: (a) Jesus cured Peter's mother-in-law of a fever. (b) He showed compassion.
1.32–39: (a) Jesus healed many people of diseases and demons. (b) He showed not only compassion but concern, by going out to find those in need.
1.40–45: (a) Jesus cured a leper, and told him to give thanks to God, but keep silent about his cure. (b) He showed pity and sternness.
2.13–17: (a) Jesus called Levi and ate with him and other tax-collectors, and told the Scribes that sinners are just as valuable to God as the 'righteous'. (b) He showed His acceptance of *all* people, and His one-ness with them.

12 Perhaps 1 Peter 1.3–9; 1 Peter 2.18–21; James 2.1–5.

Chapter 7

1 See pp. 115, 116, section headed 'Counselling as a process'; and pp. 125, 126, section headed 'Some methods of counselling'.

2 See p. 134, last para.; p. 135; and p. 136, lines 1–5.

3 See p. 119, 1st 2 paras.

4 Perhaps: Sharing, helping, revealing.

5 See p. 116, list, lines numbered (a)–(e).

6 See pp. 121 and 122.

7 See p. 119.

8 (a) See p. 126, lines 8–13, centred heading, and numbered paras 1–3; p. 129, centred heading and numbered paras 1–6; p. 132, centred heading and numbered paras 1–5; and p. 137, centred heading and 4 following lines.
(b) See p. 125 last 10 lines; and p. 126, lines 1–3.

9 See p. 135, last 3 paras; and p. 136, 1st 4 paras.

10 (a) See p. 137, 2nd para.
(b) See p. 128, whole page apart from Examples; and p. 129, lines 1–8.

11 (a) The need for care: our words as well as our deeds will be judged.
(b) We should 'speak no evil', but only what is fitting and edifying. Words can either harm, or be a means of grace.
(c) Words have immense power for good or evil. Words can turn people in one direction or another, as the rudder steers a ship, or a bit guides a horse.

12 (a) (i) (b) (i). (c) (ii). (d) (ii). (e) (ii) or (iii). (f) (iii).

13 (a) We are all members of Christ, and of each other, as 'one body'.
(b) The strong should give way to the 'weaker brother' – all for peace.
(c) The pastor should be 'all things to all men' – in order to *share* the gospel with his flock.
(d) All human beings are weak, and so they need to share each other's burdens – and all are subject to temptation.
(e) The pastor should 'be for others as a servant'.

Chapter 8

1 See p. 143, last 2 paras; p. 144; and p. 145.

2 See p. 162, 3 paras following heading 'Counselling and evangelism'; p. 163, last 5 lines; and p. 164, 1st 3 paras.

3 Dedication, obedience, service, support.

4 See p. 142; and p. 143, lines 1–22.

5 See p. 143, lines 10–22.

6 See pp. 154–157, section headed 'The fellowship of the Church'; and read Mark 10.17–45 and 12.28–34.

7 See p. 146, paras (a)–(f).

8 (a)(i) When a member of the Roman army showed his faith in Jesus's power to heal, Jesus used familiar passages from Psalms and Isaiah in pointing out this 'good example' to the Jewish bystanders. (ii) Today, too, people will respond when stories or legends familiar to them are used to illustrate a point of teaching or preaching – and people still need to be shown the good points in those they regard as enemies.

(b)(i) When Jesus received John the Baptist's message asking if He really was the expected Christ, He confirmed this by referring to the prophecies of Habakkuk which John himself had quoted in preparing people for Christ's coming. (ii) Scripture can often be used in this way to strengthen and confirm people's belief.

(c)(i) The Scribes and Pharisees had added many petty rules to the laws which God gave Moses for the priests who served in the Temple at Jerusalem. When these leaders accused the disciples of breaking some of these minor rules, Jesus pointed out that the Scribes and Pharisees themselves were guilty of breaking God's own laws, by oppressing and deceiving the people instead of looking after their welfare. (ii) Today too Scripture can be used to show people what is wrong in their lives.

(d)(i) Again, when the Pharisees accused Jesus and the disciples of breaking the Sabbath, He quoted a passage telling how King David himself had broken the rules for the Sabbath in order to feed the hungry. (ii) And Scripture can be used to reassure those who feel guilty about breaking 'religious' rules, that loving one's neighbour and serving human need is sometimes more important than keeping the letter of the law.

(e)(i) When the Sadducees tried to trap Jesus by interpreting a passage of Scripture about the life to come as if it applied to this life, He pointed to another passage which made the true meaning clear. (ii) People often mistake the meaning of Scripture because they interpret a single passage too literally, or forget the circumstances to which it refers. A pastor can help them to understand it better, by suggesting other passages which will make the meaning clearer.

(h)(i) When Jesus was asked to judge between a man and his brother, He used the occasion to preach against covetousness by means of a parable in which he echoed the words of Scripture. (ii) Preaching and teaching can often be strengthened by introducing Bible themes that are familiar to the hearers.

(f)(i) When the devil tempted Jesus to use His divine power for His own satisfaction and glory, Jesus quoted God's word to refute the devil's wiles and strengthen His own resolve to overcome each temptation. (ii) In the same way, reminding people of God's word can help them to overcome temptation today.

(g)(i) Again when Pharisees and lawyers accused Jesus of breaking petty regulations which they pretended had scriptural authority, He showed them that they were interpreting Scripture for their own benefit and glory rather than God's, and were misleading and oppressing the people they were supposed to be serving. (ii) Church leaders and pastors themselves need to make sure they are not misinterpreting Scripture, or using the Bible as a 'stick to beat people with'.

9 Perhaps: That it was an *ongoing* relationship in which Paul continued to remember and pray for the Christians at Ephesus. That he was eager to keep in touch by receiving their messages, and also by offering his own suffering to God as a sacrifice on their behalf. That he loved them and wanted them to share the knowledge and love of Christ which he himself experienced.

10 *Psalms*: That, whatever anyone may say, prayer is effective. God does answer, especially when people try their best to obey Him. That thankful praise and repentance for sin are more acceptable to God than any outward sacrifice or show of religious observance.
Matthew: God knows all our needs: we should not offer Him boastful public prayer or pious phrases that we do not really mean, but quiet, loving private prayer and *conversation*, as to a loving friend. What God gives in answer to true prayer is always for our good: He knows our need better than we do.
John: True prayer shared can be a means of evangelism.
Acts: If God so wills it, the prayer of deep faith can sometimes achieve what we might call 'miracles'.
Philippians: Prayer is one way of expressing our thanksgiving to God. It can be an effective way of helping people and sharing experience with them in the Spirit.

Chapter 9

1 (a) See p. 171, last 2 lines; p. 172; and p. 174, lines 1–10.
(b) See p. 178, para. (a).

2 See p. 171, last 2 lines; and p. 172, lines 1–3.

3 For an example, compare the description of traditional marriage customs and ideas on pp. 175–177 with that of Christian ideas and customs on pp. 178, 180, 181, and 182, 1st 2 paras.

4 See p. 174, section headed 'Universal Factors', 1st 5 paras.

5 See pp. 185, 186, paras (a)–(d).

6 See p. 188, numbered paras 1–5 (lines 1–15).

7 (a) The difference lies in v.9 of the passage in Matthew's Gospel, where 'unchastity' is given as the one legitimate cause for divorce.
(b) Here as elsewhere Matthew's Gospel gives fuller teaching than Mark's, perhaps in this instance because Jewish law required the divorce of an adulterous wife, or perhaps because by that time the early Church permitted separation for such a cause.

8 The teaching seems to be that whatever wife a man chooses can be regarded as a blessing from God – and especially so if she is one who manages his household well.

11 (a) Simon Peter (or Cephas, the 'rock' on whom Christ founded His Church) must have been married, since according to Mark he had a

mother-in-law, and according to Paul he was 'accompanied' by his wife.
(b) The Lord's brothers were married.
(c) It seems that Paul was single (though some scholars have interpreted
1 Cor. 7.8 as suggesting that he was a widower who had chosen not to
remarry).
(d) It seems that Barnabas, like Paul, was single, or Paul would have
included him with (e) the 'other apostles' who had their wives with them.

12 (a) The single state and the married state are both of value in God's sight.
(b) Within the marriage partnership husband and wife have equal rights,
and within the sexual relationship each is to respect the wishes of the
other.

13 (a) The problem is that married people may become so devoted to each
other that they forget about the devotion they owe to God.
(b) There need be no conflict if the couple *together* commit their lives –
and their marriage – to Christ.

Chapter 10

1 See p. 203, lines 13–3 from foot.

2 Probably: Wellbeing, soundness, wholeness.

3 Some examples might be; Sickness, illness, unhealthiness, disease,
weakness, injury, suffering, sin, wickedness.

4 (a) See p. 206, line (e); and p. 207, from line 4 to end; p. 208; and p. 209,
lines 1–6 (i.e. whole section headed 'Sickness and sin').
(b) See p. 206, para. (a) (and see also p. 213, last para.; p. 215, 1st 2
paras; and Example 43);.

5 See p. 206, last para.; and p. 207, lines 1–3.

6 See p. 209, last 2 paras; p. 210; p. 211; and p. 212, 1st 2 lines (mainly
section headed 'Understanding the individual').

7 Jesus's words suggest that though sin is often the cause of sickness, this is
not always the case. Similarly they suggest that in many cases healing is
only possible if the sick person repents. But sometimes even when a
person repents, or when no repentance is necessary, physical healing is
not part of God's will for that person.

8 (a) Failure to obey God's law. (b) Worship of false gods.
(c) Hannah's 'sickness' – i.e. her 'barrenness' – was said to be God's will.
(d) An evil spirit 'sent from God'. (e) A person's own sin.
(f) A demon. (g) A 'Legion' of demons. (h) The sin of Adam.

9 See p. 200, last 4 lines; p. 201; p. 202; and p. 203, 1st 4 paras. (It may be
helpful to prepare for this question by reading Isa. 11.1–9; 28.18,19;
35.5,6; 61.1,2; Lam. 3.1–6; 4.19,20; Ezek. 34.1–5,11,12,15,16,23–34.)

10 (a) That leaders in the early Church took seriously the ministry of healing
'in the name of Jesus', saying that it was 'His name' and the sick person's
faith in His name which brought perfect health.
(b) That when the Church takes the ministry of healing seriously, this is
also a way of bringing believers to the Lord.
(c) That even false prophets and sorcerers may be brought to Christ when
Christians add works of healing to their preaching of God's word.
(d) That the ministry of healing can be a way by which Christians earn
their living, provided, of course, that their *motive* for healing is a loving
and compassionate one, and not merely the desire for money.

Chapter 11

1 (a) See p. 222, lines 9–6 from foot.

2 *Idealize*: Admire, honour, esteem.
  Idolize: Worship, deify, hallow.

3 See p. 212, lines 11–2 from foot.

4 (a) and (b) See p. 242, last 2 paras; and p. 243, lines 1–6.
  (c) See p. 242, 1st para. (d) See p. 243, lines 7–end.

5 See p. 222, subsection headed 'Death as loss'; and p. 223, para. following Exercise B.

6 (a) See p. 224, numbered paras 1–3.
  (b) See p. 224, last 3 lines; p. 225; p. 226; and p. 228, 1st 2 paras of subsection headed 'Reorganization'.

7 (a) See p. 229, numbered paras 1–4.
  (b) See pp. 252–255, section headed 'Arranging and conducting funerals'.

8 See p. 246, last 2 paras; p. 247, Example 53; and p. 248, 1st 3 paras.

9 See pp. 251 and 252, section headed 'Practical support for the bereaved'.

10 (a) Knowing that He risked arrest and death, Jesus experienced distress, and even prayed that God might spare Him, and He expressed his feelings of sorrow and disappointment when the three disciples slept instead of watching with Him.
  (b) He suffered taunts and mockery from the priests and elders, and blows from the guards who took Him prisoner.
  (c) He suffered hunger like any other man.
  (d) He was mocked, insulted, blindfolded and beaten by the guards after His arrest.
  (e) On the cross He suffered not only pain but also thirst.

11 Ps. 23: As a reminder that God is with us always, even when we feel most bereft and alone, and that those we have lost through death are alive with Him, as we may hope to be.
  John 11.32–36: For those who feel guilty about grieving, as a seeming lack of faith – that it is natural to grieve, and Jesus Himself grieved with His friends, even while assuring them that those we love 'never die'.
  Rom. 8,35–39: For those who feel lost and forsaken by God – that nothing can separate us from the love of God in Christ.

12 (a) Peter grieved for the loss of his courage which caused him to fail the master he loved, and for the loss of his self-respect because he had broken his promise to die rather than deny Jesus.
  (b) The ruler's household grieved for the loss of the girl whom they believed to be dead.
  (c) Mary and the others wept for the loss of Lazarus who seemed to be dead (and Jesus Himself wept in sympathy although He had already said that Lazarus would live again).
  (d) The elders from Ephesus wept for the loss of Paul's presence among them as preacher, teacher, and leader.

13 OT: That after death all men's spirits go to *Sheol*, where there is no knowledge of God, nor any experience of life as such.
  NT: That Christ has 'abolished death' for the faithful, who after this life are raised to enjoy immortality with Him.

15 (a) That all comfort comes from God, and that by sharing in Christ's suffering we are better able to experience the comfort He gives, and to comfort one another. (See also pp. 229, 230: section headed 'Understanding the background'.)

Chapter 12

1 The examples you give should show that 'correct' (in this context) means 'socially acceptable' according to the customs or laws of a particular clan, tribe, nation, etc.; e.g. in Europe it is 'correct' to shake hands when meeting someone for the first time, whilst among the Maori people of New Zealand it is 'correct' to rub noses on similar occasions. And in England and elsewhere it is 'correct' to drive on the left-hand side of the road whilst in many other countries it is 'correct' to drive on the right. The examples should show that 'right' means 'morally acceptable' according to the ethical code of a particular clan, nation, etc.; e.g. it is everywhere considered 'wrong' to kill another person without cause, or to steal from one's friends, or to have sexual intercourse with another man's wife without his permission. But some actions are considered 'wrong' by one nation, and 'right' by another.

2 See p. 261, 2nd complete para.

3 See p. 270, last para.; and p. 271 1st para.

4 See p. 271, 2nd para.; and items (a), (b), and (c).

5 See p. 267, and Examples 62 and 63.

Index